本书获"2021年河海大学研究生精品教材建设项目资助"

中西文化对比
（第二版）

A Contrastive Study of Chinese and Western Cultures

祝吉芳　祝加贝　◎编著
Dr. Tracy L. Steele, Gladys Evertsen　◎审校

北京大学出版社
PEKING UNIVERSITY PRESS

图书在版编目 (CIP) 数据

中西文化对比：英文 / 祝吉芳，祝加贝编著 . —2 版 . —北京：北京大学出版社，2023.10
ISBN 978-7-301-34514-6

Ⅰ . ①中… Ⅱ . ①祝… ②祝… Ⅲ . ①比较文化 – 研究 – 中国、西方国家 – 英文 Ⅳ . ① G04

中国国家版本馆 CIP 数据核字 (2023) 第 196606 号

书　　　名	中西文化对比（第二版） ZHONGXI WENHUA DUIBI (DI-ER BAN)
著作责任者	祝吉芳　祝加贝　编著
责 任 编 辑	李　娜
标 准 书 号	ISBN 978-7-301-34514-6
出 版 发 行	北京大学出版社
地　　　址	北京市海淀区成府路 205 号　100871
网　　　址	http://www.pup.cn　新浪微博 :@ 北京大学出版社
电 子 邮 箱	编辑部 pupwaiwen@pup.cn　总编室 zpup@pup.cn
电　　　话	邮购部 010-62752015　发行部 010-62750672　编辑部 010-62759634
印 刷 者	北京溢漾印刷有限公司
经 销 者	新华书店 720 毫米 ×1020 毫米　16 开本　23 印张　540 千字 2016 年 7 月第 1 版 2023 年 10 月第 2 版　2023 年 10 月第 1 次印刷
定　　　价	88.00 元

未经许可，不得以任何方式复制或抄袭本书之部分或全部内容。
版权所有，侵权必究
举报电话：010-62752024　电子邮箱：fd@pup.cn
图书如有印装质量问题，请与出版部联系，电话：010-62756370

第二版前言

本书为英语教材《冲突、碰撞与趋同下的中西文化》第二版。

熟悉第一版的人很快就能看出，第二版虽然并没有做大的结构或者内容上的改变，但文字有了一定程度改进。除了修订全书的文字，在每个章节几乎都补充了新的材料。与此同时，为更客观、更全面地比较传统的中西文化，特别邀请曾在澳大利亚求学和工作多年并有法语文化生活经验的祝加贝对第一版文字进行了优化，为本书增添更多的视角和跨文化交际案例。

借助再版的机会，本书还将个别章节进行了压缩，同时将第一版中一些表达欠妥之处进行了删减。由于压缩和删减内容比较零碎，不在此一一指出。

一如既往，我们对从事中西文化研究的前辈先学，对从事高校跨文化交际、中西文化对比、翻译等课程教学的同行们充满感激之情，没有他们的先期研究，就没有此书的开展。感谢赐予更正或观点的南京大学、河海大学、Sam Houston State University和University of Queensland的同事和朋友；感谢Tracy L. Steele博士，Gladys Evertsen及其先生Harry的校正；感谢杜辉教授的审读；感谢北京大学出版社编辑李娜老师的支持。当然，书中出现的任何问题由我负责，并会在今后一一加以纠正。

祝吉芳

2023年6月25日

Foreword

Since the reform and opening up, the Chinese have come to know the Western world, yet the current Western world still doesn't have enough knowledge about China. Like our students, we sometimes are frustrated by Western prejudices and snide remarks about China, although we understand most of these are rooted in ignorance of China and Chinese culture. "If we can help them see China and its culture as we do," we think to ourselves, "chances are that they too will come to love the place, the people as well as the culture." So in writing these pages, we have an ambitious goal: We hope we could display to readers that most often the cultural differences are just differences of degree, and that acknowledging the cultural differences will lead one to re-examine not only a foreign culture but also his own culture. For this reason, this book is to focus on cultural comparison and contrast and try to identify cultural differences as well as reasons behind the explicit or hidden discrepancies, seeking to show how Chinese and Western philosophy, geography, history, administration, economics and art are intimately connected to those cultural differences.

In the past nearly 50 years of reform and opening up, we have learnt a lot from Western societies. Likewise, Western culture has changed a lot over the years through interactions with other cultures in the global community. Therefore, we should take a new look at different cultures and their recent changes, and get hold of the latest information about them. But given the limited space of this book and the great difficulty of comparing the ever-changing and dynamic cultural elements, we are to confine our attention to what is traditional and hence stable about Chinese and Western cultures.

The chapters of this book are arranged under five headings–East and West, Cultural Differences in Silent Language, Cultural Differences in Thinking, Different Cultural Orientations, and Different Cultural Standards.

While this book was informed and enhanced by our international colleagues in Nanjing who have helped to make this a better book than it would otherwise have been, friends at Hohai University, Nanjing University, Queensland University and Sam Houston State University who have given us much food for thought, and academics who have studied and published their researches, we owe a lot of thanks to our late friends in particular: Dr. Tracy L. Steele and Mr. Fernando Mercier, who offered us invaluable help. We are also greatly indebted to Professor Du Hui and our family friend Gladys Evertsen and her husband Harry. This book has benefited enormously from their comments, suggestions, and corrections.

Zhu Jifang (Ph.D) and Zhu Jiabei

Nanjing

September 2022

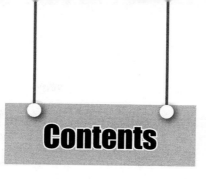

Contents

Part I East and West

Unit 1 Why Contrasting Chinese and Western Cultures? 3
I. Ancient Civilizations and Cultures 3
II. Cross-cultural Comparative Studies in China 5
III. Imperatives to Contrast Chinese and Western Cultures 9
IV. A Note on Some Key Concepts 15

Unit 2 Characteristics of Traditional Chinese and Western Cultures
.... 19
I. "There Are All Kinds of Birds in a Large Forest" 19
II. Traditional Chinese Cultural Characteristics 22
III. Traditional Western Cultural Characteristics 32

Unit 3 Affinities Across Cultures 37
I. Two Unexpected Affinities 38
II. Reading for More Cultural Affinities 39
III. A Note on Some Key Concepts 51

Part II Cultural Differences in Silent Language

Unit 4 Time 59
I. Time in China and the West 60
II. Two Time Modes 65
III. Past-oriented Societies vs. Future-oriented Societies 73
IV. Two Time Orientations 76

Unit 5 Space 80
I. What Is Space? 81
II. Spatial Language 82
III. Spatial Language and Culture 86
IV. Spatial Language and Life 93

Unit 6 Smiles, Nods and Silence 97
I. Smiles in Intercultural Communication 97
II. Nods in Intercultural Communication 103
III. Silence in Intercultural Communication 105

Part III Cultural Differences in Thinking

Unit 7 Intuitive vs. Logical Thinking 115
I. Definitions of Intuitive and Logical Thinking 116
II. Philosophy and Thinking 117
III. Application of the Two Thinking Modes 121

IV. Impact of Thinking Modes on Writings 126

V. Logic in China and Intuition in the West 128

Unit 8 Dialectical vs. Analytical Thinking 132

I. Proverb Preferences Across Cultures 133

II. Dialectical Thinking 134

III. Analytical Thinking 139

IV. More about the Two Modes 143

Unit 9 Holistic vs. Atomistic Visions 146

I. A Detention Room Incident 147

II. Prominent Attributes of Holistic and Atomistic Visions 147

III. Vision and Cognition 156

IV. Vision and Language 157

V. Zhengshan Xiaozhong and Lipton Black Tea 164

Unit 10 Categorizing Objects by Relationships vs. by Attributes 167

I. Two Ways to Categorize Objects 168

II. Principles to Categorize Objects 169

III. How to Categorize Objects and Why 172

IV. Impacts of Different Ways of Categorization 175

V. Causal Attribution Patterns Caused by Different Categorization Ways 178

Unit 11 Non-controllers vs. Controllers 182

I. Too Early to Tell 183

II. Why So Different Stances Towards Life? 184

III. "Being" and "Doing" Cultures 190

IV. Manifestations of "Being" Culture and "Doing" Culture 194

Part IV   Different Cultural Orientations

Unit 12   The Introvert-oriented vs. the Extrovert-oriented 205

I. Personality Types 206

II. Personality Types of Cultures 208

III. Effects of Personality Types on Pattern Preferences 213

IV. A Contrast of Some Cultural Phenomena 219

Unit 13   Collectivism vs. Individualism 225

I. An Embarrassing Custom 225

II. Collectivism and Individualism as Cultural Orientations 227

III. Collectivism and Individualism in Cultural Anthropology 233

IV. Collectivist and Individualist Perspectives of "Self" 236

V. Interdependence vs. Independence 241

Unit 14   Advocacy of *Jing* vs. *Dong* 245

I. Introduction to Two Concepts 246

II. Chinese Advocacy of *Jing* 248

III. Western Advocacy of *Dong* 258

IV. Differences and Discomforts 263

Unit 15 Implicitness vs. Explicitness 267
I. "Half a Story" 268
II. Implicitness vs. Explicitness of Language 270
III. Implicit Traditional Chinese 276
IV. Explicit Westerners 284
V. High-context vs. Low-context 287
VI. "Chicken and Duck Talk" 291

Part V Different Cultural Standards

Unit 16 Peace vs. Conflict 299
I. Great Names and Different Cultural Standards 300
II. External Factors and Cultural Standards 305
III. Cultural Standards and Their Unique Products 308
IV. Better Ways to Know Each Other 313

Unit 17 Egalitarian vs. Inegalitarian Distribution 316
I. Hate-the-rich Mentality 316
II. Traditional Chinese-style Egalitarianism 318
III. Western-style Inegalitarianism 321
IV. Egalitarianism and Inegalitarianism in China and the West ... 323

Unit 18 Good vs. Evil Human Nature 326
I. Definition of Two Concepts 326
II. Human Nature and Education 328

III. Theorization of Assumptions about Human Nature 331

IV. Human Nature Theories and the Rule of Ethics vs. Law 337

Unit 19 Rule of Individuals vs. Rule of Law 339

I. Rule of Individuals in Traditional Chinese Thought 339

II. Rule of Law in Traditional Western Thought 345

III. Rule of Law in China Today 350

Part I
East and West

"Oh, East is East, and West is West, and never the twain shall meet." The opening line of "The Ballad of East and West" by the famous English poet Rudyard Kipling (1865–1936) is often quoted to underline that two things are so different that they can never come together or agree. But, the fact is the "twain (two)" did meet.

In this part, the question about why we should compare Chinese and Western cultures is answered in Unit 1 after a brief introduction to the two civilizations and a review of cultural comparative studies in China. Traditional characteristics which may help to identify Chinese and Western cultures are then discussed in Unit 2. Unit 3 offers a reappraisal of the affinities or similarities that unite cultural traditions in the East and West.

Unit 1   Why Contrasting Chinese and Western Cultures?

I do not want my house to be walled on all sides and my windows to be stuffed. I want the cultures of all lands to be blown about my house as freely as possible. But I refuse to be blown off my feet by any.

—Mahatma Gandhi

If you were having a face-to-face talk with the famous Indian politician, what would you say to him? Do you love meeting people from other cultures?

Stop to smell the roses along the way.

—An old English saying

For further study: Look for more similar catchphrases in Chinese.

I. Ancient Civilizations and Cultures

To illustrate why we should compare and contrast Chinese and Western cultures, it might be a good idea to start with the two major civilizations on earth–the Chinese inland civilization and the Western sea civilization.

1. Chinese Civilization and Culture

Surrounded by land on three sides, ancient China with the Central Plains Region (中原地区) as the source of its civilization has long been isolated. This geographical isolation, together with its unique natural environment and ecology has endowed the nation with a unique cultural tradition and a distinctive social psychology. The self-reliant and self-supporting rural-based agrarian economy born out of this isolated land caused greater isolation in dire need of the spirit of openness and adventure.

Encouraging people to stick to their homeland, be content with their simple life, follow the ***dao*** (Way or Tao), happily labor at sunrise and rest at sunset, orthodox Confucianism, a product of this civilization, contributed much to the development of the isolated and hence inward-bound Chinese culture. Its doctrine of "the integration of Heaven, earth and man (天人合一)" pushed Chinese culture further down the road of introversion or inward-seeking (内求). The cardinal Confucian virtues of humanity and righteousness urged the ruler to "lovingly care for his people (仁爱)" and "regulate human relationships (正人伦)". Guided by the thought of "applying theory to reality (经世致用)" which emphasizes scholarship, ancient Chinese read not for knowledge or skills but for the ***dao*** by practicing "seriousness to straighten the internal life and righteousness to square the external life (君子主敬以直其内，守义以方其外)". They had little interest in pursuing "investigation of the things (格物致知)" into the realms of what we call natural or social sciences. The inward seek, so to speak, was what the ancient Chinese pursued.

As a consequence, a culture of introversion or inward-orientation was gradually formed in this inland civilization, and nurtured many generations of Chinese marked by their home-orientation, non-action, tolerance, pacifism, lack of competing tradition, and absence of explicit time concepts.

2. Western Civilization and Culture

Ancient Greece as one of the sources of Western civilization is of a long irregular coastline with many fine harbors, because of which foreign trade developed early in this nation. The ecology of this place, consisting as it does mostly of mountains descending to the sea, favors occupations that require little cooperation with others such as hunting, herding, fishing, sea trade, sea transportation, and even piracy. With the exception of trade the economic activities do not strictly require living in the same community for a long time, which made ancient Greeks outward-bound. It is the outward-bound that ushered in the rise of natural sciences characterized by transcendence, conquer, and creation, which in turn inspired people to be more open and more outward-oriented. It is because of its outward-orientation that settled agriculture which requires cooperation and stability came to this civilization later than inland civilizations, but quickly became commercial.

Gradually outward-bound Western culture was formed in this blue sea civilization surrounded by water on three sides.

II. Cross-cultural Comparative Studies in China

Before the Sino-British Opium War (1840–1842), Chinese and Western cultures developed like two streams running side by side on their own by following their own courses. But the Qing dynasty's defeat in the war first opened the eyes and ears of the Chinese to the rising Western world. And the dynasty's subsequent defeat in the Sino-Japanese War of 1894–1895 (甲午战争) turned our attention also to Japan which was assumed to be fast developing because people there had learned from the West.

1. Studies During the Reform Movement of 1898

After the Opium War and shortly after the Sino-Japanese War, the Western powers began to occupy various ports of China by force, which badly upset Chinese people who had felt disappointed and disheartened. To bring new hope to them, the leaders of the Reform Movement of 1898 (维新运动) such as Kang Youwei (1858–1927), Liang Qichao (1873–1929), and Tan Sitong (1865–1898) translated Western works to spread the Bourgeois ideology of Europe, and wrote articles to compare Chinese and Western cultures so as to found the theory of Constitutional Reform and Modernization. Although the Reform Movement didn't last long and failed in the end, it might be said to have made preparations for more systematic studies on Chinese and Western cultures during the 1919 May 4th Movement.

2. Studies During the May 4th Movement of 1919

The aggressive invasion of Westerners and Japanese against China led Chinese intellectuals to assume that the humiliation and backwardness of China were due to the useless rigid obsolete Confucianism.

In May 1918, Lu Xun (1881–1936) used his pen name for the first time and published his first short story in vernacular *A Madman's Diary*, a scathing criticism of outdated Chinese traditions that were supposed to be "gnawing" at the Chinese. The impact of Lu Xun and other revolutionaries such as Cai Yuanpei (1868–1940) and Hu Shi (1891–1962) was undeniably immense, given the fact that the whole young generation was transformed. During the tumultuous days of 1919, students in Beijing marched on the streets protesting the unequal treaty with Japan and blaming Confucianism for such an injustice. They angrily shouted "Down with Confucianism" and opened their arms and hearts to new ideas of science from the West. In short, the message sent by the Movement was clear: Up with Western scientism and down with Confucianism.

However, an objective voice could still be heard, for instance from Liang Qichao, a political activist and academician. Before he went to Europe, Liang Qichao's views were identical to those of the New Culture Movement which launched a ruthless attack on Confucianism. After returning from Europe, he acquired a new basis for critical reflection on modernity, and published *Journey to Europe* (《欧游心影录》), in which Liang refuted his previous views completely, advocating borrowing the spirit and methods of Western science to reassess and reorganize the national cultural heritage in order to develop a new one.

Echoing Liang Qichao's theories in his *East and West: Their Civilizations and Philosophies* (《东西文化及其哲学》), Liang Shuming (梁漱溟) foretold that Western civilization would be doomed to eventual failure. Although he disfavored complete reform and adoption of Western institutions, Liang believed that reform in China was necessary. Soon there appeared a debate between "Old Learning (Chinese)" and "New Learning (Western)". Although the contention lingered on in the following years, the latter had forced its way into prominence while the former gradually withdrew into obscurity.

Against this larger social background, Wang Guowei (1877–1927) advocated "going beyond the distinction between Chinese and Occidental Learning (学无中西)", while Lu Xun recommended his strategy of "looking for new voices in foreign cultures (别求新声于异邦)". Those views turned out to be so prevailing that all sorts of Western theories and ideologies flooded into China through translated versions.

3. Studies after the May 4th Movement

Faced with "the Complete Westernization" as a trend of thought and the deteriorating economic situation, some professors in Shanghai jointly published a manifesto in 1935, openly advocating the necessity of constructing native Chinese culture.

With respect to "Westernization" or "construction of native culture", Zhang

Dainian (张岱年) and other scholars came up with a proposition of "synthetic creation (综合创新论)". This proposal emphasized that, in dealing with cultural issues, equal attention should be paid to what is the best both in Western culture and Chinese culture. Later on, Zhang introduced "cultural creationism" and uplifted the realistic significance of "synthetic creation" to the level of actualizing the rebirth of Chinese culture and national rejuvenation.

Similar proposals like those greatly encouraged and inspired Chinese scholars who attended to the construction of Chinese culture and consciously took up the responsibility for the future of the nation and its people.

4. Studies in the 1980s

In the 1980s, much attention was cast on comparative and contrastive studies of Chinese and Western cultures again. Some television series elaborated that compared to the sea civilization, the inland civilization had advantages as well as disadvantages. These television series initiated a whirlwind of discussion and debate when they were first broadcast nationwide. CCTV statistics claimed that over 300 million people watched at least one of them, making the series the most popular one that year. Their scripts were published in the newspapers and in book form, which started a new wave of cultural comparative studies.

5. Studies in the New Century

The first few years of the 21st century witnessed a decrease in traditional values and the appearance of some social ills–a result of the accelerated economic growth, the cultural invasion of the West, and the tragic collapse of Confucianism. More tragically, it seemed that no principle, no law, and no morality could offer help. People became confused. Then the Lecture Room of CCTV 10 initiated a sudden revival of Confucianism and other fine traditions in 2006. Today Confucian classics are no longer regarded as fossils, but as a way to address the social problems, since for more than 2,500 years the Confucian doctrines of humanity, righteousness, filial piety, etc. were the guiding principles of life and governance in China. Confucianism is back in fashion again. As far as we know, about five to six million Chinese students are currently studying *The Analects* (《论语》). Some companies are using Confucianism as a management tool. The government is also promoting the Confucian values of ethics, fairness, and honesty, regarding Confucianism as the backbone of Chinese culture.

With the revival of Confucianism, cultural comparative studies, particularly East-West studies, appear so important that many scholars have engaged in it and many colleges and universities have added relevant courses to their curriculum.

In 2019, President Xi Jinping called upon scholars in the country to consolidate cultural confidence and create works featuring notable Chinese elements in an article published in the 12th issue of the *Qiushi* Journal, identifying a new way for cultural comparative studies.

III. Imperatives to Contrast Chinese and Western Cultures

China is not like the West. It will remain in very fundamental respects very different from the West. Now the big question is: How shall we make sense of modern China and the West? Why should we try to correctly understand them? Here we want to offer you nine of the imperatives for trying to understand what China is like and what the West is like by contrasting their cultures.

1. The Harmonious Imperative

Though it has tried its utmost to build a harmonious and friendly relationship with other countries since its reform and opening up in 1979, China has to face trade conflicts, disputes over the issues of the South China Sea, Diaoyu Islands and Taiwan, cultural discomforts in the international context and even what it deems "containment, suppression, and attack from the mighty Western discourse". The reasons for this state of affairs are many and varied, some of them are beyond the control of anything China might do to try to correct them, but some are not. Take the very way we show our good intentions and politeness for instance. When presented with a present, the polite way for us is to decline three times before accepting it seemingly unwillingly and then putting it away without opening it or telling the giver how much I love the gift and how much I appreciate his kindness. This custom is incompatible with the so-called international practice, but it is something within our control and can be adjusted so that our good intentions can be better understood by foreign friends.

It is not our argument that the Chinese should be universally loved. Given the fact that communication breakdowns often occur in our interaction with others, there is no harm in learning more about differences between cultures in order to live more harmoniously in a world community that is becoming smaller and smaller.

2. The Peace Imperative

In this world there are always people who can be unreasonable, illogical and self-centered. And when different cultures encounter, there are often misunderstandings, bigotry, hostility, conflicts and even wars. The Japanese of 1543 called the Portuguese who landed on their shores "Southern Barbarians" since they arrived mostly from the south. It would be naive to assume that merely understanding different cultures would end wars, conflicts or misunderstandings, although peace problems do underscore the need for individuals to learn more about groups of which they are not members so that ultimately peoples, not countries, negotiate and sign peace treaties. In today's global community struggling for peaceful coexistence, to learn some dynamic intercultural communication techniques based on a contrastive study of Chinese and Western cultures may transform potential conflicts into peaceful dialogues and create compassionate connections with people from other parts of the earth.

3. The Ethical Imperative

Intercultural communication presents challenging ethical issues. Ethics may be thought of as principles of conduct that help govern the behavior of individuals and groups. These principles often arise from communities' perspectives on what is good or bad. Some are stated very explicitly. For example, the concept of "filial piety" teaches us that it is wrong not to honor one's parents. Many other principles may be less explicit at least for some Chinese people born in the 1940s or 1950s–for example, everyone, old or young, should be independent.

Ethical principles are often culture-bound, and intercultural conflicts often arise from varying notions of what is ethical behavior. For instance, in terms of supporting the aged, some Chinese consider it unethical for Westerners to send their weak or disabled parents to retirement homes or to allow them to stay there for we have the tradition of rearing children for old age and accumulating grains for famine in China.

This contrastive study is expected to provide insights into ethical issues so that we can estimate what is ethical and unethical according to variations in cultural priorities and identify guidelines for ethical behavior in intercultural contexts where ethics clash.

4. The Economic Imperative

On December 11, 2001, China formally joined the World Trade Organization. Since then both China and the rest of the world have had to run faster. This is because China's joining the WTO took China and the world to a new level of "offshoring"–with more companies (mostly Western ones) shifting production offshore and then integrating it into their global supply chains, for instance, a company takes one of its factories that it is operating in Iowa, America and moves the whole factory offshore to Lianyungang, China. There, it produces the very same product in the very same way, only with cheaper labor, lower taxes, subsidized energy, and lower health-care costs. However, such companies are partly responsible for Chinese environmental pollution while bringing economic prosperity or employment opportunities. Therefore, we need to understand how business operates in other countries, especially in the West. We need to be able to negotiate deals that are advantageous to Chinese long-term development.

5. The Technological Imperative

Today we are connected via the internet, cell phones, e-mail, QQ, Skype, WeChat and TikTok to strangers. This change has affected the ways we form or maintain social relationships. In the past centuries, social relationships were confined to the distance of an easy walk. Now we can be "accessed" in many ways and be involved simultaneously in many different relationships, even without real face-to-face contact. What does this have to do with cultural comparison?

Through high-tech communication tools we come in contact with people very different from us, often in ways we are not aware of. For instance, persons we talk to or students we teach on TikTok may speak languages different from our own, come from different countries, be of different ethnic backgrounds, and have quite different life experiences. As a consequence, miscommunication may arise from a lack of mutual understanding, and increasing technology means, as it were, we cannot afford to be culturally illiterate in this shrinking interdependent world.

6. The Interactive Imperative

American civil rights leader Dr. Martin Luther King Jr. said, "People fail to get along because they fear each other; they fear each other because they don't know each other; they don't know each other because they have not communicated with each other." Communication proves that big cultural differences can cause problems interpreting what the other person is doing. For example, a great majority of people from the U.S. and other Western cultures expect those with whom they are communicating to "look them in the eye", but direct eye contact is not a custom throughout the world. In some rural areas of China, children are taught not to look at another in the eye but somewhere around the Adam's apple. To them too much eye contact is a sign of bad manners. For another example, when a good-mannered Chinese businessman tells his Norwegian client that he is uninterested in an offer by saying "That will be very difficult", the Norwegian may eagerly ask how he can help. The Chinese may be mystified. To him, saying something is difficult is a polite way of saying indirectly "No way".

"Westerners value their privacy and manners in interactions", so some people say. But when we commuted into Melbourne during our stay in this Australian metropolis, there were certainly plenty of people conversing on their mobile phones–sometimes too loudly–discussing and sharing personal details with a friend. It's surprising that they talked as though the person was sitting next to them and that they didn't even acknowledge the person who was actually sitting beside them. Don't they value privacy and manners? There are countless examples like these, which prove the complexity and difficulty of intercultural interaction.

7. The Work Imperative

As is known to many, the rule of the market economy is that if somewhere has the richest human resources and the cheapest labor, the enterprises and businesses will naturally rush there and receive a warm welcome there. Employment competition will be predictably worldwide and hence tougher. That's why the noted American economist Thomas L. Friedman reminded his daughters, "Girls, when I was growing up, my parents used to say to me, 'Tom, finish your dinner–people in China and India are starving.' My advice to you is: Girls, finish your homework–people in China and India are starving for your jobs." To get employed today, one really has to become more experienced in marketing himself.

8. The Imperative to Present China Stories (讲好中国故事)

Under the current international situation which continues to undergo profound and complicated changes, we need more people to tell China stories well in foreign languages. It is believed that only in this way can we effectively influence international public opinion and win understanding and support for China's development from the international community. But according to some American scholars exposed to American culture, if we are to be effective, we have to do more than just tell China's story, we must sell China's story. As the Scottish novelist Robert Louis Stevenson (1850–1894) wrote in 1892 in *Across the Plains*, "Everyone lives by selling something." It may take time and patience to "sell" foreigners a perspective of China that is different from the one that they've been spoon-fed by Western media for decades or years. So it is necessary to plan carefully not just what we say but how we say it, trying to put ourselves in our listeners' shoes since they probably have not had the opportunity to experience China. Our highly educated and well-traveled landlord during our stay in America in 2007 would be a good example. He did not even know that China had modern medicine!

9. "Fortune Favors the Prepared Mind"

Some of those who find it impossible for them to work abroad or in a joint venture have questioned whether the yoking together of English learning and cultural comparative study has much meaning, "What's this got to do with me?" This point touches on the ultimate purpose of this book, which finds expression in the broad extent to which different cultures control our lives. Culture is not an exotic notion studied by a select group of scholars. It is a mold in which we are all cast, and it underpins our daily lives in many unsuspected ways. By nature all men are alike, but by education widely different (性相近，习相远). The best reason for the layman to spend time comparing Chinese and Western cultures is that he can learn something useful and enlightening about himself. This can be an interesting process, at times harrowing but ultimately rewarding. One of the most effective ways to learn about oneself is by taking seriously the culture of others. It forces you to pay attention to those details of life which differentiate them from you. "Fortune favors the prepared mind."(Louis Pasteur) If you want to be competitive and have a bright future, you have to be fully prepared.

IV. A Note on Some Key Concepts

1. Chinese Culture

The reference to Chinese culture covers at least three subcultures: the fine traditional Chinese culture, the culture of revolution, and the advanced culture of socialism. In this book, we are going to mainly talk about the first one, which, with a long history, is the root and soul of the Chinese nation. Meanwhile, we are to think about whether the fine traditional Chinese culture still has its vitality and what new contributions it can offer in building a community of common destiny for all humankind.

2. Cultural Stereotypes

Chinese wear white for mourning, whereas Westerners wear black; Chinese honor dragons as symbols of prosperity and auspiciousness while Westerners think of them as vicious monsters. Such stereotypes are right and may sharpen our cultural sensitivity.

Chinese throw female babies into the river; North Americans do not care about elderly people. Such stereotypes are insulting and can upset people.

It is necessary to note here that the terminology both Chinese and Westerners use to indicate a people belonging to a particular cultural group—cultural stereotypes (i.e. ideas about people of other cultural groups based primarily on membership in that group), is unfit for all in a particular culture. Even if we make stereotypes of other cultures, we should inform ourselves about what is true and what is not because we could be wrong and offend others. Each person is different, and that is what life is about.

3. Cultural Shock

Cultural or culture shock is a multifaceted experience resulting from numerous stressors occurring in contact with a different culture. It is an important source of interpersonal stress and conflict for many foreign students. Because our society is becoming increasingly multicultural, we all experience varying degrees of cultural shock in unfamiliar cultural or sub-cultural settings. Effectively dealing with cultural shock requires recognition of cultural shock occurrences and implementing behaviors to overcome cultural shock with stable adaptations. Awareness of the nature of cultural shock and the typical reactions fosters constructive intervention by providing the basis for recognizing our own ongoing cultural shock experiences and for reframing the situations with adaptive responses and problem-solving strategies. That awareness is sufficient for us to normalize our experience, to reappraise our situations, and to respond in a more productive and less stressed manner.

4. Keeping up with the Times

China has undergone drastic changes over the years. Meanwhile, Western culture has changed a lot through communication with other cultures, too. We should keep up with the times in our cultural comparative studies. But given the great difficulty of comparing the rapidly changing cultural elements, this book is to pay special attention to what is traditional and thus stable about both cultures under discussion.

5. Multiculturalism

Western civilization is no doubt suitable for Westerners, but it will probably mean ruin for China if we try to copy it blindly. Such a view was held by German poet and novelist Hermann Hesse (1877–1962), too, as he said many years ago, "Every age, every culture, every custom and tradition has its own character, its own weakness and its own strength, its beauties and cruelties; it accepts certain sufferings as matters of course, and puts up patiently with certain evils. Human life is reduced to real suffering, to hell, only when two ages, two cultures and religions overlap." So it is important to advocate "multiculturalism" in modern society and to let it known to the young generation exposed to both Chinese and Western influences that nobody else can protect our own culture. We are obliged to protect it ourselves.

6. A Community of Shared Future for Mankind

In 1954 Chinese government proposed the principles of its foreign policy which are expressed in the Five Principles of Peaceful Coexistence: mutual respect for sovereignty and territorial integrity, mutual non-aggression, non-interference in each other's internal affairs, equality and mutual benefit, and peaceful coexistence. A recent expression of this idea is the concept of "building a community of shared future for mankind" articulated by President Xi Jinping. This idea means that all countries have equal sovereignty–none can intervene in the internal affairs of others; that countries should jointly manage global affairs democratically; that countries should engage in "win-win cooperation" to "build a world of common prosperity"; and that countries should treat the diversity of civilizations not as "a source of global conflict but as an engine driving the advance of human civilizations."

Further Reading

1. Aldridge, O. (1993). *The Dragon and the Eagle: The Presence of China in the American Enlightenment*. Detroit, Michigan: the Wayne State University Press.
2. Anderson, W. T. (1990). *Reality Isn't What It Used to Be*. New York: Harper & Row.
3. Friedman, T. L. (2005). *The World Is Flat: A Brief History of the Twenty-First Century*. New York: Farrar, Straus and Giroux.
4. Hall, E. T. (1990). *Understanding Cultural Differences*. Yarmouth, Maine: Intercultural Press.
5. Stevenson, R. L. (2010). *Across the Plains*. LittleWhiteEbook.com.
6. Zhang, Y. J. (1998). *China in a Polycentric World: Essays in Chinese Comparative Literature*. CA: Stanford University Press.
7. 费孝通著，方李莉编 (2013)，《全球化与文化自觉——费孝通晚年文选》，北京：外语教学与研究出版社。
8. 侯建新主编 (2022)，《中西文明十九讲》，北京：商务印书馆。

Unit 2　Characteristics of Traditional Chinese and Western Cultures

God gave every people a cup, cup of clay, and from this cup they drank life… They all dipped in the water, but their cups were different.

—**Ruth Benedict**

For further study: Look for more hints that can help to account for cultural differences.

I. "There Are All Kinds of Birds in a Large Forest"

Undeniably Chinese are different from one another and so are Westerners, just as the saying goes, "There are all kinds of birds in a large forest (i.e. People come in all varieties)."

1. Different Chinese

A culture's geography may affect its people's personality traits. The impact of the material environment on the making of man is also great. People nurtured in different parts of China, for example, different in temperament, physique, and habits, which has been vividly depicted in *My Country and My People* by Lin Yutang (1895–1976), a world-famous literary translator, bilingual writer, and outstanding linguist.

According to Lin,

…we have the northern Chinese, acclimatized to simple thinking and hard living, tall and stalwart, hale, hearty and humorous, onion-eating and fun-loving, children of Heaven, who are in every way more Mongolic and more conservative than the conglomeration of peoples near Shanghai and who suggest nothing of their loss of racial vigor. They are the Honan boxers, the Shantung (Shandong) bandits and the imperial brigands who have furnished China with all the native imperial dynasties, the raw material from which the characters of Chinese novels of wars and adventure are drawn.

Down the southeast coast, south of the Yangtse (Yangtze), one meets a different type, inured to ease and culture and sophistication, mentally developed but physically retrograde, loving their poetry and their comforts, sleek undergrown men and slim neurasthenic women, fed on birds'-nest soup and lotus seeds, shrewd in business, gifted in *belles-lettres*, and cowardly in war, ready to roll on the ground and cry for mamma before the lifted fist descends, offsprings of the cultured Chinese families who crossed the Yangtse with their books and paintings during the end of the Jin dynasty, when China was overrun by barbaric invaders.

South in Kwangtung (Guangdong), one meets again a different people, where racial vigor is again in evidence, where people eat like men and work like men, enterprising, carefree, spendthrift, pugnacious, adventurous, progressive and quick-tempered, where beneath the Chinese culture a snake-eating aborigines tradition persists, revealing a strong admixture of the blood of the ancient Yupeh (Yue) inhabitants of southern China. North and south of Hankow, in the middle of China, the loud-swearing and intrigue-loving Hupeh (Hubei) people exist, who are compared by the people of other provinces to "nine-headed birds in heaven" because they never say die, and who think pepper not hot enough to eat until they have fried it in oil; while the Hunan people, noted for their soldiery and their dogged

Unit 2 Characteristics of Traditional Chinese and Western Cultures

persistence, offer a pleasanter variety of these descendants of the ancient Ch'u (Chu) warriors.

Many Chinese sayings are in agreement with Lin Yutang's observance and meanwhile, further prove the great impact of the material environment on the making of man, e.g., "It takes all sorts to make a world (一种米养百样人)," "The material environment of a place nurtures a peculiar group of people (一方水土养一方人)," and "Every man has his taste (萝卜白菜，各有所爱)."

Indeed not all ethnically Chinese are the same. The two most famous Tang poets, for instance, are typecast as having contrasting personalities and capabilities. Li Bai was the romantic, drunken vagabond with inimitable, innate talent; Du Fu was the earnest Confucian scholar with impeccable technique. In any event, the two men were not rivals but friends.

2. Different Westerners

Westerners (primarily Europeans, Americans and citizens of the British Commonwealth) differ from each other. Their differences are exhibited to some extent in what people jokingly say about Europeans:

> In an ideal world the policemen would be English, the car mechanics would be German, the cooks would be French, the innkeepers would be Swiss, and the lovers would be Italian. But in a living hell, the policemen would be German, the car mechanics would be French, the cooks would be English, the innkeepers would be Italian, and the lovers would be Swiss.

The jokes above may be regarded as stereotypes which can be misleading and upsetting sometimes, but may help us develop sensitivity to sub-cultural differences (亚文化差异) and individual discrepancies.

3. A Note on "Comparison"

Through comparison and careful examination, we can note that even persons from the same family are different in a variety of ways, including different ways of looking at things, different ways of dressing, different ways of expressing personality and goodness. So we hold this truth to be self-evident that comparison is very basic to human understanding; without comparison we cannot recognize anything.

II. Traditional Chinese Cultural Characteristics

However bewilderingly different the Beijing native in northern China is from the Nanjing local in the south, the cultural integration and unity of thousands of years expose them to one culture with the following distinct characteristics.

1. Oneness

a. One Territory, One Ideology, and One Politics

In 221 BC the state of Qin "swallowed up" the other feudal states. With this unification came measures for the standardization of weights, measures and writing script, the destruction of all feudal barriers between regions and the construction of better roads and communications. Great masses of people were forcibly moved to new areas for purposes of defense or resettlement, and labor gangs were sent to work constructing the Great Wall out of smaller defensive walls of the old feudal states. Never before had China been so unified in the territory.

The vast land, held together by the terror of Qin's laws and the personal power of its first emperor, quickly disintegrated with the fall of the dynasty. However, the Han dynasty worked gradually to build it up again, unifying, organizing and standardizing the land brought under its control. This effort at standardization extended even to the realm of thought which again the Han

Unit 2 Characteristics of Traditional Chinese and Western Cultures

succeeded in accomplishing by gradual and peaceful means. Emperor Wu (156 BC–87 BC) of the Han made Confucianism the orthodox doctrine of the nation while other schools of philosophy including the Daoist and Legalist schools were deemed heretical. From then on Confucianism has been the mainstream of Chinese philosophy for more than 2,000 years.

Accepting Confucianism as the statecraft in the Han dynasty generated one ideology and one political system. In the later dynasties, Confucianism continued to unify ideology and political system largely through the imperial examination system (科举制度)–the only bridge to political success for young men. China remains coherent and stays undivided with one territory, one ideology, one politics, and one central government.

b. One Tradition of Three Teachings

Many of us profess ourselves to be Daoists, Buddhists, Muslims, or Christians, but seldom have we ceased at the same time to be Confucianists, for Confucianism since the time of its general acceptance has been more than a creed to be accepted; it has become an inseparable part of Chinese society and thought as well as of what it means to be a Chinese. Next to Confucianism, the most important and influential native philosophy has undoubtedly been that of the Daoist school. In many ways the doctrines of Confucianism and Daoism complement each other, running side by side like two powerful streams through all later Chinese thought and literature. There is an adage holding that every Chinese is a Confucianist when he is young, healthy, and successful, a Daoist when he is old, poor in health, and a failure, and a Buddhist when he needs mental comfort and a favor.

The introduction of Buddhism to China is an event with far-reaching results in the development of Chinese thought and culture. After a long and difficult period of localization, this new teaching managed to establish itself as a major system of thought, contributing greatly to the enrichment of Chinese philosophy, and as a major system of religious practice that has an enduring influence on Chinese popular religion. Indeed, it came to be spoken of along with the native traditions, Confucianism and Daoism, as one of the Three Teachings or Three Religions, thus achieving a status of equality with the two native beliefs.

Although the key difference between the Three Teachings lies in the fact that Confucianism is humanistic, Daoism naturalistic, and Buddhism spiritualistic, there exist in China sayings such as "The Three Teachings are one," "Three Teachings return to one," "The Three Teachings share one body," and "The Three Teachings merge into one."

c. One Roof for the 56 Ethnic Groups

The richness of Chinese culture finds expression in its great variety. China has always been a country of many ethnic groups. Its people live under the same roof, peacefully co-existing together.

d. Education as the Only Bridge to Success

Confucius (551 BC–479 BC) made great contributions to education in China. Before him, only the children of nobles had the opportunity to get a formal education. It is Confucius who took the lead in Chinese history to bring education to all the people. For thousands of years getting an education has been the only bridge to success, wealth, a good life and family prosperity, especially for boys from poor families. No wonder Emperor Renzong (1010–1063) of the Song dynasty wrote, "Study hard and you will become successful and able to afford a big house. Study hard and you will become so successful that a beautiful woman wants to marry you (书中自有黄金屋，书中自有颜如玉)."

Unit 2 Characteristics of Traditional Chinese and Western Cultures

e. One Writing Script

The Chinese writing system was developed more than 4,000 years ago; the oldest extant examples of Chinese characters such as 日 (sun) and 月 (moon) which date back to the 14th or the 15th century BC when the Shang dynasty flourished, are still used today. Chinese writing consists of an individual character for every syllable, each character representing a word or an idea rather than merely a sound; thus problems caused by homonyms in spoken Chinese are not a problem in written Chinese. The written language is a unifying factor culturally, for although the spoken language and dialects may not be mutually comprehensible in many instances, the written form is universal. Those who invented the writing script were extremely clever. For instance, they drew three horizontal lines and connected them with a vertical line through the middle, calling the character 王 (*wang*, i.e. king). The three horizontal lines refer to Heaven, Earth and Man, and that vertical line which passes through the middle joins the Ways of all three. Occupying the center of Heaven, Earth and Man, passing through and joining all three–if he is not a king, who else could he be?

f. Oneness of Heaven, Earth and Man

The Chinese idea of integrating Heaven (*tian*), earth and man originates from the notion of the Way or *dao* in the proposition that *dao* consists of *yin* and *yang* in the *Book of Changes*. Laozi who lived about 500 years before Jesus Christ further illustrated the concept of *dao* in Chapter 42 of his book *Dao De Jing* or *Laozi*, "Dao gives birth to One (i.e. chaos); one gives birth to Two (i.e. Heaven and Earth); Two gives birth to Three (i.e. *yin-yang* and harmony); three gives birth to the myriad things (道生一，一生二，二生三，三生万物)."

Two centuries after Laozi, Zhuangzi (369 BC–286 BC) proposed that the perfect man has no self (至人无己) for "he has transcended the finite and identified himself with the universe (天地与我并生，万物与我为一)." Gradually the theory that man is a part of the universe became rooted in Chinese thought.

Dong Zhongshu (179 BC–104 BC), a Confucianist and politician of the Western Han dynasty, further developed the worldview of oneness. He assumed that "the energy of Heaven and the energy of earth are unified, which consists of *yin* and *yang* and is manifested in four seasons and five agents (五行)." A number of Chinese sayings mirror the same idea of integrating man with Heaven and Earth rather than separating them, e.g. "Heaven affects human affairs and human behavior finds a response in Heaven (天人感应)", "The law of Heaven and the feelings of humanity are in unison (天理人情)", "Heaven accords with human wishes (天遂人愿)", "Heaven is angry and people are resentful (天怒人怨)", "Heaven's will brings about human affinity (天依人愿)", and "Heaven and humankind turn to one (天与人归)".

The Chinese character "天 (*tian*)" is translated as "Heaven" in the above paragraph, although *tian* carries a wider sense than the English word "Heaven". ***Tian***, Earth and ***Ren*** (man) always react to and comply with each other. They can never be separated. Such a worldview of oneness is also reflected in the ancient Chinese axiom of living in an environment with a rockery, a pond, flowers, and a lawn.

2. Continuity

China is of the world's longest continuous civilization. It is true that there were times of division, but the division was transient. There seem to be cycles of division and unification, but unification has outlived division. During its thousand years of development, China has undergone various ordeals. On the one hand, it withstood a number of foreign intrusions such as the Huns' harassment in the Qin and the Han dynasties, and the invasion of Western powers in the late

Unit 2 Characteristics of Traditional Chinese and Western Cultures

19th century and early 20th century. On the other hand, it also suffered from domestic suppression by the autocracy such as the First Qin Emperor who had many precious books burned and Confucian scholars buried alive (焚书坑儒). Having experienced so much misery and ordeal, the traditional Chinese culture survives and becomes enriched and consolidated with time.

The major reason why traditional Chinese culture has so much vitality and continuity of life lies in its magnanimity and inclusiveness. As Oriental Studies Master Professor Ji Xianlin (1911–2009) said after he received a lifetime achievement award for translation, "The fact that our culture has been able to remain consistent and rich with 5,000 years of history owes much to translation. Translations from other cultures have helped to infuse new blood into this culture." And the principle of fidelity that all Chinese translators are required to follow displays Chinese inclusiveness.

3. Inclusiveness

Traditional Chinese culture is a learning culture that has assimilated and incorporated various foreign cultures.

Initial Chinese culture originated mainly from Western Xia (西夏) and Eastern Yi (东夷) cultures. Yangshao (仰韶) culture was the representative of Western Xia culture; Longshan culture, was that of the Eastern Yi. The convergence of the Eastern and Western clan cultures laid a foundation for the Chinese culture which was of multiple resources. In the Spring and Autumn period and the Warring States period, the culture of the feudal states of Qin, Jin, Wu, Yue, Qi, Yan, Zhao and Lu was respectively blossoming in splendor and eventually grew into the culture of the Han nationality with Qilu culture as its core. In the later years Chinese culture continued to assimilate the cultures of ethnic minorities mainly from the West and the North, such as the Huns (匈奴),

the Qiang (羌), Xianbei (鲜卑), Rouran (柔然), Gaoche (高车), Tujue (突厥), Huihe (回鹘), Qidan (契丹), Nuzhen (女真), Mongolia, and Manchu, and in the South, Baiyue (百越) and Bashu's (巴蜀) cultures; it has also assimilated Indian Buddhist culture, Arabian culture, Persian culture, and now Western culture. This extensive inclusiveness is very rare in the history of world culture. It typically reflects Chinese cultural spirit of magnanimity, self-confidence as well as inclusiveness.

4. Atheism

By the standards of most religions, China has always been a godless country. To the extent that early Chinese thought can be considered religious, it was based on what might be deemed a spiritualist tradition. One had to worship one's ancestor spirits, and nature too was alive with spirits. Every river, lake, pool and spring, for instance, was associated with some spirit or deity. The story of the evil Yellow River deity He Bo has long been familiar to most Chinese children. In the Shang dynasty, a "Lord on High" or **Shangdi** was considered to control the rain and clouds. But throughout the Zhou dynasty **Shangdi** was equated simply with the ***tian***, a supreme, impersonal force. The Jade Emperor was, crudely speaking, a Daoist equivalent of **Shangdi**–or identified as his assistant and successor **Yuhuang Dadi**. These godlike beings did as emperors did by battling evil external forces like monsters and demons, looking after their people, and observing the ***dao***. They didn't play the role of a moral guardian; neither did they imbue the cosmos with meaning.

So basically, China is a non-religious nation. Common people here care little about the differences between religious and philosophical schools. They simply believe that deities personify justice and protect their interests. To them, there is no strict delineation between deities and human beings. Deities must come from somewhere and some of them are the sages of mankind. For instance, in his life on earth, Guan Yu was a great general and an upright man of the Three Kingdoms period. Upon his death he has been worshipped as the god of war.

5. Ethics as a Top Priority

More than 2500 years ago, philosopher Laozi wrote: "Water is the highest good. The goodness of water is that it benefits the ten thousand creatures, yet itself does not scramble, but is content with the places that all men disdain…." Today even illiterate people realize the importance of the Daoist principle of "water-like" behaviour, i.e. not striving to get on top or to the fore. Water, a daily necessity like the air, thus becomes a virtuous substance, bearing a force of daily moral instruction in China where ethics has long been valued.

The core value of traditional Chinese culture is to achieve moral excellence and improve one's spiritual state. The determination to be morally good is displayed in the aphorism "In the morning one hears the *dao*, so he can die in the evening without regret (朝闻道，夕可死矣)". To the virtuous ancient Chinese, personal interests and desires were of less importance and hence not worth pursuing–"What a gentleman worries about is not poverty but whether there are right principles throughout the country (君子忧道不忧贫)". During the Song and Ming dynasties there arose Confucian arguments over whether human desires or heavenly principles should be chosen and slogans like "Survive on heavenly principles; root out human desires (存天理，灭人欲)" which emphasizes the supreme position of ethics in Chinese society were put forward. The famous poem composed by notable Tang poet Liu Yuxi (772–842) explicitly displays the significance of ethics. It goes:

A mountain needn't be high;

It is famous so long as there is a deity in it.

A lake needn't be deep;

It has supernatural power so long as there is a dragon in it.

My house is humble,

But it enjoys the fame of virtue so long as I live in it.

6. Introversion

Initially, the Chinese assumed that there was a world or *tianxia* (literally, under Heavens) with an indefinite perimeter, and thereafter the cultures at the borders were absorbed inwardly by the powerful influence of Chinese culture. In contrast, Western culture tended to diffuse more outwards from a single center. The inward-looking Chinese culture mainly depended on internal forces for development while the expansion of Western culture relied on the forces of religion, colonization, and military might; Chinese culture allowed for the integration of all ethnic groups both within China and along its borders while Westerners engaged in numerous wars in order to gain commercial benefits. In short, a contrast of the historical development of China and the West reveals the inward-orientation of Chinese culture.

7. The Peace-loving

Traditionally Chinese people are peace-loving, kind, grateful and thus tolerant, accustomed to hardship and injustice for peace (believed to be impossible without families that are harmonious, happy and civilized.) or gratitude (found in idioms like "**A favor of a drop of water received should be repaid with a surging spring**"). Rarely do we give vent to our feelings by resorting to violence such as fighting, killing, beating, and wars because an emphasis on peace and harmony is an essential feature of this culture. The search for moderation and the beauty of harmony have, since ancient times, always been at the core of traditional philosophical thinking. The thinkers, together with

Unit 2   Characteristics of Traditional Chinese and Western Cultures

philosophers and educators of various dynasties, studied and expounded the dimensions of peace and harmony, their significance and the pathways to their fulfillment, which has formed a comprehensive system of thought of moderation and harmony or *zhonghe*, exerting a great influence on the morals, ethics and values of many generations of Chinese.

8. Fellow-townsmen Complex

No matter where we go, our heart is linked by an invisible silk thread to our hometown. Even in modern society, the phrase "seek roots" is not outdated, and looking for fellow-townsmen and establishing the association or the community of fellow-townsmen (老乡会) are still popular on the college campus and at workplaces. Chinese community abroad is also overflowed with the sentiment of homeland. According to them, "we were, after all, members of the 'same family' 500 years ago and the same accent represents a very good starting-point to develop a friendship."

In "The Land of My Ancestors", the famous Chinese woman author Bing Xin (1900–1999) describes this fellow-townsmen complex (老乡情结) as generally warm and says, "I did not visit all the local attractions in Fuzhou. Everywhere we could find historical relics as well as villages and towns inhabited by relatives of overseas Chinese and returned overseas Chinese. Fujianese expatriates are found all over the world. They have mostly started from scratch by the sweat of their brow. When I met some of them on my visits to Asian, African, European and American countries, they all expressed warm feelings towards me while shaking my hands. As I ate Fuzhou food and sipped jasmine tea in their homes or shops, I felt that being a Fujianese, I could make myself at home wherever I travelled in the world."

III. Traditional Western Cultural Characteristics

Western Christian heritage, scientific outlook, humanitarian elements, distinctive points of view in terms of the rights of the individual, etc., endow Western culture with the following traits.

1. Religiosity

Religion occupies an important position in ordinary Westerners' lives. Even political figures don't conceal their religious mentality in public speeches. In her speech made on 25 December 2021 Queen Elizabeth II said, "It is this simplicity of the Christmas story that makes it so universally appealing: simple happenings that formed the starting point of the life of Jesus–a man whose teachings have been handed down from generation to generation, and have been the bedrock of my faith. His birth marked a new beginning. As the carol says, 'The hopes and fears of all the years are met in thee tonight'."

2. Pursuit of Science

The pursuit of science is closely associated with curiosity which characterized the ancient Greeks, predecessors of some of today's Westerners. Aristotle (384 BC–322 BC), one of "The Three Greek Philosophers", held that curiosity is the uniquely defining property of human beings. When talking about the Athenians of a later era, St. Luke, the famous evangelist said, "They spend their time on nothing else but to tell or to hear some new things." The Greeks, far more than their contemporaries, speculated about the world they found themselves in and created models of it. They constructed these models by categorizing objects and events and generating rules about them that were sufficiently precise for systematic description and explanation. Therefore, they did very well in scientific fields like those of physics, astronomy, axiomatic geometry, formal logic, rational philosophy, natural history, and ethnography. This pursuit of science could be found in Italian scientists Copernicus, Bruno and Galileo, who suffered from the persecution by the Inquisition in the Middle Ages. The Westerners might not be the first in the world to take up science, but certainly were the first to put science in such a primary position of application to promote the development of human fundamental needs. Thus the West has been foremost in pioneering in the combination of theoretical research with practical applications. In a sense, it is the continuation of the practical spirit advocated by Greek thinkers like Aristotle, although such progress was checked during the Medieval Times. The rise of science and technology should also be ascribed partly to the European Renaissance and the Enlightenment Movement, which provided the necessary environment and encouragement to those great figures who ignored the authoritative religious forbiddance and freely and passionately pursued science.

3. Constitutional Liberties

One of the possible reasons why the West has developed quickly in modern times is its dedication to constitutional liberties. Living as free men and women, Westerners have been creative in every area of human life and the best among them have understood how much of what they cherish as progressive has come by the limitation of power, and by the release of personal energy from authority. And of course, there is no other culture on earth that worships violence and has gone to great lengths to make it with whatever means a tool to take away the freedom from non-Westerners to rise economically.

4. Practical Spirit

Western culture, with the admission of Christianity to its ranks alongside Greek and Roman cultures, became integrated and established long ago. What's curious about this culture is that its three cultural sources were diverse, and sometimes hostile. As is known to all, Romans tried to suppress Christianity and the Vatican was hostile towards Jewish migrants and their culture. One feels puzzled at the paradoxical events or phenomena arising out of the historical process of Western civilization in association with its three cultural sources. Tolerant attitudes as well as the practical spirit of Western culture, as in the conversion of Constantine the Great (c.280–337) to Christianity, are helpful guides to seeing the positive side of this religion. Practical spirit is thus a virtue Western culture fostered in its early days.

5. Critical Spirit

The critical spirit, ushered in by the European Renaissance, is highly encouraged by today's Western educational system.

As is known to many, the significance of the Renaissance lies in its confirmation and manifestation of humanist thinking and application. This movement supplies great inspiration to Westerners in creative work and builds up their confidence in bringing about more achievements in art, literature and science. More important than the surface accomplishment is perhaps the critical spirit the European thinkers and practitioners fostered during the Renaissance. This critical spearhead was directed particularly against scholasticism as a core of theology at the time. Consequently, it paved the way for the development of science and secular culture. One example is the Reformation which largely changed the religious structure and content of Christianity, based on the whole on the revaluation and criticism of the Christian ideas represented by the Roman church and the Papacy.

6. Dichotomies

Greek philosophers such as Thales, Heraclitus, Plato and Aristotle advocated

Unit 2　Characteristics of Traditional Chinese and Western Cultures

dividing the world into two opposing parts: element and soul, reality and reason, matter and form. Their theories laid the foundation for the further development of the concept of dichotomy or the dividing-one-into-two view adopted by Western culture. Apart from his physical skill, Archimedes is remembered as saying more than two thousand years ago, "Give me but one firm spot on which to stand, and I will move the earth," applying philosophical thought to scientific research. A dichotomy is also reflected in English proverbs such as "Heaven is conquered by obeying her." Conquering or obeying, Westerners have no alternative but to make a choice between them.

7. Conflicts as a Cultural Standard

Given the fact that dichotomies are common in Western thought, it is not surprising to find that the conflict has become a Western cultural standard (文化本位) revealed in various aspects of society such as presidential campaign speeches characterized by a warlike atmosphere in which the winning side has truth (like a trophy). In such speeches, the middle alternatives are virtually ignored. The presidential campaign, aggressive, original, challenging and ambitious, exemplifies the preference for conflicts. The formation of this cultural standard probably owes much to famous philosophers in Western history (see Unit 17).

8. Extroversion

As one of the "three pillars of Western culture," ancient Greece was surrounded on three sides by water, including the Aegean Sea to the east, the Ionian Sea to the West and the Mediterranean to the south. Blessed with excellent fishing opportunities and efficient travel routes, the ancient Greeks began to sail to other areas around the Mediterranean and the Aegean Sea and develop their economy. As a result, the overseas trade and commodity economy of ancient

Greece grew rapidly, which helped make its people more and more extroverted.

Moreover, Westerners used to live in a big space composed of many smaller ones. They were not isolated by geography, developing and unavoidably conflicting with one another. Therefore, they had a very strong sense of competition. Since their life style was open, they were disposed to be sociable, paying attention to their own individual roles and looking outward. This orientation has decided their focus–the world outside, which is displayed in their incessant outward expansion. An outward-looking or extroverted culture is thus developed.

Further Reading

1. Holcombe, C. B. (1999). *The Real Chinaman*. New York: Dodd, Mead & Company.
2. Russell, B. (1945). The *History of Western Philosophy*. New York: Simon & Schuster.
3. 辜鸿铭 (2010),《中国人的精神》,李晨曦译. 上海:上海三联书店。
4. 梁漱溟 (2010),《东西文化及其哲学》,北京:商务印书馆。
5. 林语堂 (2000),《吾国与吾民》,北京:外语教学与研究出版社。
6. 饶尚宽译注 (2006),《老子》,北京:中华书局。
7. 芮陶庵 (Andrew T. Roy) (2017),《芮陶庵中国生活回忆录》(*Never a Dull Moment: A Memoir of Family and China*),南京:南京大学出版社。
8. 杨伯峻译注 (1958),《论语》,北京:中华书局。

Unit 3　Affinities Across Cultures

Our most basic common link is that we all inhabit this planet. We all breathe the same air. We all cherish our children's future. And we are all mortal.

—J. F. Kennedy

Are you on the same page as former U.S. President J. F. Kennedy? If yes, why?

Some literary critics say that Chinese literati, especially poets, are mostly disposed to be decadent, which accounts for predominance of Chinese works singing the praises of autumn. Well, the same is true of foreign poets, isn't it? I haven't read much of foreign poetry and prose, nor do I want to enumerate autumn-related poems and essays in foreign literature. But if you browse through collected works of English, German, French or Italian poets, or various countries' anthologies of poetry or prose, you can always come across a great many literary pieces eulogizing or lamenting autumn. Long pastoral poems or songs about the four seasons by renowned poets are mostly distinguished by beautiful moving lines in autumn. All that goes to show that all live creatures and sensitive humans alike are prone to the feeling of depth, remoteness, severity and bleakness. Not only poets, even convicts in prison, I suppose, have deep sentiments in autumn in spite of themselves. Autumn treats all humans alike, regardless of nationality, race or class.

—Yu Dafu

Personally speaking, Yu Dafu's arguments are very sound and presented clearly. For further thought: Can you give more examples to illustrate the affinities between Chinese and Western literature?

… since we are alike under the skin, what touches the human heart in one country touches all.

—Lin Yutang

For more affinities, please read more across cultures.

I. Two Unexpected Affinities

In a lot of languages, the word for "mother" seems often either to be mama, or mom and mum. When it comes to European languages closely related to English, like the Germanic ones, the similarity isn't so surprising. After all, these languages are children of what was once one language called Proto-Into-European. So if French has maman, and Italian has mamma, and Norwegian has mamma, then maybe that's just a family matter. But the point is Chinese, so different from English, French, Italian and Norwegian, has mama, too. What's more, in Africa, Swahilli has mama. Koasati, spoken in Louisiana and Texas in the U.S., turns out to have mamma. Why "mama"? Linguist Roman Jakobson points out that the first syllable babies are usually capable of making "ah" or "mah". These are usually the first sounds babies reach for because they don't require complex mouth positions or the use of tongue or teethe. Moreover, "mah" is associated with the murmuring sound a baby makes when it's breastfeeding.

The answer to the question of why lots of languages have "mama" for the word "mother" is so simple, which somehow reminds us of another unexpected affinity. One day about fifteen years ago we happened to catch sight of American black woman writer Zora Neale Hurston's grave in the segregated cemetery Garden of Heavenly Rest in Ft. Pierce on one of our trips around the U.S. We were surprised to notice a few pennies scattered on the vault. Our friend Dr. Tammy Shadel smiled and explained, "That's a superstition, to throw coins on the gravesite, so the dead won't be broke." As we thought about Hurston's persistent money woes, Tammy added, "She died penniless in 1960, you know." By a remarkable coincidence, we use almost the same way to make sure our beloved ones could enjoy a rich life after death, with the difference that we burn joss paper which we make believe are large notes issued by the so-called Hell Bank and stamped by the legendary King Yama. Thereupon we can see this custom of expressing good wishes for our deceased beloved ones is both Western and Chinese. After all, we are human beings. Though exposed to different cultures we share some of the life experiences and feelings.

II. Reading for More Cultural Affinities

Every day we do lots of reading in Chinese and English, not only for improving our language level, but also for a good mastery of cultural differences as well as affinities such as "A hungry man is an angry man (饿汉易怒)", an English proverb which specifically talks about a man, but actually applies to all people–Chinese and Westerners included. In this unit, the latter is addressed.

1. Affinities in Textual Details

It is crucial that we should pay attention to concrete details in different texts, because differences as well as similarities become prominent on the level of concrete details. Most often we recognize the details and their distinctions in a text by comparing them.

For clarity and convenience, let us consider the official slogan of the 2022 Beijing Winter Olympic Games "Together for a Shared Future (一起向未来)". The Chinese catchphrase carries the Beijing Winter Olympics's expectation of a beautiful future for the world, highlights the sports spirit of indomitability, promotes the Olympic values of unity and peace, and demonstrates the faith and determination in defeating the Covid-19 pandemic together. Although the Chinese verb "*xiang* (向)" is converted into the proposition "for" and "shared" is added to the translation, the English message is as clear as its Chinese version and connotations, expressing support for the world's solidarity and opposition to political confrontation, advocating cooperation while opposing isolationism, encouraging diversity and inclusiveness while opposing populism, and depoliticizing sports while opposing the imposition of ideology in global governance.

2. Thematic Affinities in the Myths

On the ground level of textual details, differences as well as affinities appear prominent, and on the level of total meaning of texts and literary traditions, thematic patterns also emerge to display affinities. Therefore, we never lose anything in comparison insofar as we do not pay attention to thematic patterns at the expense of textual details, or vice versa. Now consider thematic affinities in the water myths of ancient China and the three origins of Western civilization– ancient Greece, Rome and Hebrew. Although Chinese myths form an incoherent corpus, existing in several versions that overlap and conflict, they are no different from the myths of ancient Greece, Rome and Hebrew.

a. Flood Myths

It's common knowledge that flood myths are universal–every culture has one which offers a Year Zero for the construction of genealogies.

Unit 3   Affinities Across Cultures

b. Cultural Heroes in the Flood Myths

Chinese and Western flood myths alike contain at least a culture hero who strives to tame the flood or ensure a rebirth.

It is recorded that the Yellow River flooded during the reign of Emperor Yao and Shun, and people were forced to abandon their villages, and live in trees or on mountaintops. Emperor Yao appointed Gun to harness the flood. Gun built dikes to keep back the water (堵), but failed, and he was sentenced to death. After Gun died, Gun's son Yu was appointed to continue with the flood-harnessing work. Yu adopted the dredging method (疏) to lead the flood waters to flow along river courses into the sea. He worked very hard. It was said that during the 13 years he spent taming the floods, he passed his home three times, but did not enter until his task was completed. As a result of his successful efforts, people bestowed on him the title "Yu the Great (大禹)" and Shun chose Yu as his successor.

However, in the face of the flood, Western ancestors adopted a different attitude. God told Noah to build an ark. Noah did so, and took aboard his family and pairs of all kinds of animals. For 40 days and nights, floodwaters came from the heavens and the deeps until the highest mountains were covered. After a year and 10 days from the start of the flood, everyone and everything emerged from the ark. Noah sacrificed some clean animals and birds to God, and God, pleased with this, promised never again to destroy all living creatures with a flood, giving the rainbow as a sign of this covenant. Animals became wild and some of them became suitable food, and Noah and his family were told to repopulate the earth.

c. A Moral Agency in Floods

In both Chinese and Western flood myths the uncontrolled waters have a moral agency.

In the Noah legend, their message is clear: the waters descend as God's punishment for humankind's wickedness, and only the virtuous man and his family could escape this retribution.

In China, the nature of water itself holds a particularly instructive message. That which causes the flood is violent, untamed, and chaotic: it is "bad" water. And it gets to be this way by a misdeed, a rebellious and criminal act. The stability of society depended on bringing this water under control: channelling and pacifying it, making it orderly and "good". Whoever could do this would be, virtually by definition, a virtuous person. In this way, the taming of the great flood becomes a moral issue: a successful system of control becomes not just a useful but an exemplary action, and the person responsible for this strategy demonstrates a right to rule.

d. Powerful Symbolic Function of the Flood

The image of the flood carries a powerful symbolic function in Chinese and Western mythical stories. In contrast to the creation myths that begin before humans exist and which have an essential role in establishing a universe of gods and heavens, the flood wipes the slate, animal bones or tortoise shells clean for the emergence of human societies and institutions. It supplies a rationale for the mythmakers themselves and a motivation for the establishment of a new covenant between heaven and earth, gods and humankind.

e. Meditations on the Right to Rule

Biblical narrative not only commands the listener to observe proper respect for God's authority, but also imputes a moral superiority, and therefore a right to rule, to the descendants of the survivors.

Every aspect of the Chinese flood myths converged in meditations on the nature of the ruler and the justification of his authority. Fear of disorder and chaos has always haunted China's rulers, but it's understandable that relevant myths were formalized when social order in a time of turmoil turned into a dream.

f. Gods of Water

In Chinese and Greek mythical stories, there are gods of water.

Gong Gong (共工), for instance, is honored as the God of Water and believed to be the earliest flood-control hero. He led people to combat floods bravely and put floods under control by "blocking", rather than "dredging". Though he failed to tackle the root causes, he had accumulated a lot of experience in flood control for later generations. He was also an expert in agriculture and invented the method of "building embankments for water storage" (筑堤蓄水), improving farming productivity. In the Sui and Tang dynasties, dragons responsible for the raining were worshipped as the God of Water, which ruled the seas and other water bodies.

In the ancient Greek myth, Oceanus (俄刻阿诺斯) is worshipped as the God of water. One theory depicts him as the first-born child of Uranus (天宇之神) and Gaea (大地女神), for the formation of the ocean involves the rains from the sky and the streams flowing on the earth, a combined influence of Uranus and Gaea.

g. Sacrifices to the Sea Gods and River Gods

People in coastal areas of China have the tradition of offering sacrifices to Matsu and placing their hope on the Sea Goddess for protection from dangers and a safe voyage. And people in rice-planting culture are always longing for water and worship river gods. For many Chinese people every river has a god or deity, to which sacrifices are offered on a regular basis in case they should be angry. To please them, even human sacrifices were offered, which is recorded in the famous story of "Ximen Bao" which tells about how Ximen Bao stops a superstition of annually offering a young and beautiful girl to the river god known as the Earl of the River as a "bride", otherwise he would flood, destroying crops and houses. Among the numerous river gods that were worshipped by the officials and ordinary people, the four golden dragon kings were the most popular and prevailed. The worship of river gods was regarded by ancient officials as an important method to govern Yellow River floods, and after one river engineering project was finished, building a river god temple with the horizontal inscribed board awarded became an important measure to thank the god.

Ancient Greeks have the same tradition. Whichever theory it is, Oceanus married his sister Tethys, Goddess of the Sea, who gave birth to the three great rivers known to the Greeks, including the Nile in Egypt. They had more than three thousand other children. Each became the minor god or goddess of a river, stream, spring, lake, or pond, accepting prayers and offerings from local people during a memorial event.

3. Allegorical Interpretation of Canonical Works

In the ancient world physical love and sexuality were thought to be detrimental to moral cultivation and social stability. That is why love poems in canonical works have to be interpreted as about anything but physical love. Therefore, when we read about the seemingly passionate love in the "Song of Solomon" of the *Bible*, the Rabbis and Christian fathers would tell us that the text has nothing to do with love between a man and a woman, but the spiritual love between God and Israel, or between God and His Son, Jesus Christ. Verse 1 of the "Song of Solomon" goes:

    This is the greatest song Solomon ever wrote.

    A Shulammite woman says to King Solomon,

Unit 3 Affinities Across Cultures

"I long for your lips to kiss me!

Your love makes me happier than wine does.

The lotion you have on pleases me. Your name is like perfume that is poured out.

No wonder the young women love you!

Take me away with you. Let us hurry!

King Solomon, bring me into your palace!"

The other woman says,

"King Solomon, you fill us with joy. You make us happy.

We praise your love more than we praise wine."

The woman says to the king,

"It is right for them to love you!

Women of Jerusalem,

My skin is dark but lovely,

It is dark like the tents in Kedar.

It's like the curtains of Solomon's tent.

Don't stare at me because I'm dark.

The sun has made my skin look like this.

My brothers burned with anger against me.

They made me take care of the vineyards.

I haven't even taken care of my own vineyard.

King Solomon, I love you.

So tell me where you take care of your flock.

Tell me where you rest your sheep at noon.

Why should I have to act like a prostitute near the flocks of your friends?"

The other women say,

"You are the most beautiful woman of all.

Don't you know where to find the king?

Follow the tracks the sheep make.

Take care of your young goats near the tents of the shepherds."

King Solomon says to the Shulammite woman,

"You are my love.

You are like a mare that pulls one of Pharaoh's chariots.

Your earrings make your cheeks even more beautiful.

Your strings of jewels make your neck even more lovely."

…

The poetry is obviously about the love story of a man and a woman, but many Christian commentators interpret it as a picture of the Church as the Bride of Christ. God loves His only Son and has called out and prepared for him a beautiful virgin bride, "without spot or blemish." If not, how could Solomon who had 700 wives and 300 concubines be the faithful and passionate lover this poem portrays?

When a text is canonized as all-important and providing guidance to truth and proper behavior, it is often necessary to interpret it allegorically to defend it against possible challenges to its canonical status. This is not only true of the "Song of Solomon" in the West, but also of the Confucian classics in China. Take, for instance, the first poem "Cooing and Wooing" in *Shi Jing* or the *Book of Poetry*, one of the five Confucian classics:

By the riverside are cooing

A pair of turtledoves;

A good young man is wooing

A pretty maiden he loves.

Water flows left and right
Of cress long here, short there;
The youth yearns day and night
For the good maiden fair.

His yearning grows so strong,
He cannot fall asleep,
But tosses all night long,
So deep in love, so deep!

Now gather left and right
Cress long or short and tender!
O lute, play music bright
For the bride sweet and slender!

Feast friends at left and right
On cress cooked till tender!
O bells and drums, delight
The bride so sweet and slender!

(Tr. by Xu Yuanchong)

When we read "Cooing and Wooing" about the cry of a lovebird in the islet of a river and a young man wooing a pretty girl, Confucian scholars would tell us that the poem is not about love between a man and a woman, but about the virtue of a good queen whose only desire is to find people with virtue and talents and have all of them serve her king.

4. Incorporation of the Material World into the Rhetoric Device

All cultures tend to incorporate their material world into the rhetoric they use for living, and natural elements like water, fire and plants are particularly rich and versatile media for doing so. Take metaphor for instance. Metaphors involve talking and thinking about one thing in terms of another, on the basis of perceived similarities or correspondences between them. We use them to make sense of and communicate about new, complex, abstract and sensitive experiences in terms of more familiar, simpler and accessible ones. For example, the unrealistic desire has been described as a flood or water to be tamed.

a. Water Metaphors

"Water! Oh, water!" Confucius exclaimed. But what did he mean by it? What was so admirable about water? Mencius, the most celebrated of the great master's interpreters, tried to explain it as describing the quality of a ***junzi*** or gentleman who is ashamed of an exaggerated reputation. Water for the Chinese is itself a virtuous substance, bearing a force of moral instruction. "Water is the highest good," wrote Laozi in the *Dao De Jing*, the foundational work of Daoism. Not only did daily experience of water provide metaphors for Chinese philosophical thought, but also the philosophy in turn influenced practical affairs: There evolved an intimate connection between hydraulic engineering, governance, moral rectitude and metaphysical speculation.

This situation in itself is not unique to China. French philosopher Gaston Bachelard has identified many of water's mythic associations: it cleanses, purifies, nurtures and destroys. Narcissus loses himself in the water's placid mirror. It is a deathly embrace. "Too much of water hast thou, poor Ophelia," Laertes laments in *The Tragedy of Hamlet, Prince of Denmark* by William

Shakespeare. Nothing in all this seems to distinguish Chinese thought as unusual in its readiness to reach for water images.

b. Fire Metaphors

There exist abundant metaphorical expressions which make use of the concept of fire in both English and Chinese.

According to physiology, there exist some physical and psychological changes when people get angry: the face turns red, the breath becomes short, the heart beats fast, the body temperature rises, the blood runs faster and the blood pressure even gets higher. All these changes lead to intense heat in an angry one's body as if he or she were on fire. Besides, a fire rises in an upward direction. Thus there are **fire up** and **flame up** in English and *maohuo* (冒火 to describe anger), *huomaosanzhang* (火冒三丈 to describe how one flies into a rage), *wuming zhihuo* (无名之火 to describe a nameless anger), and *nuhuo zhongshao* (怒火中烧to describe how one bursts into anger) in Chinese. In addition to these examples, there are many idioms in both English and Chinese, such as **sexual desire is fire** and **intensity of a fire** in English and *yuhuo zhongshao* (欲火中烧 to describe a strong sexual desire), *ganchai liehuo* (干柴烈火 to describe the strong sexual desire between men and women) and *tianlei dihuo* (天雷地火 to describe the great degree of love in the lovers) in Chinese.

c. Plant Metaphors

Many abstract concepts are conveyed through plant metaphors in Chinese and English. For example, **The spoken word is often flowery and vague**. In Chinese, there is *huashao* (花哨) used to describe the spoken language which is complicated, rhetoric and elaborated with decorative details. Besides, there are metaphoric expressions such as **the investment woods** and **in full bloom** in English, and **tree of life** (生命之树) and **flower of love** (爱情之花) in Chinese.

In ancient Nanjing, there was once such a practice. If their friends were to walk southward out of the city, locals would see them off to Changganli where they would pick a willow branch as a parting gift to show their unwillingness to leave each other. The convention of "picking willow branches at Changganli (长干折柳)" has something to do with the metaphoric meaning of willow branches. In the English context, the idiom "weeping willow" means "to lose a lover", which is a metaphorical meaning derived from the British custom of wearing wicker hats to express sorrow.

5. Depiction of Evil Characters in Literature

The approximately similar depiction of evil characters has been found in stories, for instance, about stepmothers who are given a negative connotation in both Chinese and Western literature. Contrasts in personality and physical traits between the biological daughter and the stepmother often appear to be an element in many Chinese and Western folktales like *Cinderella* where Cinderella is beautiful and soft-featured compared to the persnickety stepmother. The stepmother not only looks mean, but also has much sharper features. By and large, stepmothers are portrayed as evil and self-centered. They lack self-control, exhibiting hostility and acting on their passions without regard for anyone else's concern.

Stepmothers in Chinese and Western stories are also depicted as torturers of their stepchildren. Snow White's evil stepmother tried every means to kill her. Minzi (闵子), one of Confucius' students was maltreated by his evil stepmother when he was little. In winter, the stepmother and her biological son were well-fed and clothed, but Minzi had to go to bed on an empty stomach and had nothing to keep himself warm.

It is interesting that stepfathers in both Chinese and Western folktales possess an opposite character in contrast to the wicked stepmother. The kind stepfather gracefully accepts his stepchildren and treats them as his own. With loving arms, he mercifully takes in his new wife, often an unwed-mother and her illegitimate children.

III. A Note on Some Key Concepts

1. "Affinities Across Cultures"

Far from simply calling for respect for our culture and other cultures, scholars have scrutinized texts in both Chinese and English and tried to forge links between the two cultures. This effort may first of all provide readers with a new perspective on multicultural issues–with appreciation and understanding rather than tolerance or hatred. Cultural commensurability provides a solid ground for the mutual respect of different cultures and unites cultural traditions.

Secondly, a focus on affinities across Chinese and Western cultures may help the reader to appreciate the essence of human creativity and the richness of human imagination as well as expressions beyond the gaps of language, race, time, and space.

Thirdly, the comparison and contrast made with the intention to see the commonality between Chinese and Western cultures may serve as a springboard for readers to study the cultural and textual encounters between China and the West. Similar efforts in the future will surely uncover many other unexpected affinities of concepts, expressions, themes and character depictions that are drowned in different texts.

2. "Uniqueness", "Differences", "Similarities" and "Frictions"

a. "Uniqueness"

The idea of uniqueness is very useful because uniqueness means being the only one of its kind, having no parallels or comparisons, although it is very difficult to find anything culturally significant that qualifies as something truly unique.

b. "Differences"

Difference is another matter, for it does not imply the only one in the universe, simply not exactly the same. In this sense, we do find many significant differences between East and West. Culinary art, for example, is obviously different. From ingredients and cooking methods to the way food is prepared, presented and served on the table there are remarkable differences. This is by no means a trivial case, because food is perhaps more culturally specific than anything else in our daily life. The fact that food is a basic necessity in our daily life helps us realize that differences become prominent on the level of concrete details of things in reality rather than the conceptual level of ideas and themes. In China people often share the dishes at the table, but Westerners have their own plates individually. Not that there can be no sharing in the West, nor that individualism does not exist in China, but the way food is served may help us reflect on the different ways individualism and collectivism manifest themselves in China and the West. As long as we do not draw extreme conclusions from comparison, we may get some insight into different degrees of emphasis in different cultures.

c. "Differences and Similarities"

We can talk about differences only when we put things together in comparison, which means that differences and similarities are inseparable and always mutually implicated.

There are of course more differences on a more concrete level. For example, it is believed that classical Chinese literature does not have long epic poems and most dramas tend to have happy endings unlike many Western tragedies. In folk literature and oral traditions, however, long heroic epics do exist in some of China's minority cultures; it is too simplified to say that tragedy with unhappy endings is uniquely Western. For instance, Greek tragedies do not necessarily end in death or suffering. We can talk about the tragic in a broad sense, that is, the sense of being in a position to bring about suffering and death not totally of one's own doing, like a building driven away by a flood because of its height. If so, we may find many works in Chinese literature that give expression to precisely that sense of the tragic. For instance, the untimely death of Zhou Yu, the famous general of the state of Wu during the Three Kingdoms period, is a result of his narrow-mindedness.

We need to closely examine what seems to be, on the surface, very different between two cultures, look for thematic affinities and conceptual similarities under those differences, and then we will find some points of convergence as a point of departure in intercultural communication.

d. "Differences and Frictions"

It is indisputable that there are huge differences between civilizations, which have occasionally engendered frictions. But it is misleading and dangerous to magnify such frictions into world political clashes and wars. After all, one man's meat is another man's poison (各花入各眼).

In a diversified world, it is only natural that different civilizations should co-exist. Chinese scholars have been stressing complementarities among different cultures, holding that it is necessary to draw on each other's strong points so as to make progress together. Just as the official Chinese document *Outline for Strengthening Patriotic Education in the New Era* (《新时代爱国主义教育实施纲要》) states when it elaborates on patriotism, "Patriotism is not narrow nationalism. We need not only to inherit and develop the fine heritages of the Chinese people, but also to study and absorb the civilizations created by other nations, including capitalist nations. Only by so doing can the Chinese people make their due contributions to world peace and human progress along with other nations."

While acknowledging cultural differences makes it clear that "this is a difference of degree, not of kind," it should be emphasized that there is a common cultural ground on which people from West and East can stand, make meaningful comparisons and hence communicate effectively on an equal footing. In a fluid world, all nations should show appreciation and respect for each other and develop together. Each of us must keep an open mind, listen to other parties, and be ready to accept what is true. This should be the case not only of interpersonal dialogue, but of intercultural communication as well.

3. Ethnocentrism

Ethnocentrism refers to the attitude that one's own group, ethnicity, or nationality is superior to others. Cultures train their members to use the categories of their own cultural experiences when judging the experiences of people from other cultures and thus they tend to believe that their culture is the center of the world and their standard should be the role model for the rest of the world.

According to British sinologist Martin Jacques in his TED speech of 2011, "Our attitude towards China is that of a kind of little Westerner mentality. It's kind of arrogant in the sense that we think that we are the best and therefore we have the universal measure. And secondly it's ignorance. We refuse to really address the issue of differences; the West thinks of itself as probably the most cosmopolitan of all cultures. But it is not. In many ways, it's the most parochial because for 200 years the West has been so dominant in the world that it is not really needed to understand other cultures because at the end of the day it could, if necessary, by force get its own way."

Further Reading

1. Bradford, R. (1994). *Roman Jakobson: Life, Language and Art.* London: Routledge.
2. Churchill, W. S. & Gilbert, M. (2016). *Churchill: The Power of Words.* New York: Bantam.
3. Goatly, A. (1997). *The Language of Metaphors.* London: Rutledge.
4. Lakoff, G. & Johnson, M. (1980). *Metaphors We Live By.* Chicago, IL: University of Chicago Press.
5. Zhang, L.X. (2007). *Unexpected Affinities: Reading Across Cultures.* Toronto: University of Toronto Press.
6. 辜正坤 (2007),《中西文化比较导论》,北京：北京大学出版社。
7. 梁漱溟 (1987),《中国文化要义》,上海：学林出版社。
8. 许渊冲译 (2004),《汉英对照中国古诗精品三百首》,北京：北京大学出版社。

Part II
Cultural Differences in Silent Language

Language is spoken verbally or non-verbally. The language which is spoken non-verbally through time, space, and the information sender's body movements such as smiling, nodding, frowning and silence is known as silent language. Even silent materials in nature like water are probably telling us more than they seem. Rooted in daily life, water in China does much more than symbolize yearning, loss and sorrow; it speaks to the highest aspirations and ideas.

Silent language is subjective, so it is probably the hardest language to learn. You may assume it is easy to become part of the culture when you go to Germany if you are fluent in German. But even if you can speak perfect German, sometimes you find yourself unable to express yourself non-verbally in ways that the locals understand and carry in business and personal transactions. This causes communication breakdowns and misunderstandings in your interaction with locals because you speak a different silent language–although you speak perfect German.

How fluent can you be in a silent foreign language, then? The good news is: It is a learned art. The bad news is: There is no course that could help. As with all things, practice is the secret to getting better and becoming more sensitive to cultural differences in silent languages.

In this part, time which often talks silently but differently in different cultures will be explored in Unit 4; different cultural expressions in the spatial language employed in social interaction and architecture will be discussed in Unit 5; body movements like smiles, nods and silence in different cultures will be investigated in Unit 6.

Unit 4 Time

Empires come and go, but the rivers and mountains remain.

—**A Chinese saying**

Many cultures have made a stream or river a symbol of time–of change and transience, but also of longevity and permanence. Chinese poets and philosophers were humbled by the knowledge that the great rivers had flowed from their source to the seas since long before they walked on earth, and would do so long after they had gone. For further personal exploration and enlightenment: Look for Chinese proverbs that are at variance with the above saying.

American born, Zhu Diwen is of course a very "Americanized" scientist. He impresses others with his self-confident, humorous and witty conversation, while remaining refined and cultivated. With his informal attire and satchel clasped behind his back, Zhu looks no different from other young men. His amiable and witty style of conversation has closed the gap between master and the students. Throughout the past half month of media events, Zhu was seen dressed in Western-style clothes only when he met Jiang Zemin.

—**A news report in 1997**

Zhu Diwen, a Nobel-prize winner, struck people as informally dressed, but when meeting with important officials he was formally dressed to show respect, as he wished to act, dress and be perceived as a professional.

Suppose you are advising a friend who is going to spend some time abroad, explain to him what changes he will need to make in his dressing when interacting with different kinds of people and why.

I. Time in China and the West

Time, though a silent language, often talks loudly but differently in different cultures.

1. Chinese Time and Western Time

Unlike the discrete and clearly-defined Western system of time, traditionally there were no very specific rules for time in China. Even if there were some in some cases, they would not be listened to very seriously.

a. Chinese Time

Traditional Chinese time springs from inside. It is an inside force that helps people plan their lives, which is revealed in the aphorism, "One who does not work hard in youth will grieve in vain in old age." It is widely believed that if all day is spent merely chatting idly, saying unreasonable things and showing off his cleverness, one will accomplish little and have a miserable life when old. In spite of that, time is seldom experienced as "wasted". Instead, the "wasted" time is usually regarded as taking a break, catching a breath, making preparations or accumulating energy so that one day when one's chance comes he will seize it and become successful and world-famous overnight, just as the idiom goes, "An insignificant person who appears to be wasting his time will amaze the world with his successful maiden efforts (不飞则已，一飞冲天；不鸣则已，一鸣惊人)."

In such a culture, time is therefore not accurately calculated and carefully considered. Strictly speaking, there is no time concept at all at times. So after he has had a conversation with a person, a Chinese scholar would say with a sigh, "Talking with you for one night is better than studying books for ten years." *Chan* (禅宗), practiced by many Chinese, aims to attune the Buddhist disciple's self inside himself to nature by suggesting "eating when hungry and sleeping when tired", not encouraging himself to accurately plan his time. And the ideal life which has been aspired for thousands of years is to "labor at sunrise and rest at sunset".

Because of the inexact calculation of time, promptness is not valued so highly in traditional China, which is reflected in imperatives like **Eat slowly** at dinner table, partings like **Walk slowly**, and comforting like **Study slowly** and **Take your time** when comforting students who have been suffering academic setbacks. So to speak, promptness sometimes refers to immaturity, recklessness, and danger.

Preoccupied with leisurely life, traditional Chinese associate the past with the future, which explains why Chinese time has been treated very much like a mirror. One can observe himself in it and check up on his outfit, hair and face to see if anything goes wrong. On the other hand, one can see his past in it and remind himself to avoid repeating mistakes in the future, just as Emperor Taizong of the Tang dynasty said, "Using history as a mirror allows one to see the future trends."

In a culture which pays so special attention to the past, forgetting one's past nearly means negating one's past. Chinese are used to looking back. For many of us the past is the best teacher: What happened in the past is still relevant today. Since very ancient times, the Chinese have possessed an unusual passion and respect for the past. According to historical records even the earliest dynasties appointed historian officials. The Chinese historian official was believed to be very trustworthy, because he was trained and required to be objective and he based what he wrote on government files of memorials, edicts, court decisions and other papers, and since he worked in an official capacity he had access to the dependable first-hand written material. If he wished to write down his own judgments, which he seldom did, he usually marked them so that the reader could readily recognize them. Like the royal houses, Confucianism encouraged and developed a sense of history and respect for the past. Two of the five Confucian classics, the *Book of History* (《尚书》) and the *Spring and Autumn Annals* (《春秋》), supposedly compiled and edited by Confucius himself, are history works, transmit information and give moral lessons. Since ancient times, the study of history has always been a major part of Chinese education and citing historical examples has traditionally been among the principal techniques of Chinese argumentation and persuasion.

Meanwhile, history is regarded as a cyclical succession of eras arranged in a fixed order by the Chinese philosophy of history, which is also deeply influenced by Daoist theories. Not only eras, but also all of the history changes, grow and decay in the form of a cyclical succession. This view is shared by many, just as famous Hong Kong entertainer Andy Lou (i.e. Liu Dehua) sings, "The flower has withered, but it will blossom again next year as usual." In other words, time is handled as if it were part of a rotating circle, coming and going on a regular basis.

b. Western Time

In Western society time is imposed from outside. As an outside force, it helps people to organize their lives, for instance, there are schedules to tell them what to do and when. In this culture, those who cannot schedule time are thought of as impractical.

Unit 4　Time

For Westerners, time is a line that has segments kept discrete for "one thing at a time", moving ceaselessly forward. Therefore, Westerners tend to look ahead and are oriented almost entirely toward the future.

As late as even today, the ancient Greek sense of curiosity about the future is still very striking. Ancient Greeks liked new things and were preoccupied with change and the future. They wanted to know how to overcome resistance to change the future so much so that scientific theories and even some pseudo-scientific ones were often given much attention. Gradually, they came to realize that the desire for change needs to be satisfied by segmenting time and handling it like a single perishable material.

Since time is treated as if it were a perishable material, it can be earned, saved, spent, squandered, wasted, killed, run short or out of. Therefore, it should be accurately calculated and carefully considered. And it is sort of immoral, rude or improper to have two things going on at once on many occasions. In China the popularity of specialties such as instant-boiled mutton, Sichuan spicy hotpot and Guangdong seafood hotpot owes much to "more than one thing at a time"– allowing or requiring eaters to cook while eating, talking and having fun.

Promptness, though disfavored in traditional China, is therefore highly valued in Western life, which is conveyed in dictums like "Punctuality is the politeness of kings" and "Punctuality is the soul of business." If people are not prompt or punctual, the unpunctuality or non-promptness is often taken either as an insult or as an indication that they are not quite responsible, which makes them deem it necessary to put activities into a time frame for they are time-bound.

Westerners feel so strongly about time that they have stressed this aspect of culture and developed it to a point unmatched anywhere in the world, especially in America, Switzerland and Germany. No wonder their handling of time is much criticized and many people attribute ulcers, diabetes, and hypertension to the pressure engendered by such a time system.

2. Two Views on Time

a. The Circular View

Traditional Chinese look upon time as the rotation of a circle, going round and round ceaselessly. This circular outlook on time is revealed in classical literary writings. Qu Yuan, a noted patriotic poet of the Warring States period, wrote in his masterpiece *The Lament* (《离骚》), "The sun alternates with the moon; autumn returns after spring soon (日月忽其不淹兮，春与秋其代序)." For him time is not a one-way ticket, but a back-and-forth rotation like the endless cycle of the four seasons. Many Chinese scholars also lament that time goes quickly just as Confucius, standing by the river, said "Time passes by like this, flowing away day and night (子在川上曰：逝者如斯夫，不舍昼夜)", but meanwhile they believe that it will come back soon as spring and autumn do. The circular view results in a sense of the abundance of time and accordingly doing things in an unhurried manner and making up for the lost time as time rotates is encouraged. Although we also sigh over "time waiting for no one (Tao Yuanming)" and feel "regret for the negligent loss of time (Han Yu)", yet we expect the favor of the time cycle and the shift from bad to good luck.

We hold the view of time as a cycle, and naturally cherish and revere the past. Hence we have been taught to keep diaries to record what has been done in the past even each day in order "to engage in introspection every day on three points". So we constantly reflect on our past behavior and try to find out whether we have done anything offending or shunned our responsibilities so that we could improve ourselves the next day.

On the whole, the circular view encourages respect for the past, an unhurried leisurely life style, and the practice of doing more than one thing at a time.

b. The Linear View

Westerners tend to look upon time as a line moving towards the future and never returning, and therefore hold the future in high regard and carefully plan for it.

Just because they hold a linear view of time, Westerners have a strong sense of the shortage of time. They say time flies; they say time and tide wait for no man and thus quicken their pace of life and habitually look ahead. That explains why Westerners are used to marking in their calendars what is to be done in the future and focusing much of their attention on planning for themselves. Future-oriented, they are inclined to defy authorities and enjoy working on something new instead of following the established routine.

On the whole, the linear view encourages respect for the future and the practice of doing one thing at a time.

II. Two Time Modes

Based on his study, American anthropologist Edward T. Hall has termed doing more than one thing at a time "Polychronic" or "P-time". Inspired by Hall's research, we group Chinese time into the category of Polychronic time since the Chinese system involves several things at once. Hall has termed doing one thing at a time "Monochronic" or "M-time". Since M-time emphasizes schedules, segmentation and promptness, the North American time system is classified by Hall as a Monochronic one. The two time modes are logically and empirically quite distinct.

1. P-time

a. Polychronic Chinese

In China, there are some typical environments such as the food stand on the street corner, where the stand owner is often seen trying to serve a group of people at once. Usually there is no recognizable order as to who is to be served next, no queue or sequence to indicate whose order has not been handled. For first-time Western visitors, it appears a riot is breaking out. However, it is normal in China that some people don't form lines. Instead they form "huddles" around the stand owner, ticket booth, or office clerks since Polychronic people are used to interacting with several persons at one time and are continually involved with each other whether at home or in the workplace. Tight scheduling or scheduling ahead of time is therefore difficult in some cases.

b. Cultural Features of the P-time Mode

This mode or "more than one thing at a time" system has affected the flow of information, the shape and form of the networks connecting people, and even helped to develop a host of important cultural phenomena such as **one item with multiple functions, one organization with multiple obligations**, and **a jacket for different occasions**. A middle-aged professor recalled in her classroom one day that "There was only one knife in my mother's kitchen when I was little. My mother used it to peel potatoes and sugar canes, slice pork and fish, cut noodle dough and firewood, and even sharpen pencils." Today some Chinese, though no longer poor and isolated from the outside world, are seen to be formally dressed in suits, ties and leather shoes when they do sports, go sightseeing or fishing. And some of us use the dishwasher as a dish rack and eat three meals a day in the kitchen where we prepare food and cook.

The most striking feature of the P-time mode is the "killing-two-birds-with-one-arrow" mentality. For instance, we used to use jam jars as drinking glasses or vases and whip eggs with chopsticks. Take for another instance the age-old advice about cooking which says: "When you prepare a dish, you must keep three things in mind: It must be pleasing to the eye, the aroma must be appealing, and it must be appetizing." For this reason, you can expect that each Chinese dish, whether the most economical or the most elaborate, will always be colorful, have a delightful aroma or at least taste delicious. And we sincerely believe in the old proverb "Good food brings happiness". What is implied is that food not only satisfies our hunger, but also serves as an excuse for people to socialize together, an occasion for family members to communicate, and an opportunity for a good chef to show off.

The third characteristic that might have arisen out of the Polychronic "more than one thing at a time" is the practice of "a clever-rabbit-digs-three-holes-for-future-use". For instance, we love to store goods just like we keep a thermos of hot water available at all times. Similar practice can guarantee at least one way out even if the most terrible thing should happen.

The fourth characteristic is that Polychronic individuals are oriented toward people, human relationships and family. In this culture, scheduling is not so valued since all the members have to be considered and what's more, anything might happen to any member at any moment. Caden is an American of Chinese descent. Six months ago he got a job in Nanjing. His relatives in Changzhou told him he was welcome to visit them at any time and the intercity high-speed rail network would make it convenient and fast for him to commute between the two cities. He stayed with them for two weekends but did not enjoy himself. He found it hard to spend his time with his relatives because he never knew what was planned until he was hurried to go out to eat or visit some places. He did not like to "be kept in the dark". Nurtured in Western culture, Caden failed to know that his relatives didn't tell him their plan because time cannot be considered carefully and thus things are so constantly changing in a medium-sized city like Changzhou that sometimes plans are found unable to be realized until the last second. In this sense, their silence about their weekend plan had nothing to do with their intention to keep him in the dark. Planning something early in China does not really mean that it is to happen since time is not handled so seriously that things are very likely to be out of our control. As a result, we Chinese are accustomed to planning late in our daily lives so that the plan can be realized.

2. M-time

a. Monochronic Westerners

"God has made man himself a creature of time." Time is so thoroughly integrated into Western society that it is treated as though it were the only natural and logical way of organizing life. For instance, people don't make an early morning call unless it is about a matter of utmost importance and extreme urgency; they don't make a phone call during sleeping hours unless the message involves a terrible secret or life and death.

Monochronism means doing one thing at a time. For most Westerners the ideal world is where they can center their attention first on one thing and then move on to the next. Scheduling makes it possible for them to concentrate on one thing at a time. Karl May is a German conducting business in Nanjing. When his meeting with a high-ranking official in the office was constantly interrupted, he felt upset and started wondering whether the official was as important as he was led to believe, and he even started to doubt how seriously his business was being taken. In his culture, such a meeting is usually uninterrupted for it is usually held in a closed office or a secluded place for privacy.

The "one thing at a time" system has deeply affected the Western division of time. To save energy and make better use of daylight in summer, New Zealand time uses "Daylight Saving", with clocks put forward one hour to GMT+13. To make it easy to calculate and plan their time, Americans have divided their country into nine standard time zones covering all the states and their possessions. The time zone boundaries are under the authority of the Department of Transportation. Official and highly precise time keeping services are provided by two federal time agencies: a department of commerce agency, the National Institute of Standards and Technology (NIST), and its military counterpart, the United States Naval Observatory (USNO). The clocks run by these services are kept highly synchronized with each other as well as with those of international time keeping organizations.

b. Cultural Features of the M-time Mode

The M-time mode has extended beyond the field of time. Take, for instance, the social world where people often have many friends at one time. Friendships in this mode are usually tied to specific circumstances or activities, so there are car-pool friends, leisure activity friends, neighborhood friends, etc. When they change circumstances and activities, they change friends.

The second feature that might have arisen out of the Monochronic "one thing at a time" mode is the existence of a "one-to-one" relationship. For example, in the Western kitchen a utensil is usually invented or bought for one purpose. Hence there is the fruit knife, the bread knife, the vegetable knife, the pizza knife, the pencil sharpener, etc., quite contrary to the traditional Chinese use of a kitchen knife for cutting, peeling or sharpening almost everything in sight.

The "one thing at a time" mode has found its way into such organizations as factories. The assembly line invented in America in the early 20th century is still striking today. The assembly line in the factory refers to a manufacturing process in which interchangeable parts are added to a product in a sequential manner, greatly reducing labor costs and thus contributing a lot to Western prosperity. Without the mode of M-time, Western societies might not be what they are today.

Another characteristic that might come out of the "one thing at a time" mode is that people make appointments for almost everything, for instance, with their doctors for a session, professors for problems or even hairdressers for hair beauty. Hypothetically, a Monochronic reporter has made an appointment to interview a Polychronic businessman at 1 pm. At 1 pm precisely she will call at his house and will probably be surprised to find that several members of the businessman's family are visiting him. In circumstances like this, the businessman will feel compelled to invite the reporter to join the party. As a result, the reporter who has scheduled her time very carefully will feel annoyed– she wants to conduct the planned interview straight away. The man has no alternative because if he does not entertain his family regardless of the schedule, the result might be endless criticism from his family. As a consequence, he will have to lose a good opportunity to promote his business.

The fourth characteristic is that time is handled as if it were an opportunity that might never come back again. Questions like "**How often do you see Warren Buffett on the street**" are asked when emphasizing the importance of opportunities. To seize the opportunity, people are taught how to make their case in 30 seconds or less because "the 30-second parameter is based on the typical attention span"(Milo O. Frank). That's a reason why the standard commercial or television "sound bite" in the West lasts 30 seconds.

3. Blending of P-time and M-time

Now all cultures with high technologies seem to incorporate both Polychronic and Monochronic functions. The point is each does it in its own way. Chinese remain Polychronic when looking inward–toward ourselves. But when dealing with Westerners, some Chinese are beginning to shift to the dominant Monochronic time mode which characterizes Western society.

Some Westerners are both Monochronic and Polychronic, too. The French are Monochronic intellectually but Polychronic in behavior. On the surface, American time is Monochronic, but in a deeper sense it is both Polychronic and Monochronic. M-time dominates the official world of business, government, entertainment, and sports. However, at home, particularly the more traditional home in which a woman is the core around which everything revolves, P-time takes over. How else can a woman raise several children, run a house, hold a job, and be a wife, mother, nurse, house maid, tutor, and chauffeur at one time?

Of course, not all M-time and P-time are exactly the same. There are tight and loose versions of each. The banks and joint ventures in Polychronic China provide an excellent example of tight M-time. The pattern is not too different from schedules for office workers in the West. The difference is that in China the tightly scheduled Monochronic pattern is applied to foreigners who are not well integrated into the Chinese time mode, where the emphasis is on developing a good working relationship and where safety is highly valued, for instance depositing and withdrawing money from the cashier, the bank counter or ATM.

4. Strengths and Weaknesses of P-time and M-time

Both M-time and P-time modes have strengths as well as weaknesses.

a. Strengths and Weaknesses of P-time

P-time culture is by its very nature people-oriented. Actually, polychronic

Chinese are so deeply immersed in each other that we feel a need to keep in touch and have a good knowledge of each other, which makes our interactions very humane and warm, greatly reducing the sense of isolation, loneliness, and depression. As a matter of fact, our relationship with others is the very core of our existence, which has naturally formed a society of acquaintances where human warmth is easily accessible.

However, we depend on having gifted people at the top, and hence are slow and clumsy when dealing with something new or different. Without talented people at the top, a P-time bureaucracy would be a disaster sometimes. Because leaders deal simultaneously with many people, most of them stay informed about what is going on. So when considering setting up organizations, people exposed to P-time modes theoretically demand a much greater centralization of power, which may give officials more power than they need.

Many scholars believe that the principal weakness of P-time is the forming of bureaucracies. As functions increase, there is a proliferation of small bureaucracies not set up to handle the problems of outsiders. Actually the outsider traveling or residing in a place outside his own society of acquaintances sometimes finds the bureaucracies cumbersome and unresponsive and assumes that one has to be an insider or have a friend or *guanxi* who can make things happen.

b. Strengths and Weaknesses of M-time

Monochronic Western culture is oriented to schedules, tasks, and procedures. Schedules can and frequently do cut things short just when they are beginning to go well. For example, investment funds run out just as the results are beginning to emerge. Orientation to tasks and procedures helps to make it likely for Monochronic organizations to become large and profitable, but the weakness is their blindness to the humanity of their members. "As anyone who has had experience with Western bureaucracies knows, tasks and procedures attach no importance to either logic or human needs, which is at least partially responsible for the reputation of American business being cut off from human beings and unwilling to recognize the importance of employee morale." (Edward T. Hall)

III. Past-oriented Societies vs. Future-oriented Societies

Different views on time and different time modes help to build two kinds of societies: One is past-oriented and the other is future-oriented.

1. Past-oriented Societies

> How many dynasties have risen and fallen
> In the course of long centuries
> And history goes on
> Endless as the swift-flowing Yangtze. (千古兴亡多少事？悠悠。不尽长江滚滚流。)

The 13th-century Song general Xin Qiji mused as he sat in retirement on Beigu Mountain in Zhenjiang, a peak celebrated in the *Romance of the Three Kingdoms*, and therefore redolent of times past.

Like Xin Qiji, Chinese people today enjoy talking about historical events that took place a hundred or even a thousand years ago. We often look back to the Tang dynasty when Chinese culture was at the height of its power and glory, and some of us like quoting honored philosophers and leaders from the past in debates or arguments. The policy-makers, when first introducing a new policy, may compare it to a historical event or support it with a quotation from a respected leader or philosopher of the past so as to give the policy more authority, because ordinary people may feel more secure when something new is defined as similar to something that occurred in the past.

The respect for the past in China is most obviously displayed in the cult of filial piety at the Han court where it was a mark of respect for the emperor to his imperial ancestors and especially to the founder of the Han dynasty that a ruler maintained intact the institutions inherited from them. Especially in the later ages of the Han dynasty, this proved a strong deterrent to institutional reform. Innovators could not easily set aside such dynastic precedents. To do so was equal to a behavior of impiety toward the emperor's forebears.

In China today, the past is kept alive not only in language, TV theatres, films, dramas, stories, music and dance, religious practice and customs, which enables people to know their history, but also in creating a park or mausoleum. More recently, a park has been built on a cliff face overlooking a Yellow River Dam. It is dedicated to Yu the Great depicted as a gigantic Hercules-like figure standing watch over China's most notorious torrent. The glorification of Yu is part of a rehabilitation of our traditional past. Every Qingming Festival, the "Grave-sweeping Day" on which ancestors are honored, celebrations in Shaoxing, said to be where Yu died and was buried, are reported to include "ancient rituals" to venerate the water hero.

2. Future-oriented Societies

In future-oriented societies, people feel less need to rewrite or reinterpret their history, probably because they believe "No man is rich enough to buy back his past" (Oscar Wilde). In these societies conquering the limitations of the past or surpassing the accomplishments of the past are good reasons for them to take a new unbeaten trail.

Western society is described as future-oriented. The past is studied by people to find trends and patterns since the causes of present and future conditions can be found in the past, and it is considered useful to investigate them in order to create a better future. With such an understanding, the Germans have been honest in their culpability: Students continue to take field trips to WWII concentration camps. But people may have negative expectations for the future and their efforts may be directed at preparing for or preventing bad times ahead. This is revealed in predictions about future consequences if financial problems are not solved or the spread of panic of an epidemic is not stopped.

Westerners usually plan for their future. They set goals and outline specific steps for reaching the goals. Children even as young as 10 years old are encouraged to plan their careers at school in their Career Class, working people plan their summer vocations or even their retirement, and managers want to know the personal plans of their employees. Their attitude is that people act today because that action is a step toward the future they are preparing for. For many of them the past is of less use and the future is something to move them forward. Just as Hillary Clinton said in her exit speech in 2008, "Every moment wasted looking back keeps us from moving forward." Her attitude implies that the future can be controlled if the past is forgotten and some actions are taken today.

3. Yasukuni Shrine Visit

In future-oriented societies time is linear, which means that it moves only in one direction–from the past to the future. In past-oriented societies people are more likely to experience time as the rotation of a circle repeating itself. They may pay more attention to daily, seasonal, and historical cycles than people from future-oriented societies do. Different sense of time makes it hard for Westerners to understand the controversy over the notorious Yasukuni shrine visit.

Yasukuni Shrine is the place where 14 Class A war criminals were enshrined after World War II. The shrine is not run by the state and it is not a cemetery. There are no bones, ashes, graves, graveyards or headstones. Only the souls of the dead are "placed" there. In a book entitled *Talk of Ancestors* published in 1946 the author Kunio Yanagita states, "After death, the soul remains eternally upon this land. It is believed that the soul does not travel to a distant world. This faith has endured for centuries until the present day…" That can explain why Japanese prime ministers' visit to ghosts enshrined in this war-linked place has been regarded to be hurting the feelings and dignity of the Asian countries which fell victim to Japanese aggression during WWII. Our strong indignation also comes from the fact that the Japanese government and its leaders have never officially said sorry to Chinese victims. Besides, some Japanese leaders have over and over again stirred up troubles on the history issue and made inappropriate remarks related to Taiwan, which has made us very concerned that the period of history might be repeated. Like Japan, Germany brought disasters to European people, but it said sorry officially and was forgiven and thus a new page was opened for European history, although their historical perspective sometimes can influence perceptions: It is reported that in Germany, one global delivery service found employees reluctant to wear the company's brown uniforms, because the Nazis wore brown uniforms, and "brown shirt" was a synonym for fascist.

IV. Two Time Orientations

Different sense of time naturally leads to two different time orientations. One is long-term, the other short-term.

1. Long-term vs. Short-term Orientations

A culture with a long-term orientation is of characteristics such as adapting traditions to the modern context, being sparing with resources, saving, accepting slow results, and respecting demands of virtue. The long-term orientation emphasizes patience and a long-term plan. People with long-term orientation believe that "worries will soon appear if one gives no thought to a long-term plan (人无远虑，必有近忧)", so they rear children for old age, and save food for crop failure.

A culture with a short-term orientation is of the following characteristics: respecting tradition, keeping up with the times, spending more and saving less, expecting quick results, seeking truth, etc. The short-term orientation emphasizes speed and efficiency. People with short-term orientation believe in the proverbs "Time is money"; "The die is cast"; "It is no use crying over spilled milk"; and "What's done can't be undone."

2. Orientations and Work Values

In traditional China, the main work values included learning, honesty, adaptability, accountability and self-discipline; leisure time was not so important; profits five years from now were important, although we privately disagreed on wide social and economic differences. Our investments in housing, **guanxi** (relationships or friendship) and education tended to be life-long; we were very saving. On the whole, we saved it for future use in case anything bad should happen. On the other hand, we remained very optimistic however hard life was for we believed what Zengzi said, "A scholar must be resolute and steadfast, for his burden is heavy and his road is long (士不可以不弘毅，任重而道远)." He means that virtuous talents with a strong sense of mission should have a long-term orientation, refusing to give in under tentative pressure.

In the West, main work values include freedom, rights, achievement, and thinking for oneself; leisure time is important; people emphasize the importance of yearly profits and agree that reward by abilities is a good system; personal loyalties vary with business needs; many persons are not so saving. What's more, people spend the future's money today.

3. Different Expectations of Friendship

Gabriel Lindman and Bao Gang first met in their history class at an American university. Bao Gang, a freshman from China, was excited to get to know an American friend. He hoped that he and Gabriel would become good friends. At first, Gabriel was very friendly. He greeted Bao Gang warmly before class. Sometimes he offered to study together with Bao Gang. He even invited Bao Gang to have lunch with him. But after the semester, Gabriel seemed distant. The two former classmates didn't see each other a lot on campus. One day Bao Gang decided to call Gabriel. Gabriel didn't seem interested in talking to him. Bao Gang felt hurt. "Gabriel said we were friends. And I said friends were friends forever." In his letter to friends at home he wrote, "Americans are fickle."

Chinese expect friendship to stay the same over a long period of time, maybe for a lifetime for we believe a true friendship is a relationship that endures through changes. Bao Gang feels upset because he doesn't know that there is no obligation for Westerners to stay friends. Even the relationship in which people feel close emotionally and tell each other their secrets and personal problems may not survive life changes such as graduation from a university or a big change in economic circumstances. Friendship, like many other relationships including marriage, depends on frequent interactions. So changing friends is normal in the West, but they still need those special pals who've known them long term. If the people involved do not see each other and interact regularly, the relationship is apt to wither or even die like a tree which has been uncared for and forgotten.

Further Reading --

1. Frank, M. O. (1990). *How to Get Your Point Across in 30 Seconds or Less*. New York: Pocket Books.

2. Hall, E. T. (1983). *The Dance of Life: The Other Dimension of Time*. New York: Doubleday.

3. Hall, E. T. (1959). *The Silent Language*. New York: Doubleday & Company.

4. Hofstede, G. (2005). *Cultures and Organizations: Software of the Mind*. New York: McGraw-Hill.

5. Lerner, G. (1997). *Why History Matters: Life and Thought*. New York & Oxford, UK: Oxford University Press.

6. Levine, R. V. (1997). *A Geography of Time: The Temporal Misadventures of a Social Psychologist*. New York: Basic Books/Harper Collins.

7. Smith, A. H. (2003). *Chinese Characteristics*. New York: Eastbridge.

8. 戴维斯 (Davis, L.) (2001),《中西文化之鉴》(*Doing Culture: Cross-Cultural Communication in Action*),北京:外语教学与研究出版社。

Unit 5　Space

18 July 2006: At last week's G-8 summit in St. Petersburg, United States President George W. Bush stepped behind German Chancellor Angela Merkel, reached for her shoulders, gave her a brief massage and then kept walking. Visibly startled and uncomfortable, Angela Merkel threw up her arms. A moment to be remembered, it seems within hours, links to photographs and video footage of the surprise neck grab were already racing across the Internet–from YouTube to Technorati. "Bush: Love-Attack on Merkel!" read the headline in the German tabloid Bild. Several Websites denounced commander in chief Bush as the "Groper in Chief." Though the neck rub happened nearly one week ago, Bush is still feeling the rub today. A vocal debate is brewing in several U.S. newspapers and blogs about whether the president has simply made a minor faux pas or whether he may even have sexually harassed his colleague. "You could use this video for sexual harassment training," Democratic Party activist Martha Whetsone told the San Francisco Chronicle newspaper. "It's something you'd show and say, 'No one in a boss' position should be doing that.'"

—A news report in 2006

What do you think of the massage? Was it a harmless bit of fun between two equally powerful leaders? Or a deeply unacceptable example of workplace sexual harassment?

Unit 5 Space

We shape our buildings and then they shape us.

—**Winston Churchill**

Churchill said this during the debate on the form that Parliament should have when it was rebuilt following the bombing of London during World War II. It is only recently, however, that space has begun to be recognized as influencing the direction as well as the outcome of behavior. For discussion: Give some examples related to the conception and use of space in the life of Chinese people.

I repeat that everything appertaining to this city is on so vast a scale, and the Great Khan's yearly revenues therefore are so immense, that it is not easy even to put it in writing, and it seems past belief to one who merely hears it told.

—**Marco Polo**

As the Venetian explorer testified, the sheer magnitude of everything about the 13th-century China confounds the imagination of the outsider. If that was true, is it even more so today?

I. What Is Space?

Space is a property of our universe that gives us a sense of the size of an object, the distance between two objects, and the direction of an object or some objects. It helps us to define the size of an object by measuring how much space the object occupies. A "larger"-sized object occupies more space while a "smaller"-sized object occupies less. If we look at a Chinese map, we will see the Dongting Lake stretching between Hunan and Hubei provinces and the

Xuanwu Lake in Nanjing occupying much less space. It also helps us to define the distance between two objects by measuring how much space there is between them. A "longer" distance means that there is more space between the two objects while a "shorter" distance less space. The Yangtze River running from the Qinghai-Tibet Plateau to the East China Sea is "longer" than the Qinhuai River which flows from Nanjing all the way eastward to the Yangtze River.

Our innate mental compass points not north-south, but east-west, and thus we articulate and imagine space differently from Westerners, which has perplexed some Westerners who don't know that the tectonic forces have created a unique sense of space for China: Westwards lie the mountains, the great Tibetan plateau as the roof of the world, pushed upwards where the Indo-Australian plate crashes into and plunges beneath the Eurasian; Eastward lies the ocean. No wonder most of us take it for granted that the mighty waterways such as the Yangtze and the Yellow Rivers flow eastward.

II. Spatial Language

We often hear people say things like **Absence makes the heart grow fonder** (小别胜新婚); **I'd give him a wide berth if I were you; He's my bosom buddy; Xiao Hong is a distant relative; She kept him at arm's length during their first meeting; The old man kept his distance from the visitor; Nobody is nearer his heart than his daughter; He was once regarded as one of Mr. May's closest advisers**. Obviously, to define our interpersonal relationships or set a limit we use space which usually refers to body distance and body touch in social interactions.

1. "Don't Cross the Line"–Social Distance

No matter how close you are with your friends or family, there are invisible boundaries that you cannot afford to cross and invisible or visible spaces you cannot get into without invitation of all cultures. In other words, there should be some physical distance. For instance, it's improper to walk with your Western friend hand-in-hand or arm-in-arm, and it is rude to touch her or him sometimes. On the other hand, it's improper to kiss your Chinese friends. Your kiss will embarrass them. And there should be speech boundaries, too. There are no friends with whom you can talk about everything or you needn't be careful in your choice of words when you talk. As language users, we know how powerful words are. They are comforting, soothing, inspiring, but sometimes hurting and killing. The point is: Don't cross the line.

2. "Don't Get so Close or Stay too Far"–Body Distance

Some people misjudge how close they should sit or stand when they are talking to strangers or acquaintances, and they may end up making a poor impression on others either because they get too close or stay too far away. Ji Wen, a young man of eighteen, likes to be with people, especially native English speakers so that he can practice his language skills. But he finds some of them turn away from him or step back when he is near them. Although they don't cover their nose or mouth, he doubts whether he makes people feel sick because of his bad breath, unaware of the fact that if you find other people keep moving further back when you stand close to them, it does not necessarily mean they don't like you because of your bad breath. It might mean that you are invading territory they consider their personal space. About the only time people willingly allow a stranger into their personal space is when they need medical treatment, a hair cut, or when they can't prevent it, such as when on a crowded bus or elevator. Of course people get very close to each other when they feel a very strong attraction.

Based on his in-depth observation, American anthropologist Edward T. Hall established four distances for American culture in 1959:

1) Intimate distance: 1-18 inches. It is reserved for intimates.

2) Personal distance: 1.5-4 feet. It is a transitional distance between 1) and 3).

3) Social distance: 4-12 feet. It is reserved for business.

4) Public distance: 12-25 feet. It is observed on formal occasions.

China is a country of propriety. The *Book of Rites* (《礼记》), the fourth one of the Five Confucian Classics before the Qin dynasty covers the most minute rules for the conduct of everyday life. But there are no written rules for what distance is proper for what kind of relationship so that we are still intuitively adjusting body distances in our daily social life.

Body space or personal space is one of the cultural differences that we first notice when dealing with people from other cultures. In general, North Americans prefer more distance than we do. Some Western Europeans, such as Scandinavians and Germans, like even more space. Differences in how close to stand are a source of misunderstanding. Mark Green, a New Yorker who teaches oral English at eastern China's Hohai University, told us about his discomfort caused by some Chinese behaviors. The other day he waited in line for his weekly nucleic acid test at a Covid-19 testing center in Nanjing. He noticed that people were impatiently standing very close to each other. He wanted to make people aware of his concern by keeping a distance from the lady in front of him. However, the people behind him urged him to move forward, which greatly upset him.

To this behavior, our explanation is that traditionally we have had the concept of shared space, particularly in public places; the concept of privacy or personal space is fairly new in China where some traditional big families deem it impolite and unacceptable for family members to shut their bedroom doors in daytime.

3. "Don't Fondle My Baby"–Body Touch

In all cultures, the closest body distance denotes body touch. But in terms of body touch, different cultures have different customs. Take hugging for instance. Hugging is a touch which has very obvious sexual connotations on most occasions in China. Only lovers or husband and wife hug–usually in private. In the West, hugging, whether at the time of meeting a friend or at the parting, usually has no sexual connotation. It is warmer, more enthusiastic, and less formal than a handshake and does not necessarily convey a romantic message. Women tend to hug each other more than men hug women. Despite the growing Western impact on Chinese life, most women and men who are friends still do not hug or kiss each other in public. Such actions would be considered something very unusual between a man and a woman if they were not lovers.

The other day we happened to log on to Jason's Blog and found a paragraph very interesting. It says:

"In China, a common complaint of Western mothers is that Chinese often fondle their babies and very small children. Such behavior–whether touching, patting, hugging or kissing–can be quite embarrassing and awkward for the mothers. They know that no harm is meant, and that such gestures are merely signs of friendliness or affection, therefore they cannot openly show their displeasure. On the other hand, such actions in their own culture would be considered rude, intrusive and offensive and could arouse a strong dislike and even repugnance. So the mothers often stand by and watch in awkward silence, with mixed emotions, even when the fondling is by their Chinese relatives, friends or acquaintances."

III. Spatial Language and Culture

In *The Silent Language* (1959), Hall elaborates on how people from different cultures orient themselves in space and classifies some cultures as high-contact and others as low-contact.

1. High-Contact Cultures

"In high-contact cultures what people sense when they are close to a person or object is most important."(Hall, 1959) Chinese culture can be classified as high-contact–at least in comparison with Western culture and its closer spatial language brings people much human warmth and kindness. On a typical Chinese campus, students of the same gender putting their arms around each other, walking arm-in-arm or even holding hands can be seen almost everywhere. Boy students often huddle around game displays in a fashion of close contact and some of them even don't mind squeezing twenty pals into one room for three on festive occasions, chatting, swiping cellphones and watching TV together. In the park, people of the same gender are seen holding hands, walking shoulder to shoulder, or touching each other a lot.

However, some close contact or touching take place not because of friendship or kindness, but because time presses or there isn't much room. For instance, when crossing the street, we sometimes brush others but keep moving on as if nothing had happened since it is so crowded and everybody is in a hurry, but if two people collide, a brief apology might be offered, and then they continue with their business. When we get on a bus, if the person behind us touches or pushes us, we will not be angry and consider it abnormal, otherwise our would be regarded to be out of our minds, since it is unavoidable to brush each other when we are rushed to get on the bus by the driver. To be honest, nobody likes this kind of unintentional touch.

 Of course, it's dangerous to generalize that Chinese culture is always high-contact. You can give some examples to refute our argument. For instance, a typical Chinese does not put his arm around his wife's waist when having a walk in the evening by the Qinhuai riverside. You can also use scenes of greeting and good-bye at any airport or train station as evidence to prove that we are not physically affectionate even to our families. There typical Chinese are seen with all the feelings expressed in the eyes and the practical things loved ones do for one another, which has been vividly described by the famous Chinese essayist Zhu Ziqing (1898–1948). In "The Sight of Father's Back" Zhu wrote, "I said, 'Dad, you might leave now.' But he looked out of the window and said, 'I'm going to buy you some tangerines. You just stay here. Don't move around.' I caught sight of several vendors waiting for customers outside the railings beyond a platform. But to reach that platform would require crossing the railway track and doing some climbing up and down. That would be a strenuous job for the father, who was fat. I wanted to do all that myself, but he stopped me, so I could do nothing but let him go. I watched him hobble towards the railway track in his black skullcap, black cloth mandarin jacket and dark blue cotton-padded cloth long gown. He had little trouble climbing down the railway track, but it was a lot more difficult for him to climb up that platform after crossing the railway track. His hands held onto the upper part of the platform, his legs huddled up and his corpulent body tipped slightly towards the left, obviously making an enormous exertion. While I was watching him from behind, tears gushed from my eyes. I quickly wiped them away lest he or others should catch me crying… When he came near the train, I hurried out to help him by hand. After boarding the train with me, he laid all the tangerines on my overcoat, and patted the dirt off his clothes, he looked somewhat relieved and said after a while, 'I must be going now. Don't forget to write me from Beijing!' I gazed after his back retreating out of the carriage. After a few steps, he looked back at me and said, 'Go back to your seat. Don't leave your things alone.' I, however, did not go back to my seat until his figure was lost among crowds of people hurrying to and fro and no longer visible. My eyes were again wet with tears." Indeed it is unlikely that typical Chinese will put their arms around the returning or departing dear one and squeeze him or her. And it is more unlikely for them to kiss their mom, dad or adult children.

Today there have appeared in China many so-called "empty-nest" families with only aging or aged parents at home and their children living abroad or in another city. Probably that's why more and more pets such as dogs and cats are seen in our community. They might be kept to satisfy the need for touch, we assume.

2. Low-Contact Cultures

During our stay in America, we were shocked to find that some children don't know who their biological father is and some women don't know who fathered their children. There is a very famous daily TV show known as "Maury Show" which helps people with those problems they need to work on. In that show, there are women who slept with different men, men who slept with different women and babies they made carelessly. The interactions among the host, audience members and the show stars are usually very unexpected, dramatic and exciting. Here is a question: Does the popularity of "Maury Show" mean that Americans are not sensitive to physical contact?

No, Americans are very sensitive to physical contact. They say "excuse me" whenever they feel they might touch somebody. "I'm sorry" is usually blurted out when they find themselves in others' way, especially when they touch somebody unintentionally, even among family members and best friends. Western culture, especially American culture, is low-contact, even lower today than anytime in American history. Why?

America is a complex country. There are people of different races, different cultures, different personalities, different backgrounds, and different incomes. This country is also widely known as a very free country. As a matter of fact, their freedom is based on many preconditions, especially in terms of freedom of sexuality. In Dec. 2021, a junior high female student of 13 years old was seen hugging both her girl friend and her girl friend's boyfriend in the hallway. The school authority decided to put her in the detention room as a punishment. Americans are learning people. From those cases, they have learnt that if they want to live in peace, they have to develop a habit of avoiding physical contact with others. It was true in the past that relatively high status people (e.g. supervisors, adults, men) could touch lower status people (e.g. workers, children, women), but the rules about this are changing. Now there is much concern about sexual harassment in the workplace and about the possibility of sexual abuse of children by caregivers such as teachers and activity leaders. This concern has resulted in further restrictions on touching in Western society. Touching lower status people by higher status people has become suspect as it could indicate a sexual intention.

On the whole, Western culture is comparatively low-contact. That explains a reason why the gesture of affection George W. Bush gave Angela Merkel stirred up a heated debate in the United States and Germany. To many of us, it is natural for close friends to massage the neck or back for each other without asking for permission. Aren't Bush and Merkel close friends? The point is that the touch took place between two Westerners. In the West, among strangers, acquaintances, and great friends, people are sensitive to body touch. Uninvited touch is regarded to be rude and offensive, a violation of personal rights. The correct way for Bush might be to ask Merkel first for permission, "Could I give you a massage?" or "Do you mind if I give you a massage?" If Merkel agreed, she would say, "Yes, I would love to have a massage." or "Sure. Why not? It is free, isn't it?"

Indeed there are too many sexual harassment cases, which make the alleged offenders lose their dignity, jobs, families, and even freedom. Indeed there is too much sex-related body contact in Western films and TV dramas, which unavoidably remind people of sexual harassment. But films and TV dramas are not about real life. The real life can only be found in real life and courtrooms. So don't touch Westerners without asking for permission.

Here comes another problem: People need touch, human warmth, and need to be part of another person's life. How do Westerners satisfy those basic human needs?

Well, don't feel sorry for them. Firstly, They have their own ways to satisfy their need for human touch. They watch people hug, kiss, touch, push, punch, strike, beat, or trample people on the internet or in films and TV dramas, which can explain a little bit why mass media is full of sex and violence. There is a hidden large market for topics concerning sex and violence.

Secondly, they keep pets. An American professor joked about herself in an interview this way, "What can you write about me? A middle-aged woman and her four cats?" Most of the pets they keep are warm-blooded animals because these animals can pass warmth. Our neighbor Kitty Green lost her husband Peter 20 years ago. Her only son doesn't live with her and she doesn't want to live with him (so-called American independence). She bought a dog and named it Peter. Peter's smile, tremble, tears, jumps, and noise have been her favorite topics. When she watches TV, Peter sits in her arms; when she sleeps, Peter sleeps beside her and it is fun to listen to him snort. Peter keeps her busy all day long. She washes him, feeds him, combs him, takes him to see his vet, dresses and undresses him, walks him, trains him, educates him to be polite, helps him to make dog friends...

Thirdly, people try their utmost to refresh their love by giving each other gifts on important occasions, praising each other, thanking each other, kissing each other, hugging each other, talking to each other... When their marriage unfortunately ends in divorce, they are not afraid of seeking new love and throwing themselves into another love affair. By new love, we mean remarriage or cohabitation. Cohabitation is popular in America: A man and a woman live together not as husband and wife but as boyfriend and girlfriend. There are many reasons behind cohabitation; keeping love fresh and alive is one of them.

Fourthly, they go to church on a regular basis. Some people don't believe in God, but often go to church. Why? Church is believed to be a place full of human warmth, a place to give and receive hugs. Mary Jefferson, our 23-year-old neighbor in the Woodlands, TX, likes being hugged, which is the only reason for her to go to church every Sunday. Usually there are two services in the church on Sunday morning. One is traditional for old and middle-aged people, the other is contemporary for young people. Mary chooses traditional service, because hugs from older people are warmer and more comfortable for her.

Fifthly, they like making new friends, entertaining friends at home and holding parties for friends and family members. Hugging is acceptable on these occasions.

Anyway, Westerners are still talking a lot about touching and especially honor the hug as expressing emotional warmth, affection and care. For instance, when we watch a ball game on TV we often see Western players hugging their teammates. In this case, we see the role of touching in creating bonds among the members of a group. So the point is not that Westerners use very little touching, but that they are relatively low touching and more sensitive to body touch.

3. Misinterpreted Contact Language

Different spatial languages may lead people into very embarrassing situations.

When Dorothy received an invitation to attend her Chinese neighbor's birthday party, she was thrilled. She has always admired the Liu family, and she is very fond of Will, the about-to-be-married son, and feels extremely close to Mrs. Liu, his widowed mother. After the beautiful party, Dorothy and Mrs. Liu soon became great friends. One day, Dorothy gave Mrs. Liu a very beautiful necklace. Mrs. Liu loved it so much that she felt she should give Dorothy something in return. So she gave Dorothy a purple clay teapot. Dorothy was very pleased. One week later, Dorothy invited Mrs. Liu to her home. They wrapped *jiaozi* together and enjoyed the meal a lot. Then they walked upstairs to watch TV–hand in hand. Then Dorothy sat beside Mrs. Liu and gently grasped her hand. Mrs. Liu lightly squeezed her hand in return while watching an interesting TV drama, feeling very happy that she could make so great a friend. Suddenly Dorothy tried to kiss Mrs. Liu, who was shocked and cried at the top of her voice, "No! I'm not a lesbian!" Dorothy was hurt. She asked accusingly, "Why didn't you tell me earlier?"

In China, it is natural for a woman to develop a close relationship with another woman. Physical intimacy like walking arm in arm, holding hands, sitting close to one another and even sharing one bed at night is standard, but kissing is abnormal. However, in America, women would hold hands only if they were lesbians or bi-sexual.

IV. Spatial Language and Life

Space finds expression in many aspects of Chinese and Western life.

1. Housing

Regarding architecture, the Chinese distinguish between what is public and what is private, what is male and what is female, what is outside and what is inside. In the inside-outside pattern, the inside is female and private while the outside is male and public. Traditional Chinese architecture features high walls and heavy gates. Walls and gates as well as gate men are more common in China than elsewhere. The front of a house that presents to the outside is plain, unwelcoming, even forbidding, and the walls are thick to protect what is inside.

If you think about this inside-outside pattern in relation to Chinese life, you may have noticed that people from other countries are commonly called *laowai* (foreigners) rather than Englishmen, Aussies or Indians. The inside-outside pattern also operates within Chinese society as can be seen in the phenomenon of "localism" in business and the Chinese characters *wai* (outside) and *nei* (inside).

Western architecture lays great stress on fences. American poet Robert Frost once said, "Good fences make good neighbors." The statement implies that Western life puts weight on privacy protection. The typical Western home requires an area of privacy, which is often formal and regimented. Physical features like doors, hedges, and fences reflect an emphasis on privacy, which is pervasive throughout Western life.

2. Classrooms

Most Chinese classrooms have large raised podiums with students sitting in rows below and in front. This design reinforces the authority of the teacher and encourages a teacher-centered style of learning. Moreover, the classroom usually has an open front door and an open back door as well as two big bright windows on both walls so that everything can be seen clearly from outside. The design is an indication of much care for the students from the teaching faculty.

Most American classrooms have movable tables and chairs that would make it easier to arrange the students into work groups so that teachers would easily move among the groups monitoring their work and offering advice as needed, because most American teachers prefer the role of a facilitator, a person who defines tasks and goals and arranges activities to achieve them. They see themselves as a coach, resource person and motivator instead of the main source of knowledge for the students. Most elementary and middle school classrooms are closed, with only one door but no window, so they have electric lights on and air-conditioners to control the temperature, which is a display of respecting students' privacy and personal development.

3. Office Buildings

In any culture, the location of one's office in a company or a governmental department has something to do with the person's position or status.

In China, the department manager's desk or office is often placed in the last row behind his subordinates'. In that location, he can have better leadership, seeing how his subordinates are working and keeping in close contact with them at the same time.

In America, those who are in higher positions usually have their offices higher in the building, with beautiful scenery outside and a quiet environment, and above all far from visitors. Those with lower ranks usually have an office lower in the building, with easy access to visitors and not so pleasant scenery to enjoy.

In Germany, people habitually close their offices so as to obtain a closed space to ensure the independence and privacy of their activity.

4. Different Interpretations of a Door Ajar

Max Krueger, a young German engineer, is Wang Ling's new next-door neighbor. After a few interactions, they become friends. One day he asked her to talk for a while in his room. Wang Ling agreed happily. She followed Max into his apartment room, deliberately leaving the door ajar. When Max found the door creaking ajar, he went to close it. Wang Ling felt so uncomfortable with the tightly closed door that she appeared very absent-minded and distracted, which made Max really uncomfortable.

In China, tradition has it that it is inappropriate for a man and a woman to be alone together, especially in a closed space, and therefore we are taught to leave the door ajar when alone with someone of the opposite sex so that outsiders would know you are not doing anything inappropriate, because the open door links the room to the outside and hence offers a shared space with outsiders. However, leaving the door unshut so that people would not be skeptical about your chastity or reputation is absurd for Germans. Even if the relationship between Max and Wang Ling did involve physical intimacy, a German like Max would believe that is no one else's business, not to mention that it is not safe to leave the door unclosed in a building occupied by so many people.

Further Reading

1. Carr, D. & Zhang, C. (2004). *Space, Time, Culture*. Dordrecht, Boston: Kluwer Academic Publishers.
2. Furnham, A. & S. Bochner (1986). *Culture Shock: Psychological Reactions to*

Unfamiliar Environments. London: Methuen.
3. Hall, E. T. (1976). *Beyond Culture*. New York: Doubleday & Company.
4. Samovar, L. & Porter, R. (1994). *Intercultural Communication: A Reader*. Belmont, CA: Wadsworth Publishing Company.
5. Wierzbicka, A. (1999). *Emotions Across Languages and Cultures: Diversity and Universals*. Cambridge, UK: Cambridge University Press.
6. Young, D.E. & Goulet, J.G. (1994). *Being Changed by Cross-Cultural Encounters*. New York: Broadview Press.
7. 马克林 (Colin Patrick Mackerras) (2013),《我看中国——1949年以来中国在西方的形象》(*China in My Eyes: Western Images of China since 1949*), 张勇先、吴迪译, 北京: 中国人民大学出版社。
8. 约翰·斯图尔特·密尔 (2013),《论自由》, 张梅梅导读, 北京: 中国人民大学出版社。
9. 周宁 (2006),《天朝遥远: 西方的中国形象研究》(上、下卷), 北京: 北京大学出版社。

Unit 6 Smiles, Nods and Silence

A smile is a curve that sets everything straight.

—Phyllis Diller

What do you say to this definition? How would you define smile?

There is language in her eyes, her cheek, her lip, Nay, her foot speaks.

—Shakespeare

How do you understand the remark made by the noted English playwright William Shakespeare?

An empty head or a blank mind leads to speechlessness–that is silence.

—Anonymous

How would you interpret silence? Would you interpret it as a refusal or look at this world with no words uttered?

Man is a speaking animal, but the bulk of information in face-to-face communication is sent or received through silent language channels such as smiles, nods, and silence.

I. Smiles in Intercultural Communication

In physiology, a smile is a facial expression formed by flexing those muscles near both ends of the mouth. It can also be found around the eyes. As a silent language, a smile talks a lot, from which we can get much information in intercultural communication.

1. Smiles in Communication

a. Classification of Smiles

There are many kinds of smiles. Three of them are arranged under different headings as follows:

1) A Put-on Smile

The put-on or fake smile is a performance smile intended to hide true feelings or mislead others. For example, when we meet someone who we think is the "one", we may deliberately attempt to manipulate the person into thinking we are relaxed, happy, and enjoying ourselves. We change the shape of our mouth, even bare our teeth but the smile doesn't properly reach our eyes or spread across our face because we merely wear a smiling mask.

2) A Genuine Smile

A genuine or felt smile transmits delight or enjoyment and draws the other person emotionally closer because the smiler appears to be saying, "I like me, I like you and I like life. I want to share this good feeling with you." In most people you'll notice a twinkle or what looks like a feeling of "amusement" or a somewhat "mischievous" expression in their eyes. A genuine smile is a natural and effective way to connect with people emotionally.

While a forced or put-on smile can be switched on and off at lightning speed, a genuine smile is hard to produce on demand because it depends on and is controlled by real-time emotions.

3) Miscellaneous

People smile for all sorts of reasons. There are the happy smile, the contempt smile, the dampened smile, the miserable smile and a number of others.

Unit 6 Smiles, Nods and Silence

Smiles have a powerful effect on humans. But not all smiles are equivalent and not all smiles enhance the smiler's likeability. For instance, when some young men in China are asked by their elders if they have a girlfriend they usually look away with a smile, which strikes non-Chinese as rude and inscrutable.

b. Chinese Smiles

A smile in China is not only a silent language of pleasure, happiness, amusement, appreciation or understanding, but also means that the smiler is polite, interested, understanding, friendly, sorry, sad, embarrassed, confused, uncomfortable, helpless, at a loss as to what to say, sympathetic, or even judging, and hence there are some smiles in China that will cause negative reactions by Westerners. To illustrate this, here are selections from a letter by an American to his friends back in the U.S. on Chinese smiles:

"In a classroom, a Chinese girl was asked to answer a question. She stood up and smiled, without making any sound. The American teacher looked at himself and didn't see anything funny. So he asked her the question again. The girl just smiled but said nothing." (Note: The teacher was angry. He didn't know that the girl smiled to cover her embarrassment because she wasn't able to answer the question.)

"In a dining room, an Aussie dropped a plate quite by accident and felt bad. The Chinese who had seen this began to laugh, compounding his discomfort and causing anger and bad feelings." (Note: In fact, the Chinese laughed not at the man or his bad luck–whether he is a foreigner or a Chinese. The laughter had several meanings: Don't take it seriously; laugh it off, it's nothing; such things can happen to any of us, etc.)

"When a Dutch woman was parking her bicycle, a Chinese boy accidentally bumped into her. She fell and was quite awkward and angered when the boy said with a smile on his face, 'Sorry. Terribly sorry! ' "(Note: A Chinese smiles when he / she apologizes and feels sorry. The tragedy is that a Dutchwoman smiles only when she is happy. So she felt very humiliated.)

As typical Chinese, we hate to see some people laugh at, for instance, a student who speaks with an accent, a person who has made a seemingly stupid mistake, a guy who improperly gets himself dressed, or the disabled. We feel upset about this judging smile, believing nobody is in a position to judge others. Unfortunately judging smiles are often seen here and there, which is neither encouraged nor criticized because it is assumed that "smile is better than cry". It is believed by many that smiles represent a positive attitude toward life or at least a response to life, and what's more, it represents a philosophy with profound connotations.

c. Western Smiles

According to Westerners, a smile often denotes pleasure, happiness, amusement, kindness or acknowledging the presence of someone. Their smiles confuse Asians on some occasions, too. One Chinese student in America told his Japanese friend, "On my way to school, a girl whom I don't know smiled at me several times. I was a little surprised." His Japanese friend echoed his words and said: "When I was walking on the campus the first day, many people smiled at me, which made me quite ashamed. I hurried to the bathroom to see if anything was wrong with my clothes. Now I'm used to all smiles." It is not unusual for Americans to exchange smiles with complete strangers. They smile at people on the street, at the airport, in restaurants, shopping malls and so on. They consider it a friendly gesture. However, generally speaking, Asians do not smile at strangers. Of course, Westerners do not always go around smiling at strangers in a corridor, elevator, or other confined space, although it is not uncommon to

Unit 6 Smiles, Nods and Silence

see this happen. Acknowledging the presence of someone else is more common when there are few or no other people around. Thus, a Westerner will walk down a crowed street in a big city and not make eye contact with anyone. However, if that person goes into an office building and gets on an elevator with one other person already in the elevator, they are likely to exchange a brief smile or nod, or maybe even a quiet "Good morning" or other greetings. People usually do not want to intrude on a stranger's privacy, but pretending they are not there by avoiding eye contact or other acknowledgement is seen as rude.

2. Misinterpreted Smiles

It is believed that the smile is universal. Yes, indeed. But it is not interpreted in the same way. Traditional Chinese believe that a smile is a sign of frivolity. If something is important and serious, you don't smile. And you were not encouraged to exchange smiles with strangers of the opposite gender. That's not true for many of us today because we have learnt that we have to smile in order to convey the right feeling.

During our stay in Australia, we smiled to everybody around us and to our happiness, this effort paid off until one day when Eva Taylor, a sweet Sweden woman from church told us that her purse was stolen. We were very sympathetic and asked her with a smile, "What is in your purse?" "A debit card, a checkbook, a bunch of keys… and my green card!" "Oh, I'm so sorry to hear that!" We said and felt really sorry for her. But we did not know what to say to comfort her, so we chuckled to hide our embarrassment–in spite of ourselves. "What's funny?" Recognizing the change in her voice, we realized we had failed to transmit the correct information to her. We lost no time to explain, "Sorry, Eva. In China, we laugh or smile when we feel sympathetic. Very often, the person caught in a helpless situation would also laugh or make a joke to ease the embarrassment."

Eva's response was, "Thank you for explaining the difference to me." We know it is hard for a Westerner to accept such a smile in such a context. She would interpret laughter or a smile in such a setting as a sign of either insensitivity or worse–pleasure that the victim had lost her purse because she was disliked. Later we were told that a typical Western response on this occasion would have been to look at her sympathetically without any smile at all and listen to her.

As mentioned above, a smile can be misinterpreted, especially when it involves people from different cultures. One day Will Smith went into a Chinese restaurant in New York. "A roast meat wanton soup, please. Will it be long?" asked Will. Li Xiao, a waiter, answered with a smile on his face, "No. It will take only two or three minutes, sir." Will sat down and looked around him. It was a very clean restaurant and there were already many diners.

Three minutes passed, then five minutes. Will was beginning to get impatient. Noticing Will's impatience, Li Xiao promised him smilingly, "It won't be long. It won't be long." Will waited for another five minutes. When Li Xiao finally put the soup on the table, Will was already very hungry. Li Xiao was very sorry about what had happened and smiled before he spoke, "I'm really sorry to keep you waiting for so long, sir. And I want you to know it will never happen again." As he said, he looked at Will with the smile he had been wearing since Will stepped into the restaurant.

Will stared at Li Xiao and said, "Are you sure you are sorry? You don't look sorry at all!"

Li Xiao's smile was frozen on his face: He never expected Will to take his apology so negatively! He became desperate and tried harder to make himself understood. "Sir," he managed to smile again, "Trust me. I really feel terribly sorry about it."

Will unhappily said, "If you're really terribly sorry, how can you smile?"

To Li Xiao, the smile is an important part of the apology since it indicates respect and embarrassment in China. However, it is very hard for Will Smith to believe that smiles can be used as a sign of respect and apology. A Westerner might be expected to look at his listener in the eye and definitely not to smile when apologizing. In this case, different perspectives on a smile made things worse.

3. Smiling–a Good Policy

To those Westerners who have never visited China or have never had any chance to get to know the Chinese culture and people, it's very easy for them to reach some stereotypical conclusions:

"When I was a child, I was taught to be careful around Chinese people, that they were the type that smiled when offended because they'll stab you in the back in revenge." This answer provides a racists's stereotype of Chinese people.

Different perspectives on a smile may cause misunderstandings and even communication breakdowns, but people are encouraged to smile more in all cultures. As the saying goes, "None will hit a smiler in the face." All the courtroom judges, Chinese and Western, are equally likely to find smilers and non-smilers guilty, but they give smilers lighter penalties, a phenomenon called the "smile-leniency effect". And scientists have found that smiling, real or fake, can trick the body into feeling better.

Smiling–is it a good policy? Of course it is. Smile more, then. Smile to the world and it will smile back.

II. Nods in Intercultural Communication

Different cultures assign different meanings to the silent body language–nodding.

1. Nods in Communication
   a. Western Nodding

In the Western concept, a nod of the head is a gesture used to indicate agreement, acceptance or acknowledgment.

"Nod" or "nodding" can also be used as a slang term to describe the physiological side effects related to consuming heroin or other opiates.

   b. Chinese Nodding

In China, nodding doesn't necessarily mean agreement, acceptance or acknowledgment. Of course it doesn't really mean disagreement. Sometimes it is an indication of listening, attention, politeness, or nothing but a "habitual movement" (Yi Zhongtian). Therefore, Chinese nodding is very difficult for foreigners to interpret sometimes.

2. Differences Between Chinese and Western Nodding

Nodding, as a silent language, means agreement, acceptance and recognition in both Chinese and Western culture. However, in China, nodding does not always carry the same meaning as Westerners assume. For instance, sometimes Chinese nodding simply suggests that the listener is listening attentively. Some traditional Chinese people (except close friends or lovers) seldom make eye contact when talking politely to each other. Therefore, to keep the conversation going, nodding serves as an indicator that "I'm listening." This difference has caused many misunderstandings. Below is a selection from a graduate student's journal:

"Our international professor Will Block has been in China for at least seven years. We thought he was more Chinese than some of the natives until one day last year. Before class that day, he came with two friends from the States and asked whether some of us could take them to a bar not far from the campus after class. Silence. Then, some of us nodded. Happily, Will started the class, assuming some of us would surely do this since we nodded. To his great disappointment, he watched us leave the classroom one by one after class as usual, leaving our two guests waiting there. Nobody went up. Even nobody said sorry or goodbye. We just left, as if we hadn't heard Will's request in the first place. This was a real embarrassment for him. He didn't know how to explain to his friends who were warmly welcomed by his students 45 minutes ago. How could this happen? Who was to blame?"

And here is another incident:

One day, a Swede went to China on business. He hired a car and a Chinese driver. When he told his driver to take him to his hotel, the Chinese nodded at once politely. The Swede was very happy that he was understood so soon. So he closed his eyes and waited for the car to move. But to his surprise the car was not moved. He opened his eyes, asked why before giving more detailed directions and got many more nods from his driver. This time he was confused because the driver seemed to have no intention to drive. He became angry and raised his voice: "Why do you nod to me and refuse to drive me to my hotel at once?" The driver nodded and answered, "Yes, yes, sir! But where are you going?" The Swede was too surprised to say a word.

Because of lack of enough knowledge about nodding or because of inadequate preparation for cultural differences, some Westerners find nodding doesn't always talk to them explicitly when they are in China.

III. Silence in Intercultural Communication

Silence refers to the absence of speech, but it is widely believed that silence not only screams, but also says a lot.

1. Silence in Communication

Silence can be employed in different situations.

a. Silence in Physiology

Physiologically, silence means hesitation, stutters, self-correction or the deliberate slowing of speech for the purpose of clarification or processing of ideas. These silences are short.

b. Silence in Debate

Silence in the debate is the rhetorical practice of saying nothing when an opponent would expect something to be said. Poorly executed, it can be very offensive, like refusing to answer a direct question. However, well-timed silence can completely throw an opponent and give the debater the upper hand.

c. Silence in a Conflict

Silence can mean anger, hostility, disinterest, or other negative emotions in Western culture.

Here is a scene: it is in a small bathroom and the time is early morning before going to work. The husband is shaving and the wife enters to blow dry her hair.

Wife: Am I disturbing you?

Husband: (silence)

Wife: (silence, walks out)

A family conflict is taking place. Driven by the principle of politeness, the husband uses silence which is self-evident to his wife, and the wife's silence not only strengthens the message sent by her husband through silence and adds another piece of information, "OK, I'll come back when you're done."

d. Silence in Law

The right to silence is a legal protection enjoyed by people undergoing police interrogation or trial in certain countries. The law is either explicit or recognized in many legal systems.

e. Silence in Spirituality

A silent mind, freed from the onslaught of thoughts and thought patterns, is both a goal and an important step in spiritual development. Inner silence is understood to bring one in contact with the divine, the natural, and the ultimate reality of this moment. All religious traditions imply the importance of being quiet and still in mind and spirit for transformative and integral spiritual growth to occur. In Christianity, there is the silence of contemplative prayer such as centering prayer and Christian meditation. In Buddhism, allowing the mind to become silent is implied as a feature of enlightenment.

f. Commemorative Silence

A common way to remember a tragic accident and the victims or casualties of war is a commemorative silence. It usually means one or three minutes of silence, in which one is supposed not to speak, but to remember and reflect on the event or the victim instead. A commemorative silence may be held at a workplace, a school, or similar institutions. Sometimes a government will advertise a commemorative silence for a specific period at a specific time, which everybody is encouraged (but not forced) to honor. For instance, at the brief remembrance ceremony three minutes of silence was announced in respect of the 109 Chinese soldiers who died during the War to Resist U.S. Aggression and Aid Korea (1950–1953) when their remains were brought back to their motherland and buried in Shenyang on Sept. 3, 2021.

g. Silence in Collective Decision-making

As is known to us, silence is employed to create suspense in public speaking and story-telling. But few have noticed the use of silence in collective decision-making. And the chairperson tends to assume that silence as "yes" and happily fall into the "assumed yes" trap. Actually silence on this occasion might mean (especially in China): **I'm still thinking about it; I may agree but am not sure yet; Yes, I agree; No, I don't agree but I'm not going to say it out loud here; No, I don't agree but I'll never admit to it.**

2. Differences Between Chinese and Western Silence

a. Western Silence

People from Western culture will feel uneasy when one party falls silent suddenly and usually try their best to fill up the silence with small talk. According to their cultural norms, silence can be interpreted as positive or negative. It can include integrity, honesty and kindness; it can stand for indifference to and detachment from fame and fortune; but it can also act as an excuse for hypocrisy, slyness and cowardice… In a Christian Methodist faith organization silence and reflection during the sermons might be appreciated by the congregation while in a Southern Baptist church, silence might mean disagreement with what is being taught or perhaps disconnectedness from the congregated community. Therefore, sometimes it is difficult to interpret the message being sent by a person who is silent (i.e. not speaking). It could mean negative emotions.

Besides, famous Western scholars such as Sigmund Freud (1856–1939) interpreted silence as resistance. Consequently, silence in an argument is sometimes regarded as "passive aggression"– making the other person look bad by pretending to be mild-mannered or even not interested.

"Silence gives consent," so runs an ancient maxim of common law. From this maxim flows a widely applied legal principle: the rule of tacit admission. Based on the theory that an innocent man would loudly deny a serious charge, a rule holds that a suspect silent in the face of an accusation has tacitly admitted the crime. And such silence can later be introduced at his trial as an indicator of guilt. So Westerners (especially North Americans) cannot stand silence. As soon as silence falls in, they will try to break it up, thus appearing to be very noisy and aggressive to some Chinese.

b. Chinese Silence

On the contrary, the Chinese choose to be silent on many occasions such as when a sensitive subject is broached, when we feel embarrassed, when we know we are wrong, when the other party is very angry, when we don't know what to say and how to say, and when somebody is speaking. The reasons for silence are summarized as follows:

First, we choose to be silent in an argument so that we will maintain face and avoid losing it. Once both parties become more reasonable, the face that can be translated to mean "dignity, prestige or reputation" might be saved. On the other hand, we hope our silence can shut up the other party. When trying to talk those involved out of an argument or a fight, Chinese pacifiers are used to quoting the saying, "If each of you says one thing less, there's nothing to argue about."

Besides, the Chinese regard silence as a respect for the speaker, which is revealed in Confucius' comment on his disciple Yan Hui's silence, "I can talk with Hui for a whole day without him making any comment on anything I said–as if he were stupid. When he retires, I examine his conduct, and find him able to illustrate my teachings. Hui is not stupid." (See the *Analect,* Book 2: 9)

Thirdly, silence is a means of learning, which is highly valued by parents and teachers.

Fourthly, silence is a symbol of good cultivation and wisdom. In China, people believe what Laozi says, "He who knows does not speak; he who speaks does not know (知者不言，言者不知)."

3. Misunderstood Silence

a. Misunderstood Silence in a Transnational Family Dispute

Different cultures might have different interpretations of silence. Michael White, a British businessman, and Li Meimei, a retired Chinese worker, have been married for very nearly three and a half years. For the first two years, they were very happy and it is only in the last 18 months that there have been problems. This is when Jenny (Meimei's only daughter who works and lives in Shanghai) began to mention Mama and Dad looking after her baby when she had one. Michael made it known that he would not live in a house with a baby. He had done that with Jennifer (his first wife) for 40 years with their four children back in England, enjoyed every minute of that time, but would not repeat it again. Meimei agreed with him and they gave Jenny some money to employ a babysitter. But since Jenny finally had a baby boy in March, Meimei has been spending most of her time babysitting in Shanghai. One day Michael couldn't help rushing to Shanghai and reminded Meimei of their agreement. Meimei said she would not go back until the baby was able to toddle around. However, Michael urged Meimei to go back with him to Nanjing leaving Jenny some money as they had agreed, but Meimei insisted she should spend another year babysitting before going back when the baby is older and stronger.

The argument soon became tense, and Meimei fell silent. She simply refused to respond to Michael's angry words, wanting very much to provide an opportunity for him to vent his anger, and calm down. However, the silence was misunderstood by Michael as a silent refusal to communicate, which made Michael more and more upset–so much so that he shouted at the top of his voice at Meimei and finally banged the door closed and left for the railway station in great anger.

Unit 6 Smiles, Nods and Silence

You may wonder why Michael was not shut up in spite of the fact that Meimei voluntarily gave in by saying no more in the argument. For Chinese, Meimei stopped saying anything in the argument, which means she knew she was wrong. Usually, when a Chinese person chooses to be silent in an argument, it would mean the person feels guilty or the person wants to stop the argument by not talking any more out of good intentions, or both. The latter often means tolerance as one intends to keep a harmonious relationship with the other. Meimei shut up, hoping that her silence could stop Michael, for she knows (according to her experience in China) if she says one thing less, there's nothing to argue about. In this sense, Meimei was actually taking the initiative to yield.

However, Michael assumed according to his experience in England that Meimei's silence was "passive aggression"– not yielding at all! As a result, they are talking about divorce now.

b. Misunderstood Silence in Class

"Raise your hands if you agree!" Dr. William N. Brown begged his Chinese graduate students.

No response.

"Then raise your hands if you disagree!"

Still nothing.

"How about raising your hands if you're awake?"

Some glanced about awkwardly, but none dared to raise their hands, or break the silent vigil they've kept since primary school.

Dr. Brown got uncomfortable. In his culture, silence can be puzzling. If people disagree with what you are saying, many of them will remain quiet. Silence may not suggest agreement; often it only means that they consider it impolite to argue further. On the contrary, the Chinese choose to be silent on many occasions like when we want to show respect to the speaker and when we are having a class. In traditional Chinese culture, questioning authority is very impolite. Thus, pushing students to ask questions could equate to encouraging them to be impolite.

Unfortunately, Dr. Brown didn't understand his Chinese students and went on to make further requests, which only made him more and more upset and his students more and more awkward.

Further Reading

1. Bull, P. (1983). *Body Movement and Interpersonal Communication*. New York: Wiley.
2. Hall, E. T. (1966). *The Hidden Dimension*. New York: Doubleday & Company.
3. Hall, E. T. (1990). *Understanding Cultural Differences*. Yarmouth, Maine: Intercultural Press.
4. Harvard Business School (2004). *Face-to-face Communications for Clarity and Impact*. Boston, MA: Harvard Business School Press.
5. 胡文仲 (1999),《跨文化交际学概论》,北京：外语教学与研究出版社。
6. 林语堂 (2000),《吾国与吾民》,北京：外语教学与研究出版社。
7. 易中天 (2006),《闲话中国人》（第三版）,上海：上海文艺出版社。
8. 余秋雨 (2019),《中国文化课》,北京：中国青年出版社。
9. 赵 林 (2008),《西方文化概论（修订版）》,北京：高等教育出版社。

Part III
Cultural Differences in Thinking

We are thinking animals. Thinking is a mental form and process, which allows us to model the world and deal with it according to our objectives, plans, ends, and desires. It proceeds in various forms and structures–concepts, statements, categories, inferences, hypotheses, theories, etc., which record and generalize the socio-historical experience of mankind.

Instruments of thinking are language and other sign systems such as the abstract symbols of Mathematics or the concrete images of art. The elements of these systems support such basic operations of thinking as abstraction, generalization and mediation. Abstraction enables us to ignore an object's inessential properties and relations and concentrate on those that are relevant to the intellectual task in question. Generalization enables us to classify large numbers of phenomena according to certain essential attributes. Meditation enables us to reach a good outcome, which is within our control.

As thinking animals, our reasoning, visions of the world, categorizing and attitude toward life are subject to thinking. Here five dimensions of thinking are to be elaborated on in this part. They are:

- Intuitive vs. Logical Thinking
- Dialectical vs. Analytical Reasoning
- Holistic vs. Atomistic Visions
- Categorizing Objects by Relationships vs. by Attributes
- Non-controllers vs. Controllers

Unit 7   Intuitive vs. Logical Thinking

The Chinese hate the phrase "logical necessity" because there is no logical necessity in human affairs.

—Lin Yutang

How did we Chinese arrange human affairs, if not in a logical way?

According to some Anglo-American observers, the Germans even drank and danced on Sundays. The Germans, however, would have it no other way, Sunday or any day of the week. "Now I began to feel rather proud of my success and my achievement," wrote Max Krueger, "and it was my intuition to attempt to transplant German cordiality and sociality in this foreign land. To this end I built a dance pavilion and bowling alley. The beer necessary for such occasions was imported from St. Louis." Later Sundays became days of relaxation in parks and beer gardens.

—Glen E. Lich

For discussion: Make a brief comment on Max Krueger's "intuition" by incorporating your own experience.

The majority of successful senior managers do not closely follow the classical rational model of first clarifying goals, assessing the problem, formulating options, estimating likelihoods of success, making a decision, and only then taking action to implement the decision. Rather, in their day-to-day tactical maneuvers, these senior executives rely on what is vaguely termed "intuition" to manage a network of interrelated problems that require them to deal with ambiguity, inconsistency, novelty, and surprises; and to integrate action into the process of thinking.

—**Anonymous**

Some practicing managers rely heavily on intuition. But what is intuition? Can we see it as the opposite of rationality? Can we view it as an excuse for capriciousness?

I. Definitions of Intuitive and Logical Thinking

Thinking is a way of reasoning or judgment, and it has a particular form, variety, or manner, known as thinking mode. Two thinking modes are to be discussed in this unit: One is intuitive and the other logical.

Intuitive thinking is considered to be creative and constructive right-brain thinking, whereas logical thinking is believed to be analytical and objective left-brain thinking.

Normally intuitive thinking is not focused and linear. It sees many things at once and views the big picture. Usually, intuition comes into its own in conditions like time pressure, dynamic conditions, and unclear differentiation between the observer and the observed. It works best where the observer has experience in a particular situation. It is difficult to teach intuition in the classroom.

In contrast, logical thinking is focused, linear, and deals with one thing at a time. It contains time, and tends to the abstract. This thinking mode is efficient in conditions like adequate time, relatively static conditions, and a clear differentiation between the observer and the observed. It is best suited for dealing with complexities, and works best where there are established criteria for analysis. Logical thinking is necessary when an explanation is required. It can be taught in the classroom.

Some anthropologists have found that traditional Chinese are oriented to think intuitively, whereas Westerners are inclined to think logically.

II. Philosophy and Thinking

It is widely assumed that traditional Chinese society is intuition-based in its way of thinking while Western society is logic-based. The difference is believed by many to be attributed to philosophy which comes from human life and in turn guides human life.

1. Traditional Chinese Philosophy and Intuitive Thinking

It should be noted that logic did exist in traditional Chinese philosophy, for instance, the Logician (名家) and Moist (墨家) doctrines of the pre-Qin period, but priority was given to intuitive thinking.

a. Mencius' Theory on Intuition

Mencius, as one of the most frequently quoted philosophers in China, has a bearing on Chinese intuitive thinking. It is known to many that Mencius is very emphatic on the nature of right and wrong. For him, nature is self-evident, which characterizes his intuitive thinking, as revealed in the paragraph below:

"I like fish and I also like bear's paws. If I cannot have the two together, I will let the fish go, and take the bear's paws. So, I like life and I also like righteousness. If I cannot keep the two together, I will let life go and choose righteousness. (鱼，我所欲也，熊掌，亦我所欲也；二者不可得兼，舍鱼而取熊掌者也。生，亦我所欲也，义，亦我所欲也；二者不可得兼，舍生而取义者也。)"

In this sense righteousness or morality is self-evident to man, and man should take care not to lose it. Then Mencius gives an example to prove that a man cannot but intuitively choose what is right:

"Here are a small basket of rice and a bowl of soup, and the case is one in which the getting of them will preserve life and the want of them will bring death; if they are offered with an insulting voice, even a tramp will not receive them, or, if you first tread upon them, even a beggar will not stoop to them (一箪食，一豆羹，得之则生，弗得则死，呼尔而与之，行道之人弗受；蹴尔而与之，乞人不屑也。)."

Mencius' intuitive theory is based on several factors: human dispositions, common approval, and decisions made during the course of one's life. This intuition, therefore, is not identical to immediate insight, though the latter is clearly a part of the whole process. Meanwhile Mencius' theory of intuition tells us that the ability possessed by men without having been acquired by learning is intuitive ability, and the knowledge possessed by them without the exercise of thought is intuitive knowledge.

Many years after Mencius' death, the Neo-Confucian school in the Song and Ming dynasties put forward the theory of "intuition as substrate and wisdom as function (直觉为体，理智为用)" to reflect a sense of intuitively emphasizing life, nature, and experience.

b. Buddhist Emphasis on Intuition

Buddhism attaches exclusive importance to meditation, a means of transforming the mind. Patriarchal Meditation (祖师禅), as taught by the Patriarch Bodhidharma (菩提达摩祖师), requires no intellectual effort, but direct intuition of the Buddha-mind. The result of this meditation is enlightenment which may come suddenly or gradually (顿悟渐悟). In other words, this major tradition has been "sudden enlightenment preceding gradual cultivation (有了顿，必先有渐)". No other school of Buddhism, like Chan, put aside scriptural studies or philosophical discussion in favor of a purely intuitive approach to enlightenment. It is because of this distaste for book-learning, Chan is known as the doctrine "not founded on words or scriptures (不立文字)". Therefore, its teaching is "transmitted from mind to mind (以心传心)", that is, directly from one master to his disciple on a one-to-one basis, without the intervention of rational and logical argumentation.

c. Limitations of Intuitive Thinking

Intuition, as a type of thinking mode, has its limitations. It can only be applied to human affairs and actions; it cannot be applied to the solution of the riddles of the universe; nor can it be employed to make a discovery systematic, scientific and thus widely promoted. For example, most people believe that the circulation of the blood in the body was discovered by the English physician William Harvey (1578–1657) and hold that it is he who first brought the idea to the attention of the world when he published his discovery in 1628. Harvey was, however, not the first one to recognize the concept, and ancient Chinese had made the discovery 2000 years before. But why is Harvey remembered as the first to discover the circulation of blood? Because ancient Chinese with the intuitive thinking mode took many things for granted, believing it was unnecessary to explain a discovery or invention in steps since it is self-evident and everyone knows it by intuition.

2. Western Philosophy and Logical Thinking

It should be noted that intuition does exist in Western philosophy, but logical thinking has been given priority by Western philosophers.

a. Aristotle's Logic

Aristotle's logic has had an unparalleled influence on the history of Western thought, especially his theory of the "Barbara" syllogism (三段论):

If A is predicated of all B, and B is predicated of all C, then A is predicated of all C.

By predicated, Aristotle means A belongs to B, or all B's are A's. We can substitute subjects and predicates in this syllogism to get:

If all mammals (B's) are warm-blooded animals (A), and all rabbits (C's) are mammals (B's), then all rabbits (C's) are warm-blooded animals (A).

b. Francis Bacon's Inductive Method

Francis Bacon (1561–1626), an English philosopher, statesman and essayist, is best known as a philosophical advocate and defender of the scientific revolution. His works established and popularized an inductive methodology for scientific inquiry. The so-called inductive method (归纳法) is a process of using observations to develop general principles about a specific subject. A group of similar specimens, events or subjects are first observed and studied; findings from the observations are then used to make broad statements about the subjects under examination. These statements may then become laws of nature or theories frequently used in the logical thinking process.

c. John Stuart Mill's 4 Methods of Induction

British philosopher John S. Mill (1806–1873) was committed to the idea that the best methods of explaining the world are those employed by the natural sciences. He focused on four different methods of experimental inquiry that attempt to single out from the circumstances that precede or follow a phenomenon, the ones that are linked to the phenomenon by an invariable law. The four methods of induction–the methods of agreement, of difference, of residues, and of concomitant variation (契合法、差异法、剩余法和共变法)–provide answers to questions by showing what we need to demonstrate in order to claim that a causal law holds, and therefore makes it useful in scientific discovery and invention. In this way John S. Mill further promoted the application of logical thinking.

III. Application of the Two Thinking Modes

1. Intuitive Thinking in China

a. Popularity of Intuitive Aphoristic Sayings

In a number of countries such as China and the UK, the ability to spontaneously produce aphoristic sayings at the right moment is a key determinant of social status. Many societies have traditional sages or respected heroes to whom aphorisms are commonly attributed, such as Confucius, Mencius, the Seven Sages of Greece, or Jesus Christ. The biggest difference between Chinese and Western aphorisms is that images are more often used in Chinese aphoristic sayings because we are used to thinking intuitively in terms of pictures or images. For instance, many years ago Confucius lamented the decaying morality by eulogizing the pines and cypresses which stand for honesty and loyalty, saying, "Only when it gets cold can we see that the leaves of pines and cypresses are the last to wither and fall (岁寒，然后知松柏之后凋也)." This intuitive way used to clarify his position can also be found in his famous remark, "Tyrannical rule is more ferocious than a tiger (苛政猛于虎)", which vividly explains why it is necessary to set up a humane government.

Emperor Taizong of the Tang dynasty greatly missed Wei Zheng, his faithful adviser, after the latter died. He stated, "Using copper as a mirror allows one to keep his clothes neat. Using history as a mirror allows one to see future trends.

Using a person as a mirror allows one to see what is right and what is wrong. When Wei Zheng died, I lost a mirror." The emperor explicitly illustrated the importance of Wei Zheng by using the image of a mirror.

Highly intuitive aphorisms are often quoted by ordinary Chinese people, educated or uneducated, because they correspond to our thinking habits and are easily accessible. For instance, to sing the praises of the collective power, we quote, "One swallow does not make a spring (一只燕子不是春)." To explain how we form a holistic view of something by observing a small sign we say, "The falling of one leaf heralds the autumn (一叶知秋)." These sayings reflect an intuitive perspective very different from the Western one which is mainly logical, e.g. **You cannot step twice into the same river because the man is different and the river is different; He is a fool who can not be angry, but he is really a wise man who will not.** Of course, we can also find some Western sayings very intuitive like **If you see the teeth of the lion, do not think that the lion is smiling at you,** and **Slowly is the fastest way to get where you want to be.**

b. Faith in the Power of Intuition

Having faith in the power of their "intuition", ancient Chinese men of letters went about explaining the mysteries of the human body and the universe. The whole science of Chinese medicine and physiology was based on the intuitive Daoist philosophy of *yin-yang* and *wuxing* (the Five Agents or Elements–metal, wood, water, fire and earth). For them the human body is in itself a symbol of the universe in its composition. The kidneys represent the water, the stomach represents the earth, the liver represents the fire, the lungs represent the metal, and the heart represents the wood. A man suffering from high blood pressure is considered to have too hot a "liver fire", while a man suffering from indigestion may be referred to as having too much earth.

The faith in their intuition led Chinese literary critics to have summarized efficient methods of writing such as **detachment of style** (淡然超脱), **lightness of touch** (轻描淡写), and **bringing out the salient point** (突出重点). Meanwhile these methods also have their respective equivalent expressions which are rather intuitive, easy to remember and thus more popular with Chinese exposed to the intuitive thinking committed to images, e.g. **the method of watching a fire across the river** (隔岸观火), **dragonflies skimming across the water surface** (蜻蜓点水), and **painting a dragon and dotting its eyes** (画龙点睛).

Unchecked by scientific imagination, intuition has a lot of free room and often borders on a naive imagination according to Lin Yutang. Some kinds of ancient Chinese medicine popular among ordinary people are based on some fantastic association. The toad that has wrinkled skin was used in the cure of human skin trouble, and there is a popular belief that a schoolboy should not eat chicken's claws lest he should develop the bad habit of scratching his books, walls, and desks.

c. Intuition and Chinese Verbs

It is believed by many that logical thinking is denoted by nouns; on the other hand, intuitive thinking mainly involves verbs. There are more verbs in a Chinese sentence. Verbs tend to come either at the beginning, in the middle or at the end of sentences, and all are in more salient locations than in English where verbs are more commonly buried in the middle, e.g. **They talked for almost eight hours, through dinner and well into the night.**

Its Chinese version is 谈了近8个小时呀，他们几个人！用餐时还在谈，一直谈到深夜. In the original there is only one verb, but in its Chinese version there are three. More nouns in English and more verbs in Chinese influence our way to relate to the world.

d. Intuitive Belief in the Power of Words

Our belief in the power of words is surprisingly great. This intuitive belief may be traced down in all aspects of life. For instance, motives for traditional Chinese artistic works such as the bat and the deer are popular because the word "bat (*fu*)" is a homophone for "luck" or "happiness" and the word "deer (*lu*)" is a homophone for "official power". Other words are evidently taken quite seriously, too. A couple will look troubled when presented with a clock (*zhong*) which suggests the end of the marriage since "clock" is a homophone for "end (*zhong*)". They won't like books as presents because "giving books (*song shu*)" sounds like "delivering defeat" in Chinese. And good-mannered people would not give their friends an umbrella because doing so literally implies that the family of the gift receiver is going to be dispersed. Many of us do not quite know whether it is true or not, but "people say", and we are not interested in conducting a survey to verify it or using logic to think about it.

e. Traditional Education

"The aim of Chinese classical education has always been the cultivation of the reasonable man as the model of culture. An educated man should, above all, be a reasonable being, who is always characterized by his common sense, his love of moderation and restraint, and his hatred of abstract theories and logical extremes." Lin Yutang went on to explain why studying by memorizing as many facts, concepts and ideas as possible is considered more important at school than studying by analyzing, debating, or discussing. According to him, scholars exposed to traditional education, without focusing their attention on logic and analysis, were more likely to live on intuition, which to some extent hindered the development of Chinese science and technology. Consider the paragraph quoted from the *Torrent Trilogy* by famous writer Ba Jin (1904–2005): "Some say that there is at first no road at all and that road is created simply by the treading of passers-by. Others say that there is at first already a road available before more and more people come to walk on it. I don't want to judge who is right or who is wrong. I am still young. I want to live on. I want to conquer life. I know the torrent of life will never stop. Let's see where it is going to carry me!" This paragraph displays how Ba Jin allowed himself to be driven by the torrent of life, intuitively maintaining that the torrent was equal to the power of positive thinking.

2. Logic Thinking in the West

a. English Grammar and Logical Thinking

To native English speakers, whatever your goals are, a grasp of English grammar–a description of logic and logical thinking process, is necessary if you want to improve your speaking and writing skills. English grammar has clearly defined rules, so studying it can encourage logical thinking and help you gain confidence in your ability to produce work of clarity and logic.

But for Chinese speakers, grammar is less important, so contextual and pragmatic cues can be the only kinds of cues the hearer or reader has to depend on. Chinese sentences thus do not stress the form, clarity or tense. They can be incomplete, and parts of speech are flexibly used, and their meaning can be solely expressed by words without caring about the logic or grammar, for example, 头发掉了一些 (literally, hair lost some; freely, you have lost some hairs) and 白菜买了一大包 (literally, cabbages bought a big bag; freely, I have bought a big bag of cabbages) have no actors; 中国队大胜日本队 (literally, the Chinese team greatly won the Japanese team) and 中国队大败日本队 (literally, the Chinese team greatly defeated the Japanese team)have actually the same meaning–the Chinese team won the football game. In the absence of restrictive linguistic logic, the Chinese writer or speaker feels free to express.

b. Popularity of Logic

"Logic" is one of the Westerner's favorite singular words, e.g. **Still don't get the logic of "She's pretty but not beautiful"**; **You need a lot of work on your logic**, and **I don't see any logic in this**.

The popularity of detective stories reveals the Western love of logic. Take for instance Sherlock Holmes, the famous fictional detective of the late 19th and early 20th centuries. As a brilliant London-based consulting detective, Holmes was famous for his intellectual prowess and renowned for his skillful use of "logical reasoning". As a matter of fact, he was so loved by readers that when his creator, Sir Arthur Conan Doyle, planned to let him die, the poor Scottish author and physician received threatening letters from his readers and was compelled to give up that decision.

Apart from detective stories, games involving logical thinking skills such as brain teasers, math stumpers and puzzles are also popular in the West.

IV. Impact of Thinking Modes on Writings

1. Impact of Intuitive Thinking on Chinese Writings

When we write we are apt to save the best for the last, intuitively moving from big to small, from far to near, from whole to part, from causes to effects, from the least important to the most important, from the general to the specific–a way of climax. So to speak, we tend to give the background, then reasons to get the readers' or listeners' sympathy, understanding, and attention (i.e. cause-effect sequence). Usually, Chinese textual structures are: Because A, and because B, and because C, therefore/ so; If…; then…; Although…, but…; The introduction of a bilingual book we read the other day begins this way: "老人家走的路多，

吃的饭多，看的书多，经的事多，享的福多，受的罪多，可谓见多识广，有丰富的经验，老人家说的话多是经验之谈，后生小子不可不听也。"

Obviously, the structure is in the sequence of cause-effect. Its English translation below retains the original writing sequence:

"Old men, who walk more roads, eat more rice, read more books, have more experiences, enjoy more happiness, and endure more sufferings, are experienced and knowledgeable, with rich life experience. Thus, what they say is mostly wise counsel, and young people should listen to them."

Some of our international students reported they felt a little bit confused when they read the beginning lines of the English version above. They didn't understand what it was about until they came to the end of the introduction– because the thinking thread runs counter to their thinking mode which is usually anticlimax in the sequence of effect-cause.

2. Impact of the Two Thinking Modes on Western Writings

a. Impact of Logic Thinking

Westerners usually start straight with the main point by putting the most important at the beginning to get the readers' or listeners' attention and consideration–a way of anticlimax, which means you are supposed to say what you want to say, then explain why. They tend to put effect at the beginning, then reasons (i.e. effect-cause sequence). In a paragraph they usually start with a topic sentence, and then continue to handle the topic views. Below is an example of an English paragraph that displays the impact of logic thinking:

"If your life isn't where you want it to be, change it. It's what successful people have done for thousands of years. You may currently be struggling and frustrated with your life but it's not going to stay like this forever, that is, unless you don't do anything to change it."

Some Chinese readers who know nothing about Western thinking would feel when they read the beginning line that the author is intentionally creating a dramatic and eye-catching effect and thus in need of sincerity.

b. Impact of Intuitive Thinking

Intuitive thinking, though less often used by Westerners in their daily life, is more often employed in their literary works. Let us make a comparison of the following English original and its two Chinese versions:

Vast lawns extend like sheets of vivid green, with here and there clumps of gigantic trees, heaping up with rich piles of foliage.

Chinese version 1: 草地宽阔，好像地上铺了鲜艳的绿绒似的毡毯，巨大树株，聚成一簇，绿叶浓密，一眼望去，草地上东一簇，西一簇，这类的大树可不少。

Chinese version 2: 宽阔的草坪宛如翠绿的地毯，成片的参天大树点缀其间，绿叶浓密，层层迭迭。

The English original begins intuitively from far to near, from big to small, from whole to part and hence paints a well-organized beautiful word painting. But in Chinese version 1, neither of the two creative thinkings–the intuitive thinking and the logical thinking are harnessed, which explains why the translation appears disorderly and confusing, just as the saying goes, "Problem solving without creative thinking is a garden without seeds." In Chinese version 2, the translator keeps the intuitive thinking mode of the original text by creatively rendering it into Chinese and allows the Chinese reader to move his eyes comfortably from far to near and from whole to part.

V. Logic in China and Intuition in the West

"The most striking difference between the traditions at the two ends of the

Unit 7 Intuitive vs. Logical Thinking

civilized world is in the destiny of logic. For the West, logic has been central and the thread of transmission has never snapped…"(Angus Graham) But logic has a different destiny in China.

1. Destiny of Logic in Ancient China and Greece

a. Early Death of Logic in Ancient China

In China there are only two short-lived movements of little influence that share the spirit of logical inquiry that has always been common in the West. They were started by the Logicians and the Moists. The Logicians in fact made little progress toward a formal logic, though they were interested in knowledge for its own sake which is reflected in the logic of "a white horse being not a horse (白马非马的逻辑命题)". The Moist tradition embraced several logical concerns, chief among them the ideas of necessary and sufficient conditions and the principle of non-contradiction. Their evangelistic approach and readiness to discuss or debate with anyone may explain why the Moist canon the *Mozi* is so much concerned with logic and dialectics. In the portions believed to represent Mozi's teaching there is a laborious, almost painful attention to step-by-step argumentation, but Mozi never formalized his system and logic died an early death in China. Except for that brief interlude, traditional China lacked logic.

b. The Popularity of Debate and Rise of Logic in Ancient Greece

The best explanation for the ancient Greeks' concern with logic is that they saw its usefulness in argumentation or debate. The Greeks had a tradition of debate. A commoner could challenge even a king and not only live to tell the tale, but occasionally sway an audience to his side. Debates occurred in the marketplace, the political assembly, or even in military settings. Homer made it very clear that a man is defined almost as much by his ability to debate as by his bravery as a warrior.

2. Logic and Intuition Today

a. "The Age of Intuition" in Modern Western Countries

Nowadays Western executives no longer scoff at intuitive thinking. Many freely admit that intuition is a key element in the mental processes that lead to conclusions and decisions. In fact, the higher a person rises in an organization, the more intuition he needs for long-range planning. Typically, creative intuitive thinking is strongest both at the top and at the bottom.

When people are undecided, they are often advised by experts, "Think not, your intuition is better." Toffler, the famous American futurist, even went so far as to coin the term "the Age of Intuition" in his book *The Third Wave*. By that he means the world has entered into a time of using intuition a lot in solving their problems.

b. A Synthesis of Logic and Intuition in Modern China

Today many scholars may refute the argument that there is a great distinction between the intuitive East and the logical West. But seeing is believing. Western visitors to China will find nowadays' China is blending different cultures from various epochs and nation-states. Modern buildings and ancient shrines are usual neighbors in China. The Western products of logic thinking such as high-rises and electrical appliances co-exist with those of intuitive thinking such as calligraphy and traditional Chinese paintings. Meanwhile, it has been widely known in China that intuition is limited where the task is complex and uncertain, where the observer lacks experience, or the observation is distorted by biases. This weakness means a tendency to produce a fixed mindset that ignores new data. Therefore, we are encouraged to use our logical thinking abilities a lot. When logical and intuitive abilities are combined, the result is naturally "holistic".

Further Reading

1. Graham, A. C. (1958). *Two Chinese Philosophers: Cheng Ming-tao and Cheng Yi-chuan*. London: Lund Humphries.
2. Lich, G. E. (1996). *The German Texans*. San Antonio, Texas: University of Texas at San Antonio Institute of Texan Cultures.
3. Marton, B. A. (2004). "Mastering the Art of Persuasion", *Face-to-face Communications for Clarity and Impact*. Boston, MA: Harvard Business School Press.
4. Toffler, A. (1980). *The Third Wave*. New York: Bantam Books.
5. Wechsler, H. J. (1974). *Mirror to the Son of Heaven: We Cheng at the Court of Tang T'ai-tsung*. New Haven: Yale University Press.
6. 胡适口述，唐德刚整理 (2012)，《胡适英文口述自传》，北京：外语教学与研究出版社。
7. 刘毅主编 (2001)，《英文谚语辞典》，Laura E. Stewart 校阅，北京：中国青年出版社。
8. 张培基译注 (1999)，《英译中国现代散文选》（汉英对照），上海：上海外语教育出版社。

Unit 8   Dialectical vs. Analytical Thinking

Sapir-Whorf hypothesis states that the structure of a language determines or greatly influences the modes of thought and behavior characteristic of the culture in which it is spoken.

—Anonymous

The hypothesis is a theory of the relationship between languages and thought expounded in its most explicit form by the American anthropological linguists Edward Sapir and Benjamin Lee Whorf, but why is it also known as "the theory of linguistic relativity"?

Medicine in the West retains the analytical, object-oriented, and interventionist approaches that were common thousands of years ago: Find the offending part or tumor and remove or alter it. Medicine in the East is far more dialectical and has never until modern times been in the least inclined toward surgery or other heroic interventions. Health is the result of a balance of favorable forces in the body; illness is due to a complex interaction of forces that must be met by equally complex, usually natural, mostly herbalist remedies and preventives.

—Anonymous

What thinking modes are separately used in traditional Chinese medicine and Western medicine?

Unit 8 Dialectical vs. Analytical Thinking

I. Proverb Preferences Across Cultures

A study of proverbs from around the world shows that some values are shared by many cultures. Take for instance the widely-quoted English proverb "A friend in need is a friend indeed". It is equivalent to "True friends are the ones who can help each other in trouble (患难见真情)" in Chinese.

Below are two sets of proverbs that appeal to many readers:

1) Misfortune comes on wings and departs on foot.

   The harder you work, the luckier you get.

   The greatest pleasure of life is love.

2) Out of the depth of misfortune comes bliss.

   Behind bad luck comes good luck.

   Too great pleasure will bring about sadness.

Proverbs of group 1 are direct in conveying their meaning and at one glance, the meaning can be understood. Proverbs of group 2 are apparently about change, and it may take more time to figure out their real meaning since dialectical thinking needs to be adopted in the process of comprehension.

Here are more interesting proverbs:

1) Sow nothing, reap nothing.

   The squeaky wheel gets the grease.

   The wealth of the mind is the only true wealth.

2) Haste makes waste.

   Words cut more than swords.

   Your strong points are your weak ones.

Proverbs of group 2 are apparently contradictory: Haste is not equivalent to waste, words cannot be cut, and strong points are not equal to weak points.

Proverbs of group 1 appear pithy, but none expresses contradiction. Actually, proverbs like those in group 2 are more common in a Chinese compendium of proverbs than in a Western collection, and Chinese prefer proverbs with contradictions while Westerners are inclined to like proverbs without them. Many scholars ascribe differences in proverb preferences solely to differences in reasoning or thinking, i.e. dialectical vs. analytical thinking.

II. Dialectical Thinking

In Western thought analytical thinking gains the upper hand while there is a mode of thinking in Chinese thought, traceable to the Zhou dynasty, which has been called dialectical thinking or synthetic reasoning.

1. Definition of Dialectical Thinking

Dialectical thinking means moving back and forth between contrary lines of reasoning, using each to cross-examine the other. This is what juries usually do in arriving at a verdict: Consider arguments and evidence for and against a case, points and counterpoints. It is a process in which opposing facts and ideas are weighed and compared for the purposes of determining the best solution, resolving differences, and coming to the most reasonable conclusion on the basis of the evidence.

Dialectical thinking focuses on contradictions as well as how to resolve or transcend them, or find the truth in both. It is best applied in resolving controversial issues and assessing opposing positions. Often there are several possible ways of resolving questions and understanding issues rather than one single right answer. This reasoning mode can be used in situations where information is incomplete, where many approaches may compete and a person has to decide which one is most reasonable based on what is known even though there is no clear-cut solution.

2. Three Principles of Dialectical Thinking

a. Principle of Change

Ancient Chinese philosophers emphasized the constantly changing nature of everything. According to them, the world is not static but dynamic and changeable. "Constant reversal is the movement of the *dao* (or Way), and being weak is the function of the *dao*. All things under Heaven come into being from visible concrete beings, and all beings come into being from the invisible *dao* (反者道之动。弱者道之用。天下万物生于有，有生于无)." Since everything is in constant flux the concepts are fluid and subjective rather than being fixed and objective. So it is believed that "When the people of the world all know beauty as beauty, there arises the recognition of ugliness; when they all know the good as good, there arises the recognition of evil. And so, being and nonbeing produce each other (天下皆知美之为美，斯恶已；皆知善之为善，斯不善已。有无相生)."

Like our predecessors, we have the same faith in the principle of change and assume that things are constantly changing, and movement in a particular direction may be a sign that events are about to reverse direction, for instance, suffering is regarded as a sign that one is to enjoy a happy life in the future, as the idiom goes "**After the bitter comes the sweet** (苦尽甘来, i.e. **April showers bring May flowers**)."

b. Principle of Contradiction

Because the world is in constant change, oppositions, paradoxes, and anomalies are continuously being created. Therefore, new and old, strong and weak, good and bad, exist in everything; opposites complete each other; the two sides of any apparent contradiction exist in an active harmony, opposed but connected and mutually controlling.

Take *xu* (虚) and *shi* (实) for instance. *Xu* and *shi* are a pair of concepts commonly used in Chinese philosophy and everyday life. ***Shi*** roughly corresponds with **solid, complete, visible, tangible,** and **exact,** whereas *xu* is roughly equivalent to **illusory, sketchy, invisible, intangible,** and **obscure.** *Xu* and *shi* are contradictory and complementary elements which form a dialectical unity. The organization of Chinese sentences is mostly a blend of *xu* and *shi* since Chinese grammar lays stress on meaning perception, which makes it possible and essential to use as few words as possible in sentence construction, e.g. 她有个表兄，住在南京，已经打过电话了，一小时后到 [literally, **She has a cousin; (he) lives in Nanjin**g; **(we) have called him, and (he) will be here in an hour.**] Although this sentence has three *xu* or invisible subjects or actors, the meaning is clear. If we replace those *xu* subjects with *shi* or visible ones (她有个表兄，他住在南京，我们已经打过电话了，他一小时后到), the sentence will look and sound very clumsy, because it does not correspond with the habitual way of expression. The emphasis on the combination of *xu* and *shi* is not only a characteristic of the Chinese language, but also shown in traditional painting, architecture, opera, etc. The principle employed in those activities is known as the principle of contradiction.

c. Principle of Relationship

Chinese thinking is also based on the principle of relationship. The strong belief in change and opposition has led us to view the world in a holistic or synthetic way: We see a lot of background events; we are good at observing relationships between events; we regard the world as complex and highly changeable and its components as interrelated; we see events as moving in cycles between extremes; we feel that control over events requires coordination with

Unit 8   Dialectical vs. Analytical Thinking

others. In one word, we see the big environment as well as objects in relation to their environments so much so that it is difficult for us to visually isolate objects from their environments.

d. Relationship Between the Three Principles

The three principles of dialectical thinking are interrelated. Change produces contradiction and contradiction causes change; constant change and contradiction imply that it is meaningless to discuss the individual part without considering its relationship with other parts and its past states. The principles also imply another important tenet of Chinese thought, which is the insistence on finding **the Middle Way** between extreme propositions. In China, there is a strong presumption that contradictions are apparent and that "A is wrong and B is not right either." This stance is explicitly revealed in the Chan Buddhist dictum that "The truth that can be said is not the truth (能够被说出来的真理不是真理)."

3. Impact of Dialectical Thinking on Writings

How does dialectical thinking influence Chinese writings? For further exploration, it is necessary to consider typical steps to write an article in Chinese. Let's take for instance an essay entitled "A Chat about Marriage" by famous Chinese author Yu Dafu.

Step 1: Introduction

We are supposed to begin the essay with one of the three options: Make an introduction to the purpose or context for the article; elaborate upon why the subject is worthwhile; define or explain key ideas, concepts, situations, controversies, etc. For example:

The other day, Mr. Lin Yutang said something to the effect that women's only career lies in matrimony.

Step 2: Thesis

Go on with one of the two options: Clearly state the thesis before presenting arguments for the thesis; describe and evaluate the reasons and supporting evidence for the thesis. For instance:

Now, an eminent French writer declared at a press interview after arriving in Shanghai that men should stay bachelors if they want to achieve success in life.

Step 3: Antithesis

Impartially present the antithesis before describing how it is contrary to the thesis or describe and evaluate the supporting arguments and evidence. For instance:

Washington Irving was a confirmed bachelor, but in his *Sketch Book* there is an article extolling the wife as a graceful and lovely life-long partner. Charles Lamb, also a single man, in *A Bachelor's Complaint of the Behavior of Married People*, one of his essays signed "Elia", speaks mockingly of married people with their inevitable postnuptial fruits–the Children.

Marriage or no marriage, which is more desirable? That sounds like the chicken-and-egg question, which, though often discussed, remains a perpetual puzzle. Generally speaking, one who has no family dependants is not supposed to rent a house, one who has no petticoat influence in the government should refrain from becoming an official, an unmarried male writer is in no position to write about "my wife". All these seem to hit at the advantages of marriage. But, to get married, you need to have five prerequisites, namely, money, leisure, employment, good looks and potentness, of which all are not always available. What is more, after your marriage, your offspring will come to this world of themselves. And in a world with overpopulation, economic crisis, educational bankruptcy and deteriorating public morals, they may, just as Charles Lamb says, through their own acts of indiscretion, be sent to the

gallows. With such a terrible misfortune befalling your family, how could you still have wedded bliss to speak of?

Step 4: Conclusion

Conclude the article with one of the three options below:

Adopt the original thesis while rejecting the antithesis; adopt and advance the antithesis while giving up the original thesis; conclude by synthesizing the best aspects of the thesis and antithesis, and find a Middle Way or negate both the original thesis and antithesis. The conclusion needs to summarize, weigh and compare the ideas, point out the significant strengths and weaknesses, advantages and disadvantages of the two positions, and explain how and why the conclusion has been reached. For instance:

Thinking about the matter over and over again, I cannot but come to the conclusion that neither matrimony nor bachelorship has anything to recommend itself.

III. Analytical Thinking

There is a dialectical tradition that has occupied a place in Western thought since the time of Immanuel Kant and Friedrich Hegel, but the Hegelian dialectic has been held to be more "aggressive" because the effort is toward obliterating contradictions. What gains the upper hand in Western thought is still analytical reasoning or thinking.

1. Definition of Analytical Thinking

In the philosophy of German philosopher Immanuel Kant (1724–1804), analytical thinking represents judgments made upon statements that are based on the virtue of the statement's own content. No particular experience, beyond an understanding of the meanings of words used, is necessary for analytical reasoning. For example, "Jane is an orphan" is a given true statement. Through analytical reasoning, one can make the judgment that Jane's parents died or dumped her when she was little. One knows this to be true since the state of being without parents is implied in the word **orphan**; no particular experience of Jane is necessary to make this judgment. To suggest that Jane lives with his mother or father–given that she is an orphan–would be self-contradictory.

2. Three Principles of Analytical Thinking

Westerners are not aware of how committed they are to analytical principles that conflict directly with the spirit of Chinese dialecticism. The analytical principles used in their reasoning process are the principle of identity, the principle of non-contradiction, and the principle of stability.

a. Principle of Identity

The principle of identity holds that an object is itself and not some other objects. In the Hollywood film *Who-am-I*, Jackie Chan (成龙), a secret agent, fell from a crashing helicopter. Waking up in a village of local natives, Jackie had no memory of who he was, thus being addressed as "Who-am-I". With no identity, Jackie was thirsty for the answer because loss of identity implies loss of life in Western thought. Luckily toward the end of the film, he gradually realized who he was through analytical reasoning and acting from the principle of identity. It happens that the Chinese folk song "For Whom" is also about identity, but we have no exact idea who the praised person is even after we finish the song probably because individual identity is interwoven with group identity and the context, in which personal identity is decided by one's relationship with others. The lyrics of the song go roughly as follows:

Your trousers are covered with mud and you are soaked with sweat.
I don't know who you are, but I know who you are fighting for. You are

fighting for the harvest in autumn, for the return of wild geese in spring… Who are you? Who are you fighting for? When will you return, my comrade-in-arms? Who are you? Who are you fighting for? So that my brothers and sisters won't cry. Who are the most beautiful and who are the most tired? My fellow villagers, my comrades-in-arms, my brothers and sisters.

b. Principle of Non-contradiction

The principle of non-contradiction holds that a position can't be both true and false: A and not-A are impossible.

Modern Chinese are of course well aware of the same analytical principles that Westerners hold dear and make use of analysis in some contexts. But in our view, the principle of non-contradiction applies only to the realm of concepts and abstractions. The differences in the two stances toward contradiction have some interesting consequences. For instance, the Chinese worship many gods (e.g. *tian*, the supreme god, **the river god**, **the moon god**, and **the sun god**) while Western Christians only believe in the power of God, regarding God as the only true God; abortion is not good for Chinese, but acceptable and necessary when the woman is unmarried or poor in health while Westerners (especially some Americans) equate abortion to feticide, the killing and murder of a human fetus; for Chinese the opposite of a great truth is also true, but Westerners believe that the opposite of a great truth is false and a lie.

c. Principle of Stability

Ancient Greek philosophers are inclined to believe that things don't change much or that if they are really changing, future change will continue in the same direction and at the same rate. And the same is true of ordinary modern Westerners who, like the ancient Greeks, see the world in a stable state; they see objects as discrete and separate from their environments; they see events as moving in a linear fashion when they move at all. Therefore, they have developed a sense of controllability.

3. Western Emphasis on Analytical Ability

Analytical thinking is very influential in every department of Western societies. That explains why analytical ability has been so highly emphasized by the Western educational system that it has been included in many kinds of level examinations. GRE or the Graduate Record Examination is a standardized test that measures the aptitude of promising graduate students. Administered by the Educational Testing Service (ETS) of the USA, the GRE takes three basic forms: the General Test, Subject Tests, and the Writing Assessment. The General Test, most often referred to as the GRE, measures verbal, quantitative, and analytical skills. The Subject Tests measure achievement in eight disciplines. And the Writing Assessment consists of two analytical writing tasks.

Undoubtedly analytical thinking is encouraged by people in authority and the whole society, which explains why people spend so much time improving their analytical reasoning ability. When they are little, Westerners are encouraged to play games that involve analytical reasoning skills. Here is a famous problem for Western children to solve: Four men (A, B, C, D) and four women (W, X, Y, Z) are going rafting in two rafts. Each raft holds exactly four people, and the groups of people in the two rafts follow these conditions:

1) There are exactly two men and two women in each raft.

2) Either A or B, but not both, must be in the first raft.

3) If W is in the first raft, then C must also be in the first raft.

4) If Y is in the first raft, then B cannot be in the first raft.

If B is in the first raft, which of the following can be the other three people in the first raft?

(A) A, X, Z

(B) C, D, W

(C) C, W, X

(D) C, X, Y

(E) D, W, Z

To solve the problem, analytical reasoning should be employed. Through practice like that, people become good at this kind of test and what's more important, people have improved their ability in analytical reasoning through repeated efforts.

IV. More about the Two Modes

1. Weaknesses of the Two Modes

The strengths and weaknesses of the two modes are self-evident. Here the focus will be on their weaknesses.

a. Weaknesses of the Analytical Thinking

As is known to many, life is not easy. Yet owing to the dialectical thinking which can stop us from feeling extremely bad about ourselves, we seem to be happier, less anxious and less depressed than Westerners. Let us take as an example different ways of dealing with some contradictory information stemming from conflicts between a mother-in-law and her daughter-in-law. In such a sensitive relationship, the Chinese are inclined to find fault on both sides and look for solutions that will move both sides to the middle because they are family. Westerners, accustomed to analytical reasoning, are in terrible need of figuring out who is right in an argument or conflict, disregarding the fact that however bad the mother-in-law and her daughter-in-law are in a relationship they are family. At the interpersonal level which involves conflicts including those among family members, you really don't need to find the truth and then blame one side for the causes of the problems and demand changes from one side to attain a solution and offer no compromise. In the same situation, the Chinese are far more inclined to reason that both sides have flaws and virtues, because we have a holistic awareness that life is full of contradictions and everything is changing.

b. Weaknesses of the Dialectical Thinking

We do not apply dialectical thinking to the physical material world, for example, we do not believe that the sun can rise in both the east and the west, although we believe A is good, and B is not bad. However, in tests of scientific thinking we, accustomed to dialectical reasoning, are really short. Asked to determine which statement is true in a survey–whether, for instance, national pay rise makes people enjoy stronger or weaker purchasing power–many Chinese respondents took the middle road, even when they believed one statement to be less true than the other. The tendency to look for the middle way has hampered our efforts to seek scientific truth through aggressive argumentation–the classical Western method of identifying true and false answers. It may also have contributed to our willingness to tolerate improper decisions to some extent.

2. "Making Use of Advantages and Bypassing Disadvantages"

In fact there is no better mode in terms of thinking or reasoning. The best way is to use both–one mode for science and another for relationship.

In recent years, more evidence has been coming out to prove that we are not concerned with contradictions in the same way as before. We have a greater preference for compromise solutions and holistic arguments and we are more willing to endorse both of the apparently contradictory arguments. On the other hand, the greater adherence to the principle of non-contradiction on the part of Westerners seems to produce no guarantee against questionable inferences. On the contrary, Western contradiction phobia may sometimes cause them to become more extreme in their judgments under conditions in which the evidence indicates they should become less extreme.

Therefore, it is necessary for us to make use of the advantages of the two thinking modes and bypass their disadvantages (扬长避短) by learning from Western analytical methods for determining scientific truth in intercultural communication.

Further Reading

1. Hegel, G.W. F. (1991). *Philosophy of Right*. Cambridge: Cambridge University Press.
2. Hofstede, G. (2005). *Cultures and Organizations: Software of the Mind*. New York: McGraw-Hill.
3. Holland, D. & Quinn, N. (1987). *Cultural Models in Language and Thought*. Cambridge, UK: Cambridge University Press.
4. Lakoff, G. & Johnson, M. (1980). *Metaphors We Live By*. Chicago, IL: University of Chicago Press.
5. Pearl, J. (1966). *Experiments in Induction*. San Francisco, CA: Morgan Kaufmann Publishers.
6. 邓晓芒 (2013)，《中西文化心理比较讲演录》，北京：人民出版社。
7. 庞万里 (2005)，《中国古典哲学通论》，北京：北京航空航天大学出版社。
8. 许倬云 (2018)，《中国文化的精神》，北京：九州出版社。
9. 张培基译注 (1999)，《英译中国现代散文选》（汉英对照），上海：上海外语教育出版社。

Unit 9 Holistic vs. Atomistic Visions

Listen to all parties and you will be enlightened.

—Wei Zheng

As a chancellor for about 13 years during the reign of Emperor Taizong of the Tang dynasty, Wei Zheng obtained far broader freedom to criticize others, particularly the emperor, than other officials. As a matter of fact he not only criticized but also gave advice to the emperor. For instance, he suggested the emperor listen to all parties. What led him to make such a suggestion?

Seize the day! Begin now! Each day is a new life. Seize it.

—David Powers

Do you think this suggestion may work for you? Why or why not?

Everything difficult under Heaven must be dealt with while it is still easy. Everything great under Heaven must be dealt with while it is still small (天下难事，必作于易；天下大事，必作于细).

—Laozi

What Laozi said more than 2000 years ago implies that there is always a process of moving from quantitative to qualitative change. How shall we put this idea into practice?

Unit 9 Holistic vs. Atomistic Visions

I. A Detention Room Incident

In many American schools, there is a detention room for children who have violated or rebelled against school rules and regulations to stay for two or three school days. Thirteen-year-old Chinese boy Minchang, an English beginner, picked up some bad language in the hallway during his first few weeks in the U.S. and practiced it in the classroom. For this, he had to stay in the detention room for three days so that, in his headmaster's words, "he can become a gentleman in the future." That man seemed to have completely forgotten what he said the other day–"Minchang is a sweet young man." Minchang's mother tried her utmost to explain Minchang's problem to his grandparents who adamantly argued that the school's decision smelled of racial prejudice because in China we focus not only on each of a boy's traits inferred from his past behavior, and situational factors influencing him will also be examined. But in the West, they are inclined to focus on each of his personal remarks, actions, and attitudes.

Minchang's detention room incident clearly illustrates two different visions of the world– the holistic and the reductionistic. On the one hand, people brought up in traditional Chinese culture are likely to synthesize parts and examine the whole, paying special attention to the whole situation or environment. On the other hand, people nurtured in Western culture tend to dissect things into parts, focusing on details and analyzing them one by one.

II. Prominent Attributes of Holistic and Atomistic Visions

1. A Brief Introduction

a. Atomistic Vision

Atomism, a theory that explains complex phenomena in terms of aggregates of fixed particles or units, has found its most successful application in natural science: according to the atomistic view, the material universe is composed of minute particles, which are considered to be relatively simple and immutable and too small to be visible. The multiplicity of visible forms in nature, then, is based upon differences in these particles and their configurations; hence, any observable changes must be reduced to changes in these configurations. The atomistic point of view prevails in Western culture. Westerners are good at classifying things and arranging them systematically. Animals, plants, and objects are clearly divided, subdivided, and further divided according to their attributes. If you glance at the title, subtitles, and topic sentences of each paragraph of an English writing, you instantly know its content. When listening to a speech, you may easily get the message by following the cohesive connectors signaling time sequence like **first**, **second**, **third**, **next**, **finally**, and so on, and words marking logical relationships such as **because**, **however**, **actually**, **supposing**, **although**, and **therefore**.

Atomistic vision is widely accepted today by scientists as well as medical practitioners. In their medical practice doctors of Western medicine treat their patients by examining parts of the body through lab tests, X-rays and other medical appliances before making a diagnosis and using chemical-based medicines and surgery.

This vision involves the frequent use of abstract concepts. Arguably, Westerners are relatively stronger in making use of abstract concepts for analytical judgment. Abstraction is synonymous with precision, exactness and clarity, which may help to explain why more theoretical works on science and technology have been produced in the West.

b. Holistic Vision

Combined logical and intuitive thinking is holistic thinking. This synthetic

Unit 9 Holistic vs. Atomistic Visions

vision predominates in traditional Chinese culture, although analysis has never been rejected. We are accustomed to observing and judging objects or people as a whole. When reading a classical Chinese article, the reader will find that the unity and harmony of the whole piece have been attached great importance and the correspondence between the introduction and conclusion and the natural transition from one point to another have been given much attention.

Synthesis holds sway in traditional Chinese society. Exposed to such a culture, many people disliked abstractions and science. Zhu Xi (1130–1200), the greatest Confucian scholar of the Song time, wrote commentaries upon almost all of the Confucian classics, engaged in political affairs, education, and agriculture. However, he had little interest in practicing his "investigation of the things (格物致知)" in the realms of natural and social sciences. Usually, a Chinese medicine practitioner approached an illness from a broader perspective, emphasizing its entirety and dialectical implication. Instead of making his judgment based on the results of lab tests on the internal organs, a traditional Chinese medical practitioner diagnosed a patient's disease by first looking at his complexion and tongue, smelling him, feeling his pulse and soliciting complaints, in order to form a correct judgment of the patient's general physical condition before prescribing herbal medicines and acupuncture. That is why some people view traditional Chinese medicine (TCM) as a holistic medicine. In contrast, a Western doctor deals directly with the symptoms. For instance, if someone has a sore throat, a Western doctor will treat it as a throat problem while a Chinese doctor might link it to the disorder of the patient's stomach.

Confucianism also holds a holistic vision of a peaceful world, which rests on a carefully integrated program of personal self-cultivation, harmonized family life, and well-ordered states. At the heart of this vision is the sense of "integration of Heaven, earth and man."

2. Attributes of the Chinese Holistic Vision

It happens that we peel an apple around and reserve the whole before biting it. Probably the secret behind this habit is associated with our holistic vision, which has the following attributes.

a. Context-dependence

Chinese thought or vision is inclined to be more context-dependent. Holistic approaches attend to the entire context or background, emphasize change, and focus less on the specific object. Take for instance tea drinking–a national pastime which employs a holistic approach. In the past, tea drinking should take place in a setting where "spring water runs on marbles," "in a monastery in misty spring" or "in the woods during sunset." Nowadays, in order to recreate such an ambience, tea houses are always decorated with traditional paintings, calligraphy and furniture, with a girl in traditional costume playing a traditional Chinese musical instrument. Usually tea drinkers are very particular about the source of water, aroma of the tea, color, shape quality and production place of tea leaves and how they look in fine teapots and cups of different shapes. While savoring a cup of tea in a quiet teahouse they are apt to imagine themselves roaming among mountains and waters and integrating with nature. In this sense, tea means life. Therefore, it is unlikely for the Chinese to crush tea leaves into powder or tiny pellets like Lipton, the biggest tea exporter in the world.

The doctrine of **_yin-yang_**, the Five Elements, the Eight Diagrams (**_bagua_**), traditional Chinese medicine, and even playing **_majiang_** employ the holistic approach, observing the changing situation and depending generally much on the context.

b. Combination of Two or More into One

The holistic vision leads ordinary Chinese to combine two or more into one. For his patients, for instance, a Chinese doctor today may recommend Western medicine for intensive treatment and traditional Chinese medicine for the recovery of his *qi* and blood. For people undergoing chemotherapy for their terminal diseases traditional Chinese medicine may be the last resort since it can not only alleviate pain but also offers a different treatment.

For both Chinese and Westerners, marriage is full of love and sometimes compromise. But *lianyin* (i.e. combining two extended families into one through marriage), a concept available only in Chinese, betrays a complicated and thus more sensitive relationship in the traditional Chinese household, where a man was a son, an elder brother, a husband and a father given certain obligations that he could never shun. Even his marriage was the duty to produce the next generation, take care of his aged parents or grandparents, and support the bigger family with four generations living under one roof.

In philosophical terms, it can be said that we Chinese tend to combine two or more into one when making sense of the world. The well-known *dao*, for instance, is simply the invisible, intangible, and indescribable whole which merges with all things in Heaven and on earth.

c. Acceptance of Contradictions

The Chinese holistic thought or vision inclines towards acceptance of contradictions. Both Chinese and Western people put emphasis on dialectics (although to different degrees). However, Chinese dialectic is different from its Western counterpart in that it places more emphasis on integration. Therefore, we are more likely to accept two obviously contradictory proposals and try to find a third way—the middle way. A common sight in China is four people playing *majiang* at a small table, surrounded by an animated and vociferous crowd of onlookers. Such settings may underline the game's status as a pastime for the masses, but some scholars go so far as to rank it as an icon of Chinese culture alongside Peking Opera. Have you ever watched people playing the game and then yearned to join them and create order out of chaos based on random drawings of tiles? *Majiang* is believed to be deep and sort of like life. We try to make a little bit of order out of the chaos of life full of orderly chaos, disorganized order, old and new, beautiful and filthy, clean and dirty, rich and poor, kindness and arrogance, cooperation and mischief-making...

And there is a particularly beautiful aspect of the *yin-yang* dialectic that runs through all of Chinese thought and artistic expression, namely the contrast of mountains and water. The (male) mountains are permanent, symbolizing space; (female) water is changeable, a symbol of time. Mountains rise, waters descend. But they are symbiotic: rivers begin in mountains, and they are the sculptors of mountains. In this way, mountains and water represent the entire cosmos.

d. Not Seeing the Trees for the Woods

The Chinese holistic vision tends to examine problems as a whole, so it is most likely to result in "not seeing the trees for the woods" when we make sense of the world. The holistic view is the guiding ideology of traditional Chinese medicine which believes that the human body is an organic whole, centered on the viscera and connected by the meridians, structurally inseparable, functionally interacting, and pathologically affecting each other. Human beings connect with nature and the social environment. Human physiology changes along with climate and living environment. And human diseases are closely related to changes in climate, geographical environment, and social environment. Based

Unit 9　Holistic vs. Atomistic Visions

on this point of view, traditional Chinese medicine comprehensively assessed the patient's existing or potential health problems by analyzing the patient's physiology, psychology, natural and social environment, and provided health care for patients by nursing based on disease differentiation, syndrome differentiation and symptom differentiation. Often more than four herbal medicines (君臣佐使) with different tastes, functions and effects are prescribed to treat one trouble of the patient.

e. Much Use of the Integration Concept

In ancient China, stress on integration or holism extended to a sense of the integration of human existence with natural and even supernatural things. There was a belief in a supreme deity *tian* (Heaven) which ruled the world and took a personal interest in the affairs of mankind, a belief in the existence and power of spirits of nature and spirits of deceased ancestors who had to be served and placated with sacrifices, a belief in the divine sanction of the political order and the great responsibility of a ruler to fulfill his **moral duties to *tian*** (i.e. *Tianming* or the mandate of Heaven) and his subjects. It is the concept of the moral responsibilities of the ruler, and the way in which the ruler should carry out these responsibilities so as not to lose the favor and protection of *tian*, which became a major concern of thinkers and one of the key problems of Chinese philosophy. For ancient Chinese, what happened on earth was believed to resonate with events in nature and Heaven. The same is true of the Chinese today. According to Daoism which is still influential, animals, plants, natural objects, and even man-made artifacts have spirits that arise from nature (灵气). Therefore, advertisements that emphasize nature are more successful in China. Some Western carmakers have discovered this fact and started their advertising campaign for their products in China with scenes of nature–with just the brand name usually appearing at the end of the sequence.

The holistic vision is also reflected in the cuisine. Chinese food which stresses color, smell and taste is usually prepared in bite-size pieces, but fish are often cooked and served whole. Whole fish culturally signifies the wholeness of things (全须全尾) as it has a proper beginning (i.e. head) with an end (i.e. tail).

3. Attributes of the Western Atomistic Vision

In contrast to holistic theories, which explain the parts in terms of qualities displayed by the whole, atomism explains the observable properties of the whole by those of its components and of their configurations. And atomist view tends to have the following features.

a. Dichotomy

A dichotomy is splitting one into two or more which are considered to be either contradictory or mutually exclusive. For example, the colors black and white represent a classic dichotomy: Either something is black, or it is white, with no room for overlap or alternatives.

Incidentally, Westerners tend to separate just as they divide an apple into parts before eating it, which is not strange given the fact that dichotomy is common in their thoughts and their vision of the world. Lipton, the famous British tea company, breaks tea leaves into tiny pellets, puts them into very standardized small bags and makes big profits. For Westerners, tea is composed of many elements that can improve human health, and drinking tea is to absorb those healthy elements before dumping the small tea bag into the garbage can instead of enjoying the aroma of the tea or admiring the shape of tea leaves in fine tea cups.

b. Not Seeing the Woods for the Trees

The Atomistic vision is inclined to regard observable forms in nature not as

Unit 9 Holistic vs. Atomistic Visions

intrinsic wholes but as aggregates of parts or components. As a result, it is most likely to result in "not seeing the woods for the trees." For example, a Western doctor deals directly with symptoms. If someone has a headache, a Western doctor may treat it as a head problem while a Chinese doctor may link it to poor blood circulation or neck trouble which can cause insufficient blood supply to the head.

c. Polarizing

The atomistic vision is apt to polarize and emphasize the debate between opposing forces so that the middle alternatives are virtually ignored. Therefore, when confronted with two apparently contradictory propositions, the Westerner tends to polarize his or her beliefs and insists on the correctness of one belief vs. another.

d. Discreteness-dependence

Western thought or vision is inclined to be discreteness-dependent. The ancient Greek philosophers saw the world as being composed of discrete objects. It is true of today's Westerners. For instance, the question "does it have a backbone?" is often used to divide species into vertebrates and invertebrates. Beginning in the late eighteenth and early nineteenth century, some Western countries, especially America, began to apply the discrete approach to improve efficiency in the world of manufacturing and commerce. They invented assembly lines, broke down the production of everything from rice-cookers to planes into the most standardized parts possible and the simplest replicable actions, analyzed each component or each action of a worker, and made it maximally efficient so that products that had taken workers or craftsmen months to produce could now be produced within a few hours or minutes. They also set up profitable niche market ventures by addressing the need for a particular product or service that was not addressed by the big providers.

III. Vision and Cognition

Cognition refers to the mental process of knowing, including aspects such as awareness, perception, reasoning, intuition, knowledge, and judgment. There is much evidence indicating that vision has much influence on human cognition.

1. Vision and Cognition of Factors Affecting Outcomes

For Chinese the factors affecting outcomes are extraordinarily complex. The practice of traditional Chinese medicine and *fengshui* (literally wind and water) for choosing building sites may have encouraged this idea, which in turn encourages the search for relationships in the context. This is quite different from the Western discrete and rule-based approaches. Consider, for example, the titles of the English books about approaches to education and self-teach–*How the Way We Talk Can Change the Way We Work: Seven Languages for Transformation* and *The Six Triggers of Persuasion*. In China, similar books are also popular but the titles betray a holistic vision, for instance, *Liu Yiting, a Harvard Girl* (《哈佛女孩刘亦婷》), *Zhang Zhaomu, a Harvard Boy* (《哈佛男孩张肇牧》), and *A Night's Talk with Sister Understanding* (《知心姐姐的话》).

Arguably, on the whole the Westerner is used to operating in a reductionistic way while the Chinese are more likely to emphasize relationships, including the environment or context. As a result, a child in the West who performs poorly in the language is likely to be regarded as having poor language ability. But in China, such a child might be viewed as needing to work harder, or perhaps his teacher and parents should work harder, or maybe the setting for learning should be improved.

2. Vision and Language Cognition

We have learnt in our grammar books that nouns are more analytical, thinking-involving and logical while verbs involve a holistic understanding of mankind and everything in nature. There are more nouns in English while there are more verbs in Chinese. It is no coincidence that Western children learn nouns faster than verbs and Chinese kids acquire verbs just as fast as nouns since, for instance, "to write" involves the hand, the movement of the hand, the paper, the ink, the color of the ink, and the marks left on the paper.

3. Vision and Information Cognition

According to atomistic, an analytical doctrine in essence, a whole should be separated into its constituent parts in order to study the parts and their relations. But in holistic vision, information cognition is usually integrated with the involved persons' own experience, intuition and creativity. When looking at the map of China, we can see that its shape appears uncannily similar to that of a rooster. The rooster's head covers the three northeast provinces, its tail includes Xinjiang and Tibet and its wings spread over the resource-rich basins of the Yangtze and the Yellow Rivers. The belly of this rooster is in the southeast, and the Hainan and Taiwan islands are its feet. When we tried to transmit the information to our friends from Calgary, Canada, they closely examined the map but few could make out the image of the rooster.

IV. Vision and Language

1. Vision and Language Differences

Different visions of the world may have helped produce different languages.

First, Chinese holism creates a highly "contextual" language. Chinese characters typically have multiple meanings and pronunciations, so to be understood they require the context of sentences. On the other hand, English words are relatively distinctive and English speakers with atomistic vision are concerned with making sure words and utterances have as little context as possible.

Second, the Chinese holistic vision allows people to look from the general to the specific and speak in a "topic-prominent" language. In Chinese, sentences have a position, typically the first position that should be filled by the current topic, e.g.这种脚，没地方买鞋穿 (literally, such feet have nowhere to buy shoes; freely, shoes are not available for such feet). While not obligatory from a grammatical standpoint, an idiomatic Chinese sentence usually starts with context, e.g.春季南京人爱去梅花山 (in spring, Nanjing natives love visiting Plum Blossom Hill). English, however, as a "subject-prominent" language with a reductionistic vision, starts with a subject. An idiomatic English sentence jumps immediately to a subject, and there must be a subject even in the sentence **It is snowing today** although **"It"** is a form subject. Obviously English is preoccupied with focal objects as opposed to context.

Third, for Chinese one should adapt himself to different situations since everything is in constant change, which is correspondent with his holistic vision. That explains why there are many different expressions for "I" or "me" in ancient Chinese, e.g. **I** (草民, literally, grass-root man) in relation to the emperor, **I** (不孝之子, literally, your unfilial son) in relation to his parents, and **I** (学生, literally, your student) in relation to his teacher. It is difficult for ancient Chinese to think of properties that only apply to **I** or **me**, but much easier for them to think of properties that apply to **I** or **me** in certain settings and in relation to particular people. For Westerners, it is the self who does the acting, e.g. **I am what I am; My name is John Smith; Call me John** (instead of saying "call your classmate John"). Therefore naming is more complicated in China. Many Chinese people, even into the 21st century, followed the widespread custom of adopting a "courtesy name" when they reached adulthood: The Tang poet Du Fu took the courtesy name Zimei, for example, while Mao Zedong was Runzhi and Dr. Sun Yat-sen was Zaizhi. The twelfth-century official Lu You meticulously records the courtesy names of all the various dignitaries whom he encountered on his travels.

The fourth difference concerns raising proper questions. For instance, when inquiring as to whether one would like more to drink, eat or take, we ask, "再喝一点 (Drink more)?" but they ask "More tea?" in English. To Chinese speakers with a holistic vision, it is obvious that it is the tea that one is talking about drinking more of, so to mention tea would be redundant since the verb "喝 (to drink)" itself involves all that contribute to the action including the action of drinking, the tea, the mouth, the hand, and the lips. To English speakers with reductionistic vision, it's crystal clear that one is talking about tea, as opposed to any other activity that might be carried out with it, so it would be rather bizarre for the questioner to refer to drinking.

2. Vision and Argumentative Writings

The holistic vision seeks integral and absolute knowledge, so it is generally qualitative (定性), not quantitative. Qualitative emphasis leads us to argue by deduction. The idea is to create a context that sounds powerful and convincing. In other words, what is said exactly is not important; it is the context or the argumentative atmosphere that is important. Thus you will find much use of phrases employed to constitute a context of debate such as **we must, we should not, it is wrong to, it is absurd, cannot be denied,** or **resolutely demand** in Chinese argumentative writings.

The atomistic vision involves both qualitative and quantitative analysis (定性定量分析), putting more emphasis on the study of the latter. The quantitative emphasis makes English writers develop their arguments in an inductive or linear way. In English argumentative writing, since context is less important and considerable stress is thus laid on making one's position clear, the tone is usually restrained, and the language is generally moderate to sound objective. In the writing process, therefore, native English writers tend to be less militant and more cautious in tone and language than traditional Chinese writers, especially those before China's reform and opening up in the 1970s. Their idea is to let the facts speak for themselves for they believe the facts themselves should be able to convince the readership.

However, in writing a thesis which involves qualitative and quantitative analysis, Chinese writers are also required to sound humble. In order to create a context of modesty, Chinese papers tend to have such titles as preceded by **A Superficial Discussion of …, An Attempt to Discuss…, Preliminary Analysis of …, or My Humble Opinions on …** To the English-speaking people all these sound uncertain and thus unconvincing.

3. Vision and Causation

Causation is a sociological term indicating the belief that events occur in predictable ways and that one event engenders the other. The influence of different visions on causation is great. Let us consider the coverage of an American campus shooting case.

In early November 1991, Lu Gang, a Chinese post-doctoral student at the University of Iowa who had received his Ph.D. in Physics from the university earlier, submitted his dissertation at an awards competition, but lost to another Chinese graduate student Shan Linhua. He subsequently failed to obtain an

Unit 9　Holistic vs. Atomistic Visions

academic job. On October 31, a snowy day, he walked into a seminar room and shot his adviser, the person who had handled his appeal, Shan Linhua who was to receive the award, several of his fellow students and bystanders, and then himself.

In this sensational case, different visions guided reporters from different cultures to focus on different aspects. The explanations for Lu's behavior in the American campus newspapers revealed an atomistic view of causes, focusing almost entirely on Lu's presumed qualities–his bad personality characteristics (e.g. he was a "**darkly disturbed man**", and had a "**very bad temper**") and wrong attitude (e.g. he had a "**strong belief that guns were an important means to redress grievances**"). Chinese reporters, on the other hand, emphasized causes associated with the context or environment to which Lu was exposed. Hence their explanations for this homicide almost entirely centered on Lu's poor people skills (e.g. **bad relationship with his adviser although he was a brilliant exchange student, envy of the slain student, isolation from the Chinese community, spoiled only-son in his family**), pressures from Chinese society (e.g. **no face to go back home to confront his family, a victim of the so-called "Top Student" educational policy in China**) and the American context (e.g. **Western violence culture** and **no gun control**).

Would Lu Gang commit the tragic murder if he had won the cut-throat competition, then?

Most of the Westerners who are used to dissecting things into parts before analyzing their relations would say, "Yes!"

"No, in many cases." would be the answer from most of us who pay special attention to the influence of context on people's behavior.

4. Vision and Communicative Behavior

Our vision controls our communicative behavior to some extent, which we cannot afford to ignore in our study.

a. Taking the Oath a Second Time

On January 21, 2009 American Chief Justice John Roberts delivered the oath to Obama at the White House again—a rare do-over. The surprise moment came in response to a much-noticed stumble on the day before when Roberts got the words of the oath a little off, which prompted Obama to do so, too.

As for the messed-up oath at the inauguration on the 20th, some constitutional experts said the Constitution is clear about the exact wording of the oath and as a result, a do-over probably wasn't necessary but also couldn't hurt. Two other previous presidents had repeated the oath because of similar issues. Some observers said that right-wing nuts would be hinting darkly that Obama wasn't really president because he had not taken the constitutionally-mandated oath as written. Now, it turns out that reasonable people believed there was a potential problem and Obama did, in fact, take the oath a second time out of what White House counsel Greg Craig called "an abundance of caution."

Regarding Obama's second oath, many Chinese scholars echoed their Western counterparts' views. But some of our friends and students said among ourselves that his legality admitted of no doubt since Obama won the much-covered presidential campaign, took the oath of office as U.S. President on the Capitol platform before the whole watching world, and above all, his group has replaced Bush's group. Yet we do understand it's a truly cautious act for Obama to take a second oath since most of his people hold a reductionistic vision.

b. "Painting the Lily"

Here is a short Chinese text about a festival:

Unit 9 Holistic vs. Atomistic Visions

彝族人民的插花节

节日期间，彝族姑娘在门上和自己身上插花以示吉祥；给老人发上插花以示健康长寿；给心上人发上插花祝福白头偕老；在田边插花以示丰收；在羊角上插花以示六畜兴旺等。所有这些，都表现出彝族人民对幸福生活的向往。

For us, this text is well-written for it tells the reader what the festival is about and what people do on that special day before ending the description with a commentary remark as a concluding sentence, thus achieving the unity of the whole piece, which tallies with Chinese holistic vision. But after reading the English version translated by one of his graduate students, an English professor suggested deleting the last sentence, pointing out that it seems to be "painting the lily." The English version is as follows:

Flower Festival of Yi Ethnic Minority

During the festival, young women paste flowers on the doors and insert some in their clothes for good luck. Old people wear flowers in their hair for health and longevity. Young men decorate their sweethearts' hair with flowers, praying for growing old together. People plant flowers by the side of the field for a good harvest and tie flowers to the sheep's horns for more domesticated animals…

All these activities show that Yi people long for a beautiful life.

Westerners tend to understand complex phenomena in terms of aggregates of fixed particles or components. For them fact speaks louder than words, and hence it upsets them to be told as if they were pupils that "all these activities show that Yi people long for a beautiful life," which has already been explicitly implied in the text.

V. Zhengshan Xiaozhong and Lipton Black Tea

During our stay in Wuyi Mountain Nature Reserve twenty years ago, we became addicted to a kind of black tea called **Zhengshan Xiaozhong** (正山小种). It has been confirmed that Lipton black tea originates from it. A story goes that one day in the 17th century a tea merchant purchased some freshly picked tea leaves, but unfortunately ran into some bandits on his way home. In a hurry, he hid his tea leaves in a safe place and ran for his life. A few days later he returned only to find his green tea leaves had turned black. As he couldn't afford the loss, instead of dumping the tea leaves into the garbage can, he processed the black tea leaves into black-colored tea never drunk before and thus not warmly accepted by tea drinkers. Later the black tea leaves were sold to some Dutch and Portuguese businessmen who sold them to British businessmen without anticipating this kind of tea would become very popular with people in Britain. Later, some Englishmen visited Fujian many times and stole the processing technique of black tea as well as tea trees, some of which were planted by them in India and Sri Lanka so the two Asian countries became big tea exporters years later.

In our home, there are some **Zhengshan Xiaozhong** black tea produced in China and Lipton black tea made in Britain. To be honest, when we first saw Lipton black tea many years ago we were surprised to notice the world famous tea consists of tiny pellets in standardized small bags. Tea in our mind used to look like tree leaves of different shapes in teapots and cups! **Zhengshan Xiaozhong** black tea leaves are black, slim, and curly as if roasted while they were still tender buds, from which we can vividly see in our mind's eye how they grow up in the mountains, bathing in the sunshine, drinking the dew drops, sleeping in the fog, dancing in the breeze... By tea we usually mean tea leaves that have retained their original shapes and aroma, but Lipton tea is composed of so tiny pellets that at first sight, some Chinese from remote areas could not assume it is tea. However, it is said that the export of Lipton each year is much bigger than that of all the tea companies in China.

Chinese black tea and Western black tea have the same origin. But why does one remain unknown to many while the other is world-famous? It is said Lipton crushes tea leaves of all grades to powder in order to erase their differences so that the company can standardize tea. As a result, the shape of tea leaves becomes invisible and black tea becomes nothing but powder incorporating all tea grades.

However, **Zhengshan Xiaozhong**, the ancestor of Lipton black tea, is still laboring in obscurity. Why don't we try breaking the leaves into powder or tiny pieces like Lipton and make big money, then?

Further Reading

1. Anderson, W. T. (1990). *Reality Isn't What It Used to Be*. New York: Harper & Row.
2. Edwards, J. (1994). *Multilingualism*. London: Routledge.
3. Holland, D. & Quinn, N. (1987). *Cultural Models in Language and Thought*. Cambridge, UK: Cambridge University Press.
4. Wechsler, H. J. (1974). *Mirror to the Son of Heaven: Wei Cheng at the Court of Tang T'ai-tsung*. New Haven and London: Yale University Press.
5. Young, D.E. & Goulet, J.G. (1994). *Being Changed by Cross-Cultural Encounters*. New York: Broadview Press.
6. 杜承南、文军主编 (1994),《中国当代翻译百论》,重庆:重庆大学出版社。

7. 孙隆基 (2015),《中国文化的深层结构》,北京:中信出版社。

8. 余秋雨 (2020),《文化苦旅》,北京:北京联合出版公司。

9. 赵 林 (2020),《天国之门:西方文化精神》,长沙:湖南人民出版社。

Unit 10   Categorizing Objects by Relationships vs. by Attributes

I would put him (President Xi) in Nelson Mandela's class of persons. A person with enormous emotional stability who does not allow his personal misfortunes or sufferings to affect his judgement. In other words, he is impressive.

—Lee Kuan Yew

Why did Lee Kuan Yew, the founding father of Singapore, put President Xi in "the Nelson Mandela class of persons" and praise him as a man who is "impressive"?

Pierre Mercier, a visiting French professor, went to a farewell tea party in honor of him. Professor Lu and his wife, whom Professor Mercier had gotten to know well, were also at the party. To his surprise, Professor Lu, two other professors and himself were arranged to sit at the same table while Professor Lu's wife sat at another!

—Anonymous

For discussion: Explain why Professor Lu and his wife were arranged to sit at different tables.

Out of clutter, find simplicity...
From discord find harmony...

In the middle of difficulty lies opportunity.

—**Albert Einstein**

Einstein was obviously not organized in the way we generally think of it. It seems the secret of being organized has nothing to do with how "neat and tidy" things are around us. Discover for yourselves what effect the previous beliefs of getting organized are having on your ability to lead an organized, productive, stress-free, and successful life.

I. Two Ways to Categorize Objects

Categorization is a cognitive process that allows us to relate to unfamiliar objects in an appropriate manner based on our familiarity with other objects that are similar to them. To live in an environment filled with many different objects, we must be able to categorize quickly. Generally speaking, we categorize objects according to their overall similarities. But in reality, similarities among objects do not always allow people from different cultures to categorize them in the same way.

Word came in December 2008 that Roger Y. Tsien won one-third of the Nobel Prize in Chemistry. The news soon produced a big sensation in China, where many people took great pride in him but soon felt a hit in the face from Roger, who was reported to have said, "I'm not Chinese, but I hope my success can inspire more young people in China." Some Chinese just couldn't understand why Roger refused to admit he was Chinese since he was Qian Xuesen's nephew, his parents were from China, and he looked Chinese. To categorize a person according to his relationship originates from Chinese radiation thinking, a pattern of holistic thinking based on the principle of relationships.

Unit 10 Categorizing Objects by Relationships vs. by Attributes

Roger Tsien, despite his Chinese decent, has been exposed to American culture where one thinks of himself first as an American, then as an American of Asian descent. Like other children of immigrants in America, his focus is more on the future, where he is going and what he will do in the future, but not on the past, nor on where his ancestors came from and what they did. What's more, Roger cannot speak good Chinese, he doesn't eat Chinese food, he lives in the American community, so it is natural for him to find a strong sense of belonging among Americans. Roger Tsien's way of defining himself arises out of rule-based thinking, a pattern of analytical thinking focusing on attributes.

II. Principles to Categorize Objects

Humans categorize objects—**persons**, **places**, **things**, or **animals**—for a great variety of reasons. Most often we group objects by following the principle of relationships, while Westerners are more likely to classify them by employing the principle of attributes.

1. Principle of Relationships

Guided by holistic thinking, a great majority of people in China judge an object to be more similar to a group with which it shares a close family resemblance, i.e. we often categorize by following the principle of relationships focusing on holism, mutual influences and change. In other words, isolated objects go into different categories, according to their relations with different things in fluid situations.

a. Focus on Holism

The principle's focus on holism supports the idea that nothing in China exists in an isolated or independent way. Instead, one thing has something to do with a multitude of different things and life is a constant passing from one state to another. To really know one object, we have to know all its relations. This principle of relationships indicates that the same thing is different in a different context and the same person is literally a different person in the family than in his role as a politician or professor.

b. Focus on Mutual Influences of Objects

According to the principle of relationships, shared attributes do not establish shared class membership. Instead, things are classed together because they are thought to influence one another through resonance. In the system of *fengshui*, metal, wood, wind, water, and earth all influence one another. Change in wind or water will affect all the others. And sometimes fire and smoke can be classed together, since there is no smoke without fire.

c. Focus on Change

This focus makes us believe that everything is changing all the time. Therefore, many of us hold that prosperity may portend poverty around the corner, and there is nothing to be happy about easy access to wealth or power, just as a proverb goes, "For this period of thirty years the region east of the Yellow River is fortunate, but for the next period, the area west of the River shall become lucky. So don't despise or bully one at his or her cruel twist of fate."(Figuratively, **The pendulum will swing back; The tables are turned.**)

2. Principle of Attributes

Guided by analytical thinking, the rule-based principle of attributes focuses on attributes, isolated objects as well as rules. In other words, following their attributes, isolated objects go to different groups according to relevant rules.

a. Focus on Attributes

Western thinking focuses on attributes. One reason why they stress attributes is that European languages, as inflectional languages, stress the importance of

Unit 10 Categorizing Objects by Relationships vs. by Attributes

grammar and form–hypotaxis (形合) instead of parataxis (意合), and encourage a focus on attributes and on turning attributes into abstractions. Take English for example. The English adjective can be granted the abstract noun status by adding a suffix *-ness*: **white** becomes **whiteness**, and **kind** becomes **kindness**. Western stress on attributes also owes much to the ancient Greeks. A routine habit of Greek philosophers was to analyze the attributes of an object and classify the object based on its abstracted attributes. It is true of Westerners today. Objects like milk and eggs available in all their markets are grouped as "**Animal Products**"; celeries, tomatoes, pepper, eggplants, carrots, cabbages, spinach, cucumbers and potatoes are displayed in the area of "**Vegetables**" where you can find celeries or tomatoes in great varieties; pears, apples, bananas and melons are available in the section of "**Fruits**" where you can find pears of different color, shapes and sizes; skin-care creams, lotions, powders, perfumes, lipsticks, fingernail and toenail polish are in the area of "**Cosmetics**" where there are many brands of creams to choose from.

b. Focus on Isolated Objects

Ancient Greek philosophers regarded the object in isolation as the focus of attention and analysis. Most of them regarded a matter as particulate and separate–formed into discrete objects–just as humans were seen as separate from one another. For them the attributes of one object are salient; the attributes are the basis of categorization; the categories constitute the basis of rule construction; and events should then be understood as the result of objects operating in accordance with rules.

c. Rule-based Orientation

As mentioned above, ancient Greeks habitually analyzed the attributes of an object and categorized the object on the basis of its attributes. They would then attempt to understand the object's nature and the cause of its actions in accordance with rules governing the categories. Rules at various levels of abstraction would be generated as hypotheses.

It is true of present-day Westerners. Categories are sometimes learned by applying rules to features or attributes. For instance, dogs are known to be mammals because a rule says that animals that nurse their young are mammals.

III. How to Categorize Objects and Why

1. How Objects Are Categorized

a. Categorization of Objects in Ancient China

For ancient Chinese, shared attributes did not establish shared class membership. Finding the features shared by objects and placing them in a class on that basis would not have seemed a very meaningful activity because the objects themselves were not the units of analysis. Instead, objects were grouped together because they were thought to influence one another. Let's take the system of the Five Elements as an example. Metal-wood-water-fire-earth are sometimes grouped in the order by which they produce one another: Wood gives rise to fire, fire gives rise to earth, earth gives rise to metal, metal gives rise to water, and water gives rise to earth; sometimes they are organized in the order by which they are conquered by one another: Fire is conquered by water, water is conquered by earth, earth is conquered by wood, wood is conquered by metal, and metal is conquered by fire.

The belief that the behavior of objects is due to the interaction of the objects with surrounding forces makes it natural for traditional Chinese to classify based on relationships. Just as what some people who understand the differences between the oriental and the occidental have recognized, maybe in many cases,

Unit 10 Categorizing Objects by Relationships vs. by Attributes

the first impression of some Westerners about China is no more than rudeness, but it is actually not that simple. What should be highlighted here are the **in-group/ out-group effects** because we believe some experts are right in saying that "rudeness to strangers is the flipside of deep bonds with loved ones."

The lack of interest in classes of objects with shared attributes was consistent with the basic scheme that the ancient Chinese had for the world. For them, the world consisted of continuous substances. That is why a part-whole dichotomy made sense to them, since the dichotomy does not encourage induction from a single case.

b. Categorization of Objects in Ancient Greece

Ancient Greeks, especially philosophers, had a passion for categories and used them as the basis for the discovery and application of rules. This addiction to the categorization runs through Western intellectual history, where there has been a conviction that it is possible to find the necessary and sufficient conditions for any category.

For ancient Greeks, objects belonged to the same category if they were describable by the same attributes. So a one-many, individual-class dichotomy made sense to them, since the Greek world was composed of discrete objects. The Greek belief in the importance of the dichotomy was central to their faith in the possibility of accurate inductive inferences: Learning that one object belonging to a class has a particular attribute means that one can assume that the other objects in the same class also have the same attribute. So to speak, if one mammal is warm-blooded, it's a good bet that all mammals are warm-blooded; since one dog is warm-blooded, all dogs are warm-blooded. A focus on the one-many, individual-class organization of knowledge encourages induction from a single case, which encouraged the age-old Greek medical practice of dissecting human bodies into their component parts, treating the head if there was a headache, and treating the foot if there was a foot ache.

2. Why People Categorize Objects Differently

When shown a family album, we tend to see a family with interrelated members while Westerners are likely to see a collection of persons with attributes that are independent of any connections with others. Why do we categorize so differently?

First, we see the world through our own eyes, but in our own different ways, just as Professor Stephen Covey said, "We see the world not as it is, but as we are." Indeed the world is composed of objects, but the point is Westerners are more disposed to objects and there are more object-dependent nouns that denote categories in Western languages. In contrast, the Chinese are more exposed to relationships. Let us take the Chinese language as an example. There are more verbs in a Chinese sentence, and the context-dependent verbs denote relationships. Relationships involve, tacitly or explicitly, verbs. Learning the meaning of a transitive verb normally involves noticing at least two objects and some kind of action that connects them in some way. For instance, "to read" means to move your eyes from left to right and meanwhile use your hand to turn over pages. The action of "to read" might be successful on the precondition that all the body members that participate in this activity should be in good relationships, supporting each other.

Second, in the process of classification, different thinking modes might be involved. We might depend on our radiation thinking mode and classify, while Westerners tend to be more rule-based and analytical.

Third, when we categorize objects, we might use different principles. Chinese may categorize based on the principle of relationships, whereas

Westerners may be focusing more on the attributes of the objects.

There might be more reasons behind the fact that we categorize so differently.

IV. Impacts of Different Ways of Categorization

Categorizing ways has influenced various aspects of human life, manipulating how objects operate. Such aspects as table manners, social life, family education as well as views of time and money are to be examined in the following sections.

1. Impact on Views of Time and Money

a. Western Time and Money as a Category

Westerners group in accordance with class membership. For example, when shown pictures of an ox, a rabbit and a carrot, they may justify their classification in terms of the shared attribute: The rabbit and the ox are animals while a carrot is root vegetable. This way of categorization leads people to put intangible time and tangible money in one category, although it appears that they have nothing in common. In Western culture, "time is money" in many visible ways: minutely telephone rates, hourly wages, monthly salaries, and yearly budgets. These practices structure everyday activities in a very profound way so that Westerners act as if time were nothing but intangible money. Thus time can be spent, wasted, budgeted, invested wisely or poorly, saved, or squandered–like money. Since money and time have the same attributes, it is natural for Westerners to place them in one category.

b. Traditional Chinese Time and Money not as a Category

For many Chinese people, time is life, so in an emergency concerning life and death time is an undisputed priority because life is priceless. What is more, as the saying goes, "**An inch of time is an inch of gold, but the inch of gold is not enough to buy an inch of time** (一寸光阴一寸金，寸金难买寸光阴)," which means that time is something more precious than money. Different definitions of time indicate that an attempt to understand time without appreciation of its context or relationships is futile in China.

2. Impact on Table Manners

At the Chinese dinner table, food is chopped into very small objects before being cooked. To send small bits of food successfully into the mouth, the hand needs support from the head, the neck, the body as well as the mouth; otherwise, the small bits may fall onto the table cloth. Although the mouth is a taker at the dinner table while the hand is a giver and the other parts are assistants, there is no clear division of labor in the actual process of eating. It is not rude for the mouth to reach for the soup when it is hot and it is not rude for the upper body to bend over bowls or plates, for sometimes it is difficult to fetch the small food objects without stretching or bending. The mouth, the body, and the hand, because they participate in the eating activity, should work together as a team. Therefore, the body parts and the steps in the process of eating are grouped into one category in China.

Westerners not only segment objects, but also segment an action into discrete parts. At the Western dinner table, the proper way is to chop food into small pieces, one-third of the mouth size before taking it all the way to the mouth which is waiting to be served. To Westerners, it is rude to spit bones and other food scraps on the table since the mouth is a taker while the hand is a giver. It is considered bad table manners for the mouth to reach for the food for that is the hand's task. The division of labor is explicit so that the actions of receiving and giving food don't go into one category.

Unit 10 Categorizing Objects by Relationships vs. by Attributes

3. Impact on Social Life

Ancient Greeks thought of themselves as individuals with distinctive properties, as units separate from others within the society, and in control of their own destinies. Their social life was independent, full of verbal contention and debates.

For ancient Chinese the world was complicated, events were interrelated, and objects and people were connected. So Chinese social life was interdependent and it was not independence but harmony that really counted—the harmony of humans and nature for the Daoists and the harmony of humans with other humans for the Confucianists. Therefore, their life was full of visits, family reunions, and parties which appeared very hot and noisy (or ***renao***).

4. Impact on Early Childhood Family Education

An emphasis on relationships encourages a concern for the feelings of others. When a Chinese mother is with her toddler, she likes using such feeling expressions as **The fire would bite and hurt you if you touch it**; **Uncle Peasant feels bad if you do not eat everything mom cooked for you**; **The flower will say "ouch" and feel painful if you pick it**, and **Brother A Fu** (i.e. the Wuxi clay figure) **is sad because you kicked him away**. Focusing on feelings and social relations helps children to anticipate the reactions of other people, with whom they will have to adjust their behaviors.

When a Western mother is with her toddler, she tends to supply information about objects, e.g. **This is a car**; **It is bigger and faster than that car**; **That is a coat**; **It is blue and warm**. Concentrating attention on objects helps to prepare children for a world in which they are expected to act independently.

V. Causal Attribution Patterns Caused by Different Categorization Ways

A "causal attribution" is defined as the perceived cause of a given event or situation. One of the greatest and most remarkable misunderstandings we have about people arises from differences present in our causal attribution patterns, established by people who have different ways of categorization.

1. Causal Attribution Differences and Attention Focuses

The Westerner prefers categories and focuses on objects when making an explanation, whereas we are more likely to emphasize relationships, depending on the environment. So it should come as no surprise that Chinese people are more inclined to attribute behavior to context and the Chain of Causation (缘起说, i.e. the process of one thing leading to another), the core of Buddhism which stresses that birth, death and rebirth that take place according to laws of karma (报应) may be repeated again and again, which process can only be stopped by achieving Nirvana, was quickly accepted when Buddhism was first introduced into China during the Eastern Han dynasty. And it is not surprising that the Westerner is more apt to attribute the same behavior to the same actor, and what captures his attention is what he is likely to regard as causally important.

There is ample evidence that the causal attribution differences mirror the attention differences. When asked to explain why he or she supports Cleveland Public Theatre, a U.S. theatregoer might explain in terms of its presumed traits (e.g. a special place, a treasure of the greater Cleveland community, a consistent space to expect the unexpected, a breath of fresh air, a unique experience that evokes thought, passion, emotion). When asked to explain why Mei Lanfang Grand Theater is so popular in China, we tend to explain in terms of contextual

Unit 10   Categorizing Objects by Relationships vs. by Attributes

factors such as the theater being named after Peking Opera master Mei Lanfang, It is a modern performance venue where Chinese tradition meets modern art, Its blending features reproduce the essence of Peking Opera, which has been inherited and passed down in its 200 years of history, and also implies the inclusiveness of the Peking Opera and the profound cultural heritage of Beijing Municipality, Besides Peking Opera, this theater also stages other forms of opera, dramas, dance, and concerts.

2. More than Preferences for Context or Objects

Differences in causal reasoning between Chinese and Westerners are broader than just preferences for environment or objects. Let us take for example how Chinese and American middle school teachers deal with historical events.

History teachers in China generally begin by describing the context of a given set of events in some detail. They then explain the important events in chronological order, making sure to link each event to its successor, i.e. putting emphasis on the initial event that serves as the impetus to subsequent events. Students are encouraged to imagine the mental and emotional states of historical figures by thinking about the analogy between their situations and situations of the students' everyday lives. The actions of historical figures are then analyzed in terms of these feelings, because the students cannot be regarded as having good ability to think historically until when they show empathy with the historical figures, including those who were Chinese enemies. Therefore "how" is frequently asked in the process of studying history. The answer to "how" presents events in cause-effect sequence, which is similar to process-oriented reasoning.

Thirteen-year-old Chinese boy Minchang did not do well in his history class during his stay in the States partly because his history teacher adopted a different way to illustrate historical facts. Unlike his history teacher in China, his American teacher would begin with the outcome (e.g. **The short history of the Texas Republic was troubled. Financing the new government proved to be difficult–foreign investors were leery about loaning money**) rather than with the initial event or catalyst. In class, the chronological sequence of events was destroyed in a presentation dominated by discussion of the causal factors assumed to be important (e.g. **The budding Texas Republic collapsed for three major reasons. The first one is…**). Students are not considered to have a good ability to reason historically until when they are capable of citing evidence to fit their causal pattern of the outcome. So "why" is asked more frequently. The answer to "why" presents events in an effect-cause sequence, which is similar to goal-oriented reasoning.

3. A Case of Miscommunication

Ian Brown, an English teacher from Canada, said the other day, "Sometimes it is very difficult for me to understand my students' writings because I don't see any causality in them, and…the relation of effect and cause is elementary logic." He showed us a written request for a leave of absence by one of his students. It goes as follows:

> Mr. Brown, I have got a phone call from my family, telling me that my grandma is ill in hospital. I was brought up by my grandma. I cannot imagine a life without her. I must go home right away to be with her (in Hunan Province). I apologize for the inconvenience my absence from your class may cause to you.
>
> Thanks!
>
> Your student: Shelly

Unit 10 Categorizing Objects by Relationships vs. by Attributes

Ian was confused: What does Shelly apologize for? Why does she think her absence may cause inconvenience? He can't see any logic in the apology! Moreover, "dear" is missing here, so Ian has the feeling that this student shows him no respect although she has used the term of humility (自谦语) "Your student" before her signature.

Further Reading

1. Bond, M. H. (1996). *Handbook of Chinese Psychology*. Hong Kong: Oxford University Press.

2. Graham, B. & Ashworth, G. J. (2000). *A Geography of Heritage: Power, Culture, and Economy*. London: Arnold, Oxford.

3. Holland, D. & Quinn, N. (1987). *Cultural Models in Language and Thought*. Cambridge, UK: Cambridge University Press.

4. Lee, K. Y. (2013). *One Man's View of the World*. Singapore: Straits Times Press Pte Ltd.

5. Said, E. (1978). *Orientalism*. NY: Pantheon Books.

6. 迪克·格罗特 (2009),《刚性排名——发挥业绩管理作用》, 祝吉芳译. 北京: 商务印书馆。

7. 伊斯顿 (Thomas A. Easton) (2014),《立场: 辩证思维训练（第一辑）: 科技与社会篇 (第10版)》, 北京: 外语教学与研究出版社。

8. 周宁编 (2007),《世界之中国: 域外中国形象研究》, 南京: 南京大学出版社。

9. 周云之主编 (2004),《中国逻辑史》, 太原: 山西教育出版社。

Unit 11   Non-controllers vs. Controllers

… For misery, happiness is leaning against it; for happiness, misery is hiding in it. Who knows whether it is misery or happiness? There is no certainty. The righteous suddenly becomes the vicious; the good suddenly becomes the bad.

—King Wen and Duke of the Zhou

In the *I Ching* or the *Book of Changes*, supposedly written by King Wen and Duke of the Zhou, there are many inspiring aphorisms. How do you understand this one?

Several years ago, after I finished reading Leo Tolstoy's *Resurrection* with tears in my eyes, I wrote on its title page, "Life itself is a tragedy." However, that is not how things are, for life is not a tragedy, but a "struggle." What do we live for? Or why do we live this life at all? The answer given by Roman Rolland is "to conquer life."

—Ba Jin

Are you satisfied with the answer given by the Nobel Prize Laureate Roman Rolland? Why or why not?

It is by acts and not by ideas that people live.

—Harry Emerson Fosdick

Are you with the famous author and clergyman Harry Emerson Fosdick or against him on how people live?

Unit 11 Non-controllers vs. Controllers

Artistic and literary expression in China focused not on deeds of individual heroism like those that were lionized in Greece but on locating humans as social beings within a well-ordered, hierarchical and bureaucratic system that carried specific duties.

—Philip Ball

As a philosophy of conduct, Confucianism shows a commendably practical concern with the business of daily life, the structure of society, and the value of a sound, open-minded education. But its emphasis is on governance and social obligation. Discover for yourself what effect this philosophy is having on your ability to live well.

I. Too Early to Tell

In China, almost everybody knows the ancient Chinese parable about an old farmer who lived in the border area of north China. Here is the story:

One day, the old borderman's only horse ran away. Knowing that the horse was the mainstay of his livelihood, his neighbors came to sympathize with him. "Who knows what's bad or good?" said the old man, turning down their sympathy. A few days later his horse returned, bringing with it a wild horse. The old man's neighbors came to congratulate him. Refusing their congratulations, the old man said, "Who knows what's bad or good?" As it happened, a few days later when the old man's son was trying to ride the wild horse, he was thrown off its back and one of his legs was broken. The neighbors came to show their sympathy because he had only one son and he was very old and in bad need of his son's help in the field. Rejecting their commiseration the old man said, "Who knows what's bad or good?" A few weeks passed. The government's army came to the village to conscript all the able-bodied men to fight a war against the invading Huns, but the old man's son was not fit to serve and thus was safe away from the bloody battlefield.

The story is interesting because nobody knows whether something is a blessing or not, which expresses a fundamental Chinese stance towards life: The world is constantly changing, full of contradictions and surprises, and hence uncontrollable.

II. Why So Different Stances Towards Life?

The parable about the old border farmer indicates that we believe in uncontrollability rather than controllability, and hence most often we make no attempt to control painstakingly. But facts like the higher rate of remarriage in the West show that Westerners are more disposed to take action and try to keep things under their control. Regarding the causes of this difference, some plausible explanations have already been provided by scholars.

1. Different Philosophies

a. Chinese Philosophical Emphasis on Change

Chinese life stance is shaped by the blending of three different schools of philosophy–Confucianism, Buddhism and Daoism. Each school is concerned with the constantly changing nature of reality.

Let's take the Daoist *yin-yang* theory for example. According to Daoism, *yin* (literally, the feminine, dark, and passive) alternates with *yang* (literally, the masculine, light, and active). *Yin* and *yang* exist because of each other, and when the world is in a *yin* state, surely it is about to be in a *yang* state. The diagram of the Great Ultimate–the sign of Chinese culture–consists of two forces in the form of a white and a black fish. The black fish contains a white dot and the white fish contains a black dot. "The truest *yang* is the *yang* that is in the *yin*; the truest *yin* is the *yin* that is in the *yang* (大阳之内必藏阴，大阴之内必有阳)." "Extreme *yin* gives rise to *yang*, while extreme *yang* gives rise to *ying* (重阴必阳，重阳必阴)." The *yin-yang* theory is the expression of the relationship that exists between opposing but interpenetrating forces that may complement each other, make each other comprehensible, or create the conditions for changing one into the other, thus making constant change possible. In this sense, the *yin-yang* doctrine is about change. Therefore, for the Daoists, the weakest can become the strongest which can become the weakest. Even the weakest female, under the greatest pressure or if treated very unfairly, might become the most vicious and commit terrible crimes.

Buddhism also stresses the need for change. According to Buddhists, an evildoer can be reformed into a kind person if he is willing to repent. They believe that a butcher can become a Buddha the moment he drops his cleaver (放下屠刀，立地成佛).

Chinese authors were also fond of declaring that everything in the world including empires comes and goes, but the rivers and mountains remain. What passes, Confucius attested, is like a river: "day and night it never lets up." Since change is constant, it is hard to keep things under control. What shall we do, then? Let's not forget what Mencius said more than two thousand years ago, "Those who follow Heaven's will survive and those who disobey Heaven's will perish (顺天者存，逆天者亡)."

b. Western Philosophical Insistence on Stability

An important aspect of Western philosophy is the belief that the world is basically unchanging and stable. Indeed, the great pre-Socratic Greek philosopher Heraclitus (540 BC–480 BC) emphasized change and famously said, "A man never steps in the same river twice because the man is different and the river is different." By the fifth century, however, the notion of change was put aside and the stability theory was established by Parmenides and other Greek philosophers who maintained that motion was impossible because they believed that the world was static. For instance, Parmenides' pupil Zeno proved in a few easy steps that change was impossible. He did this in two demonstrations. One was his famous demonstration with an arrow. The other was his demonstration with an object. Another Greek philosopher Aristotle also proved that all celestial bodies were immutable, perfect spheres and the essences of things remained unchanged, though motion occurred and events happened.

Since things generally do not change, it is easy to keep them under control by categorizing them according to their attributes, establishing rules, forecasting tendency or direction, and being future-oriented.

2. Different Views of Objects

Those who have had much cross-cultural communication are convinced that objects–persons, places, things, or animals–are literally viewed in different ways.

a. A Holistic View

An ancient Chinese farmer had to consult with *fengshui* about almost everything ranging from sowing in spring, weeding in summer, harvesting in autumn to planning in winter for the following year, or even when to hold the wedding ceremony and when to bury the dead. This made it natural for him to holistically look at objects, make efforts to impose control over objects, but believe the objects might be out of their control at any time. Such a holistic view of objects could have encouraged the ancient Chinese assumption of change as well as an assumption that things were out of their control.

Unit 11 Non-controllers vs. Controllers

Modern Chinese also view objects holistically—so much so that it can be difficult for us to visually separate things or people from their environments, which leads us to develop a sense of uncontrollability even when we are actually in control.

b. An Analytic View

An ancient Greek could plan a grape harvest, arrange for a new place to grow olive trees, or investigate whether it would be more profitable to sell wine somewhere without consulting with others. This made it natural for him to focus on the attributes of objects with an analytic view toward categorizing them and finding rules that would help to make predictions and thus exert control over their behavior. For him, results were due to attributes of objects or his own actions. Such an analytic view encouraged the Greeks to be goal-orientated and assume that change was under his control since things were stable.

Modern Westerners, like ancient Geeks, are not overly constrained by objects' relations and they view objects analytically, which leads them to have a sense of personal control, even when they are actually not in control.

3. Different Senses of Self

a. Ancient Chinese's Sense of Self

The ancient Chinese assumed that self was in a network of relationships and thus habitually looked around him before taking action, for instance, outward toward his counterparts and upward toward authorities. This assumption made it natural for him to view objects or actions in general as continuous and composed of relationships, which encouraged recognition of complexity, change and contradictions, strengthening his belief in uncontrollability. Therefore, it is not hard to understand why today's Chinese are disposed to size the situation in general and feel the need to attend to social relations—so much so that we have the inclination to think that objects or actions are uncontrollable.

b. Ancient Greeks' Sense of Self

The ancient Greeks had an impressive sense of self. They assumed that self was unique and individual. Equipped with this assumption, they endeavored to keep their own life under control and felt free to act as they chose. This sense of personal control and freedom accompanied a stronger sense of self, which made the ancient Greeks view themselves as special individuals with distinctive attributes and goals. Then with the passage of time, the sense of being personally in control gradually becomes an important source of Western well-being or happiness.

4. Different Power Distances

It is universally agreed that more power or higher status means more control, and there is no society where everyone is precisely equal to everyone else.

a. Higher Power Distance in Chinese Culture

In traditional Chinese thought, people are unequal at birth. Apart from this, orthodox Confucianism encourages a highly hierarchical way of thinking based on one's position within society. Therefore, in traditional China, those in lower positions of power simply supported their bosses' ideas and showed great respect for their bosses as well as reluctance to criticize them. They would probably think that it was natural for bosses to change their policies and decisions without consulting with people in lower positions, and the employees' task was to obey. An ideal boss was expected to be fatherly, brotherly, or at least approachable. Likewise, children at school were taught to respect and obey parents, teachers, and others in authority. Therefore, traditional Chinese culture is usually grouped in the category of higher power distance cultures, in which one might find it hard to develop a sense of controllability since there is always somebody who is more powerful.

b. Low Power Distance Cultures

In some Western countries, many people believe they are born equal. As for differences in power or status, they deem it necessary to eliminate, minimize or at least not to emphasize them. They are low power distance cultures.

In low power distance countries, those in lower positions in the hierarchy are likely to approach and criticize their boss. For them, the boss may be in a higher position, but that does not mean he deserves any privileges. As for children, they are encouraged to become adults as soon as possible by claiming the privileges of adults whenever possible and learning how to keep things under personal control when they are little. In such a system, one may find it easier to develop a sense of controllability since people are fundamentally equal and independent.

c. Power Distances and Different Approaches to Teaching and Learning

A Chinese visiting scholar at NYU was impressed by the role of her Western counterparts in the classroom. They didn't act as authority who gives final conclusions, but as a researcher looking for answers to questions together with the students. She also noticed one linguistic feature in their interaction with the students was that they used many modal verbs. When answering questions, they usually said, "This is my personal opinion and it could be wrong. It would be a good idea if you could read the book I mentioned the other day." "You could be right, but you might find this point of view also interesting." When making comments on the students' performances, the professors usually said, "There might have been greater clarity if you had incorporated some of the ideas we discussed earlier this semester."

In China, authorities are supposed to make wise decisions and give directions. They usually say, "Keep this in mind." "It's dollars to doughnuts that…" "You must…" Therefore, students always expect the professor to give a correct answer to the question. Once they get the answer, many of them are sure about it. So the professor makes far more assertions and finds it difficult to use modal verbs since the function of modal verbs is to provide room for negotiation and different ideas.

To sum up, different power distances result in different approaches to teaching and learning, which also helps to develop different stances towards life.

III. "Being" and "Doing" Cultures

If one is preoccupied with a sense of control, he will take actions, which may make him feel in control. Hence Western culture is also known as "doing" culture, since it lays emphasis on doing or actions, although too much doing can create a feeling of drowning in stress. On the contrary, there is much support in traditional Chinese culture for a human "being" rather than a human "doing."

1. "Being" Culture

When we were little, our parents used to tell us: "If life is simple, you only have to open your mouth in order to achieve something; life as simple as that is naturally controllable." However, life in reality is complex and subject to changes without advance notice, and hence not easily controlled. Rather than attempting to control situations, we try to adapt to them or just let them be. That is why we have been encouraged to be humble and modest, to live in harmony with nature and at the rhythm of nature, assuming that everything has spirit obtained from nature and what is important is to remain balanced.

An American colleague from work once commented, "Americans are more afraid of death and aging than many other people—we want to deal with it instead of accepting it." This is not the case with us exposed to the "being" culture. Our matter-of-fact approach is illustrated in proverbs like **Life is nothing but a stage over which the sun and the moon function as two spotlights** (人生一台戏，日月两盏灯); **Man has but one life; grass sees but one spring** (人生一世，草木一秋), and **People, old or young, can die** (黄泉路上无老少). Those proverbs exemplify the Chinese belief that man is born to die and that life is merely a journey from womb to tomb, a natural process that no one can escape. No matter what efforts one might make, everyone succumbs to mortality within a certain time span determined by *tian* (Heaven). Needless to say, nothing can be done other than follow the natural process from birth to death. Therefore, the best policy is to let it be (顺其自然).

In short, "being" culture produces lots of non-controllers who adapt and accept rather than take action in order to keep things under their control.

2. "Doing" Culture

Westerners, although aware of the inevitability of death, try all means to stop or put it off instead of passively and philosophically accepting it like some traditional Chinese. This kind of effort can be found in the British heavy metal band Black Sabbath who sang in 1978 "Never say die." The same maneuver is also reflected in George Washington, the first U.S. president. During the American Independence War (1775–1783), he not only established the thought of "we can do it" as an integral part of the American spirit, but also exemplified the spirit after the war: Of the nine presidents who owned slaves, only he freed his; he resisted efforts to make him a king and established the precedent that no one should serve more than two terms as President; he voluntarily did what he promoted, setting up a good example.

Like George Washington, many Westerners are bent on achieving specific goals. They develop procedures, measure results and put stress on actions; they value predictability, so they emphasize inspecting the work that has been underway and controlling the procedures for producing quality work; they want things to be correctly done, so they value accuracy and precision in those they work with.

For people exposed to this culture, **time and tide wait for no man**. As soon as former American Secretary of State Hilary Clinton failed in her presidential campaign, she lost no time to support her rival Barack Obama and made it clear in her exit speech delivered on June 7th 2008 that "life is too short, time is too precious, and the stakes are too high to dwell on what might have been. We have to work together for what still can be. And that is why I will work my heart out to make sure that Senator Obama is our next president. And I hope and pray that all of you will join me in that effort."

3. Distinctive "Being" and "Doing" Cultures

The biggest difference between "being" culture and "doing" culture, as evidence suggests, is that feeling in control is not as important for Chinese as it is for Westerners.

a. Different Definitions of Happiness

Feelings of happiness are enhanced more for us if we have other people around who might assist in providing control, whereas feelings in control of their individual lives are strongly associated with mental health for Westerners. We are satisfied that we are simply in the same boat with others, whereas Westerners are happy that they have direct, personal control.

b. Different Interpretations of Leadership

People in the West resent being told what to do or how to do it. Authorities usually make their requests as questions instead of commandments or imperatives. For example, telling a woman "Go do the laundry" even though you are the boss, will irritate her. "Could you help out?" will have the same effect without resenting her. Authoritarian leadership is more tolerated in China since leadership is traditionally hierarchical, not team-based. When a Chinese boss orders one to do something, it means he is in control and responsible, but not necessarily abusing power. Therefore, he is often heard using the imperative mood when making requests.

c. Different Ideas of Modesty and Honesty

Westerners are not necessarily being dishonest if they openly say that they are accomplished at something they don't know. They believe "it can be done as long as you do it." On the contrary, we are *keqi* (modest) about our skills, and will passively wait for someone to ask us to use our skills instead of volunteering our talents. We were told the following story years ago:

Two friends, one American and the other Chinese, were asked which one of them could fix a fountain in the hallway. The American said, "Hey, no problem. I've done it many times and I can get it running in no time." The Chinese responded "*keqily*", "I can give it a try but I am not that experienced." Undoubtedly the American got the job. He fiddled with the fountain this way and that for quite a while and then gave up. His Chinese friend then came up to the fountain, fiddled with it for a little while and got it fixed. The American got very irritated and shouted accusingly at his friend, "You are a liar!" And that brought an end to a friendship.

Keqi means considerate, polite, and well mannered. It also represents humility and modesty that look like water. Water, a source of moral instruction, displays its humility and modesty by seeking the lowest point. As Laozi puts it:

"The reason that the Yangtze River and seas rule a hundred streams is that they are good at taking a lower position to them... This is why the sage who wishes to be in authority over the people always humbles himself in his speech (江海之所以能为百谷王者，以其善下之……是以欲上民，必以言下之)." The implication is not that one should lie down, but that one should find a stable, steady morality. To be more specific, we tend to degrade ourselves to show humility and modesty in the real world by negating complimentary remarks or our own abilities. Unfortunately that made the American think of his Chinese friend as being dishonest and rude, for he wants to feel things are under control and like the other Americans he likes to make others have a sense of being in control by volunteering their talents.

IV. Manifestations of "Being" Culture and "Doing" Culture

1. Manifestations of "Being" Culture

In "being" culture, people do not try to be controllers; even though they do they will not care about the result, leaving the final decision for *tian* (i.e. Heaven) or authorities to make, which is clearly expressed in the following proverbs:

Man proposes and Heaven disposes (谋事在人，成事在天);

Submit to the will of Heaven (听天由命);

Do not feel panic if the sky should fall down, because the taller people would hold it up (天塌了，有高个子顶着).

"Being" people are very tolerant. Sometimes they are likely to take things for granted without making any complaints or efforts, which is revealed in the proverb "**There is no never ending banquet under the sun** (天下无不散之筵席)," denoting that all good things must come to an end.

To adapt themselves to reality however harsh it is, people in this culture may

Unit 11 Non-controllers vs. Controllers

say to themselves contentedly, "**We are worse off than some, better off than many** (比上不足比下有余)," and "**The table will turn in our favor** (风水轮流转)." Meanwhile, they keep encouraging themselves and saying when in trouble, "**Good happenings, results, achievements, etc. must go through many trials and tribulations** (好事多磨)." Confronted with the rapidly changing world, witnessing so many ups and downs, they manage not to be pleased by external gains, nor saddened by personal losses and struggle to live in contentment.

In one word, non-controllers or "being" people recognize the necessity of human efforts but also admit the futility of it. This dialectical attitude has a tendency to develop passive tactics such as **Great things can be reduced into small things, and small things can be reduced into nothing**. Life in "being" culture moves on, therefore, on the line of least struggle and least resistance, according to Lin Yutang. This develops a certain calmness of mind, which enables one to swallow insults and find oneself in harmony with others and not in control. However, in such a culture, there is strong hidden resistance to change, and those who pay no attention to self-cultivation are disposed to violate regulations and rules without being punished.

2. Manifestations of "Doing" Culture

Who is the original author of the aphorism "Deeds, not words" is not important now. What matters is that this much-quoted saying shows that doing is more favored than speaking in traditional Western culture. In "doing" culture, people try to be controllers, and for them doing is better than not doing. To feel themselves personally in control, controllers are not afraid of trying new things that are usually very challenging. Napoleon Bonaparte exemplified this spirit. He is remembered to have confidently said, "The man who has made up his mind to win will never say 'Impossible'."

In such a culture where action speaks louder than words, people don't judge a book by its cover, nor judge a person by his appearance. As the proverb goes, "We can't judge a person by what he says but by what he does." It is believed by them that is "easier said than done."

As is known to all, Western culture is heavily influenced by Christian culture. Many Westerners are Christians who declare to leave themselves in the hands of God, obeying Him, praising Him, and asking for everything from Him, but meanwhile "God helps those who help themselves" is one of the most-frequently-quoted aphorisms in the West.

3. Impacts of the Two Cultures on Daily Life

Differences are present in almost every aspect of our daily lives. Two cases are to be illustrated here.

a. Keeping Children Safe

When a Western and a Chinese family spend time together, the Western toddlers are allowed by their parents to run around, and when they fall down, they stand up by themselves. The Chinese toddlers, on the contrary, are not allowed to play around and are watched for the whole time by their parents or grandparents. When they fall down, they are picked up, cleaned, and comforted. Thus it can be seen that Westerners are less uncertain while Chinese are more uncertain and try their best to avoid uncertainties instead of controlling them.

In China, children from a so-called good family are not allowed to play with children of unknown origin. But in some Western countries, for instance, the Netherlands, parents are not afraid to let their kids play with unfamiliar children. Children in this culture are told to learn by making mistakes. To some conservative Chinese parents, what is different might be dangerous. But to Dutch parents, what is different is curious and interesting. Chinese people appear more passive while Westerners are more active and more willing to actively cope with differences and uncertainties.

b. Waiting at the Train Station

In China, free timetables about all arriving and leaving times of trains are available on the internet or in almost every waiting room of every railway station, but not all people check them out frequently or go and get one, expecting anything could delay the arrival or departure of a train since things are in constant change.

In Germany, there is on every train a magazine called *Zugbegeleiter*. This magazine contains all the arriving and leaving times of trains. Everybody in the station is looking at his watch and *Zugbegeleiter* when a train is arriving. They want to know precisely when a train arrives and when it leaves so that they know for sure that they won't be late for doing something. After all, much of the European train is about efficiency and comfort–leaving and arriving on time and having a comfortable seat.

4. When Chinese Meet Westerners

a. In Negotiations

As "doing" people, Western negotiators are more likely to do things such as changing their position in the middle of an argument and consulting with colleagues in the middle of a session. This flexibility can be explained as a desire to achieve the goal–an agreement or a contract. To reach the goal, the details can be changed, which makes them feel they are in control of the situation.

In "being" culture, decisions are usually made through consultation with several levels in a hierarchy, so Chinese negotiators may not be free to change their positions during actual face-to-face negotiating sessions, because they know even if they change things might not work. But after the formal session the negotiators will consult with all the important decision-makers and may change their position and some of the details in order to reach an agreement.

David Jones, our 25-year-old colleague from Canada, learned this the hard way. When he first came to China, he tried to negotiate for improved working and living conditions with his boss (immediate supervisor) and expected her to be persuaded by his reasonable arguments. When his boss said, "No, I am afraid not. I am terribly sorry," he felt upset. Later he came to realize that he would get better results by simply stating what he wanted, giving good reasons and then going away to give his boss a chance to discuss with her bosses. Often his boss would come back to him several days later with a decision–to both parties' satisfaction.

b. In Marriage

Michael White, a British businessman, married his soul mate Li Meimei in Nanjing several years ago. Despite cultural differences, he managed to have a sweet life with his Chinese wife. Unfortunately, they are now talking about a divorce. Here is an email from Michael:

> Dear Jifang,
>
> Meimei is spending a lot of her time with her daughter Jenny and her husband Tom in Shanghai and they want us to move in there and live altogether, Tom's parents and we two, something I will never agree to. So Meimei lately has been talking about a divorce and maybe it will be for the best if I let her divorce me, although on what grounds I do not know. In a house with six adults and a baby is not my idea of happiness. Not what I got married for. We had four very happy years of togetherness and then this last 16 months or so has been very upsetting since Jenny gave birth to her baby. So we shall see.

Unit 11 Non-controllers vs. Controllers

Love and Kind Wishes

Michael

Meimei is a typical Chinese woman. Traditionally a Chinese woman is not a controller of her own life: she is expected to leave everything for others to decide. By "others", we mean her father before she gets married; her husband after she gets married, and her son (or daughter) after her husband is gone. Meimei's first husband died in a car accident when her only daughter Jenny was little. She did not remarry until Jenny married Tom. Her marriage to Michael, although arranged by her daughter Jenny, had been very beautiful until 16 months ago when Jenny gave birth to a baby boy. Meimei who brought up her daughter as a single parent feels very happy to babysit her little grandson. To her great relief, her daughter and son-in-law kindly asked Michael to join their bigger family, seven now, including Tom's parents. It never occurred to Meimei that Michael, an aged step-father with many health problems, would refuse. "No! I don't want the baby to control my life," said Michael adamantly. "This is not what I got married for." Michael's response greatly perplexed Meimei and hurt her feelings. Suddenly Meimei found herself talking about divorce–in spite of herself.

c. In Job Hunting

The most effective strategies to persuade a potential employer to offer you a job vary from culture to culture. Chinese applicants often think they should say that they are hardworking, creative and easy-going. This may be acceptable to a Chinese employer with "being" culture values, but a record of what you have accomplished with your hard work, creativity and people skills is more necessary to convince a Western boss. For him, referring to your hard work is merely a statement of your strengths. He wants to know what you can do instead of what strengths you are.

d. A Pet Peeve

There is a bigger pet peeve for Westerners not just in China, but in any culture where it is considered rude to give a plain and forthright "no" in reply to a question or request. That pet peeve is when foreigners are given the reply of "maybe" or "perhaps" when they really need a yes or no. Native English speakers in particular prefer to receive a definite answer to a question even if the answer is "no." "Maybe" or "perhaps" is not an acceptable answer for them. Some Westerners even feel Chinese people often prefer to answer questions with "maybe" or "perhaps" so that they are not committed. For them, it may be that you truly do not know the answer to a question. If that is the case, just say "so." Then the listener can take action and try keeping things under control.

As a matter of fact, many people in the global community–including the Chinese, go to great lengths not to be direct. The risk of disharmony with other group members is too uncontrollable for us to be outspoken. It's better to say "maybe" or "perhaps" and negotiate with them afterward than to blatantly disagree or refuse.

Further Reading

1. Duiker, W. J. (1978). *Cultures in Collision: The Boxer Rebellion*. Novato, CA: Presidio Press.
2. Hofstede, G. (1980). *Culture's Consequences: International Differences in Work-related Value*. Beverly Hills, CA: Sage Publications.
3. Ramo, J. C. (2007). *Brand China*. London: The Foreign Policy Center.
4. Zhang, Y. (1998). *China in a Polycentric World: Essays in Chinese Comparative Literature*. CA: Stanford University Press.

5. 林语堂 (1998),《生活的艺术》, 北京: 外语教学与研究出版社。

6. 明恩溥 (2012),《中国人的气质(英汉对照)》, 刘文飞、刘晓旸译, 南京: 译林出版社。

7. 钱锺书 (2005),《钱锺书英文文集》, 北京: 外语教学与研究出版社。

Part IV
Different Cultural Orientations

Cultural orientation (文化取向) means a pattern or value system which this culture uses to respond to the world around us. It reflects the complex interaction of the values, attitudes, and behaviors displayed by the majority of the members of a particular culture. Individuals express culture and its normative qualities through the values that they hold about life and the world around them. These values, in turn, affect their attitudes about the form of behavior considered more appropriate and effective in any given situation. The continually changing patterns of individual and group behaviors eventually influence society's culture.

In this part, cultural orientation is broken down into 5 main dimensions:

- The introvert-oriented vs. the Extrovert-oriented
- Collectivism vs. Individualism
- Femininity vs. Masculinity
- Advocacy of *Jing* vs. *Dong*
- Implicitness vs. Explicitness

Unit 12 The Introvert-oriented vs. the Extrovert-oriented

Chinese people bow when they meet for they are introverted, whereas Westerners shake hands or hug when they meet for they are apt to be extroverted. The introversive Chinese reaches out to hold the other hand of his own; the extroversive Westerner extends his hand to hold others' hands. Just as using chopsticks to send food to his mouth, the Chinese exerts his force inward; just as using forks at meals, the Westerner exerts his force outward. One uses force outward, the other inward, so the symbol of Western culture is Cross, and that of Chinese culture is Diagram of the Great Ultimate.

—Yi Zhongtian

For discussion: Observe the patterns of the Diagram of the Great Ultimate and Cross, and explain why they are employed as cultural symbols or signs.

China, as everyone knows, has been an isolationist nation. While the Europeans went forth on voyages of discovery and conquest, China looked inwards and consolidated its domestic affairs to the point of stagnation.

—Philip Ball

Read *The Water Kingdom: A Secret History of China* written by Philip Ball before affirming or negating the assertion above.

As Western interventionist forces, Christianity and colonialism were crucial in establishing and maintaining political, cultural, and economic domination. Indeed, both elements of Africa's encounter with the West played pivotal roles in shaping African societies during the nineteenth and twentieth centuries.

—**Chima J. Korieh and Raphael Chijioke Njoku**

Read *Missions, States, and European Expansion in Africa* which aims to explore the ways Christianity and colonialism acted as hegemonic or counter hegemonic forces in the making of African societies before exchanging ideas with your peers about the book.

Fine feathers make fine birds.

—**An English proverb**

This English proverb is roughly equivalent to ***ren kao yizhuang, ma kao an*** (literally, a man depends on his clothes and a horse on his saddle). What do you say to the two proverbs?

I. Personality Types

There is an old saying in China which goes, "**A mother has nine sons, but the nine sons are different** (一娘生九子，九子各不同)." Why are people from the same background different?

1. Two Personality Types

The question above and much of what has happened around us can be explained in terms of the personality types, especially the notion of introvert-extrovert distinction. For instance, one of the biggest differences between

Unit 12   The Introvert-oriented vs. the Extrovert-oriented

people depends on whether they are introverts or extroverts. Extroverts are disposed to be interested and comfortable when they are working with people or things. They are incline to focus on the outer world and are the talkers. Introverts are a different kind of people: They are quiet, and tend to be more involved and comfortable when they are working with ideas and concepts. These differences are the biggest source of miscommunications, misunderstandings and communication breakdowns between people who sincerely want to get along. Extroverts tend to see introverts, because of their quietness, as closed, secretive, moody, and unresponsive. Introverts are likely to see extroverts, because of their love of being social, as exhausting, shallow, and noisy. Consequently, we get along easily with certain people while others drive us nuts.

2. A Blend of Introversion and Extroversion

Most people seem to be a blend of introversion and extroversion. One of the reasons is that there are two different ways of learning–abstract or concrete–and two different ways of making decisions–thinking and feeling. An extrovert's dominant or best-used function will be outward while an introvert's dominant function will be inward. But the extrovert will have an auxiliary second function which is introverted, and an introvert will have an auxiliary function which is extroverted.

It is important to note that while our root preferences stay the same throughout our lives, we can be affected by circumstances. An introversive child exposed to an extrovert-oriented culture may feel ridiculed and have to put on an extroverted mask while hurting inside. An outgoing child exposed to a more introverted culture may be criticized for being precocious or too noisy, and equally has to develop a protective suit. It can take years to recover from being forced to live outside one's preferences. Therefore, in reality all of us are a blend of introversion and extroversion.

II. Personality Types of Cultures

Many of the cultural differences can also be illustrated in terms of personality types, particularly the notion of introvert-extrovert distinction.

1. A Historical Fact

During the period from 1405 to 1433, a treasure fleet under the command of the eunuch admiral Zheng He made seven voyages throughout the China Seas and Indian Ocean, across the Taiwan Strait to the Persian Gulf and distant Africa. During the thirty years, China extended its sphere of influence through the Indian Ocean, half the world was in its grasp, and with such a formidable navy the other half was easily within reach—had China wanted it, but China chose not to. The Confucian officials in the imperial court had long insisted that these sea voyages were a pointless drain on finances and resources that would be better directed towards domestic water conservancy and agricultural projects. There was nothing useful, they said, that China could learn from the barbarian nations, and in any event it was not seemly to revel in luxury goods like those that the treasure ships brought back.

Shortly after the last voyage of the treasure fleet, the Chinese emperor forbade overseas travel and stopped all building and repair of oceangoing junks. Disobedient merchants and seamen were killed or severely punished. Within a hundred years the greatest navy the world had ever known willed itself into extinction and Japanese pirates ravaged the Chinese coast. The period of China's greatest outward operation in history was followed by a period of its greatest isolation.

Over 60 years later when Portuguese navigator Vasco da Gama and his fleet

Unit 12 The Introvert-oriented vs. the Extrovert-oriented

of three battered caravels rounded the Cape of Good Hope and landed in East Africa on their way to India in 1498, they met natives who sported embroidered green silk caps with fine fringe. Village elders told tales of white "ghosts" who wore silk and had visited their shores long ago in large ships. But no one knew anymore who these people had been or where they had come from. It is da Gama and the other European explorers who started the wave of outward expansion that would change the map of the world.

2. The Introverted Character of Chinese Culture

a. No Intension of Outward Expansion

Because of its introverted character (内敛性), China in the early Ming dynasty had no intention of expanding outwards at all–although it had the capability.

Even an ambitious ruler like Emperor Wu of the Han dynasty had no intention to expand outward. He just ordered his great army to enter the area where the Hun was stationed in order to stop the harassment by them to ensure his people's personal and property safety. A ruler as aggressive as the First Emperor of the Qin dynasty, instead of expanding northward to drive away foreign aggressors, had the Great Wall built to stop "the northern barbarians" who regularly raided the Chinese farming villages, leaving us a symbol of passive defense and introverted character.

b. Introverts and Extroverts in China

Traditional Chinese culture undoubtedly favors introverts. A good example would be a young man when he first visits his future parents-in-law. He is expected to speak less, listen more, and answer questions politely, clearly and briefly. In the meantime, he should sit like a bell and stand like a pine tree. So to speak, he has to appear more mature and steady so that his future parents-in-law will feel safe to let him take away their darling daughter. Most Chinese parents disfavor talkers because they appear immature and rude, and thus are not dependable or worthy of their daughter's hand. So there are many drawbacks to being an extrovert in China. He may have a harder time at school where academic success is the first concern, for he will probably enjoy socializing with others more than quietly reading books and taking notes in his classroom. It's challenging for a parent to have an extroverted school-age child because of the large amount of solitary studying. An extrovert in the office may appear very popular with his colleagues, but when it comes to promotion he will probably be "put aside" since this culture favors people who have more time for contemplation and introspection and thus can become more balanced.

c. Why Chinese Are More Introversive

First of all, orthodox Confucianism advocates introversive activities such as self-cultivation and self-criticism. For the Confucianists, self-cultivation is a lifelong process of cultivating a moral and spiritual character since the Second Sage Mencius favored "cultivating the great moral force (养吾浩然之气)". The *Great Learning*, one of the Confucian canons, attempts to establish the value of self-cultivation in terms of accepted social norms, which requires a certain amount of self-criticism. Chinese schoolchildren are therefore taught how to practice self-criticism in order to live peacefully with others and grow up healthily and happily. This stance of perfectionism through self-criticism continues throughout life.

Second, Daoism encourages people to cultivate the body by avoiding the noisy secular world and living in the mountain and by the riverside, and Buddhism, one of the three great teachings, has been used by people to nurture the mind by looking inward for they believe "You are the source of the suffering and you have to learn to look within instead of without and know yourself."

Third, the ideal climate and rapid agricultural development of ancient China provided a good foundation for the formation of an agrarian economy of self-reliance and self-support, encouraging immobility. Such an economy has determined that Chinese culture is a culture of root (有根的文化) deeply rooted in soil, blood-based relationships, and ancestor worship.

In one word, the introverted character is a legacy of more than 2,000 years of history. Here only a few of the reasons why Chinese culture tends to be introversive are mentioned, for it is hard to distinguish between cause and effect, just as it is difficult to solve the problem of what comes first, the chicken or the egg. The introverted character of Chinese culture may explain why China remains the world's longest continuous civilization in spite of various ordeals during its thousand years of development.

3. The Extroverted Character of Western Culture

a. The Inevitableness of Outward Expansion

History books tell the readership that da Gama's famous voyage was followed by the establishment of one colony after another. This kind of expanding outwards for the sake of profits and markets was inevitable given the extroverted character (外倾性) of Western culture. This orientation of Western civilization has long determined its direction of development–expanding externally, and expressing its desires through practical actions, and discouraging inactivity. Later with the development of its capitalist economy the West became more and more extrovert-oriented, transcending restrictions and obstacles on its way of development. For instance, in science scientists focus their attention on changing nature and society and benefiting from them; in medicine they use external means such as medicine and medical devices to treat patients; in politics, economy, and military, they invade, pillage and resort to arms.

b. Introverts and Extroverts in the West

From a young age, people in the West have learned the benefits of being an extrovert–those individuals who always seem to be the life and soul of a party, often engaging, exciting, outspoken, able to express their opinions easily. Besides, they are imagined to be assertive, approachable, and charming. People are taught to admire those traits early on. Kids are often encouraged to interact, play and communicate with other kids. It seems at times as though children are made to embrace a more outgoing lifestyle, with some people becoming pseudo-extroverts–introverts who mimic extrovert behaviour because society favors extroverts, despises and devalues introverts. In some countries, particularly the U.S., the extrovert is considered socially superior to the introvert who is so widely disfavored that knowing how to raise an introversive boy can be challenging for a parent.

c. Why Westerners Are More Extroversive

What has been helpful for the formation of the extroverted character of Western culture?

First, Western culture originates from ancient Greek culture, Roman culture as well as Hebrew culture. The three cultures have one thing in common, that is, they are developed on the basis of sea trade, transportation, colonization, or even piracy because of want of an ideal agricultural environment. These professions require those who are involved in them to be extroverted, outward-looking and fearless.

Second, society encourages liberty and openness and favors extroverts, which orients the culture further toward extroversion.

Third, schools of Western philosophy, eager to acquire new concepts to enrich themselves, encourage people to be extroverted, stretch out, expand, conquer, controll, and look outside. Among them social Darwinism, a belief which was popular in the late Victorian era in England, America and elsewhere states that the strongest or fittest should survive and flourish in society, while the weak and unfit should be allowed to die. It was used to justify seizing land and resources and hence applied to military actions.

Fourth, Christianity has endowed some Westerners with a strong sense of mission—spreading God's message across every corner of the world, which makes them more extrovert-oriented.

Arguably, the extroverted character is a legacy of many years of history.

III. Effects of Personality Types on Pattern Preferences

"One's fate is determined by his personality."(Heraclitus) This aphorism vividly accounts for the importance of personality. As a central dimension of human personality, introversion and extroversion also find expressions in the thinking modes—introverted thinking and extroverted thinking. The former has helped to form the circle culture with circle patterns like the Diagram of the Great Ultimate as its logo, and the latter has played an important role in the formation of the grid culture with grid patterns like the Cross as its symbol.

1. The Circle and Grid Patterns in People's Life

a. The Circle Pattern

"The empire, long divided, must unite; long united, must divide. Thus it has ever been (话说天下大势，分久必合，合久必分)." With this characterization of the inevitable cycle of ancient Chinese history, the *Romance of the Three Kingdoms* begins and meanwhile defines the circle pattern. It is really incredible how many facets of Chinese life the pattern touches. Most of the cities and towns of China, for instance, are arranged in the circle pattern. A good example would be Beijing where the urban transport is dependent upon the seven "ring roads" that successively surround the metropolis, with the Forbidden City surrounded by 10-metre high walls and a 52-metre wide moat, an area marked as the geographical centre for the ring roads. The 1st Ring Road is not officially defined. The 2nd Ring Road is fully located in Beijing's inner city areas. Ring roads tend to resemble expressways as they progressively extend outwards, with the 5th Ring Road, the 6th Ring Road and the 7th Ring Road being full-standard National expressways–linked to other roads only with interchanges. Expressways to other regions of China are generally accessible from the 3rd Ring Road outward.

In the circle pattern, important things are usually located at the center and everything else is drawn toward the center. In eastern China's Jiangsu Province, for instance, almost all major roads lead to Nanjing, the capital city, and most mileage signs tell you how far you are from Nanjing.

The circle pattern is also visible in the social and political life of China. In rural areas, Chinese farmers live in villages where the ancestral hall is at the center. In a Chinese family picture the oldest male (i.e. the patriarch) sits at the center, and you can tell how important one is in the family by how far he is from the center or whether he sits, stands, or squats on the heels. In his ward, a new patient can tell immediately who is in the authority among a group of medical staff in white who are doing their morning inspection routinely–just by observing who is surrounded by the whole team.

b. The Grid Pattern

The grid pattern touches many facets of Western life. Most of the cities and towns of the United States, for example, are arranged in a grid pattern. If

Unit 12 The Introvert-oriented vs. the Extrovert-oriented

you look at the map of Manhattan, the grid pattern is very clear: The streets running east and west are numbered in sequence. The north-south streets are also numbered in sequence but are called avenues. The naming and numbering system varies from city to city, but the basic grid pattern is the same. With a pattern like this, it is difficult to get lost, because the address of any building is in a specific place on the grid. This is a pattern that provides easy access even to strangers. A visitor does not need to rely on a knowledgeable local to find his way. We stayed for a week at #5601 Hollywood Blvd in Los Angles. In fact this place is not in the area of Hollywood, but far out close to downtown Los Angles. The grid pattern has been extended to the hotel, so anyone can easily find it.

This same pattern can be seen in the interstate highway system that covers the U.S. with a grid of regularly numbered highways. The odd numbered roads run north and south and the even numbered roads run east and west. Interstate 45, for example, will take you from Houston to Dallas and Interstate 44 will take you from west to Wichita Falls, Texas or east to St. Louis at Interstate 55. Anyone can go where he likes with the aid of a map or GPS.

The large farms of mid-western America are arranged in a similar way. After the War of Independence the United States acquired large tracts of unsettled land from England and promptly divided it into regularly shaped states, counties, townships, and farms. Each farm was a regular rectangle and one plot in each township and a larger tract in each state were set aside to meet the educational needs of the area. This pattern encouraged settlers to move west, as the grid provided a path for them to follow. It civilized the wilderness. From the airplane you can easily notice that the boundaries of many states are straight lines. And you can also find the same pattern in the characteristic American suburban sprawl. Those who rise in social class and income move out from the city into newer and more expensive housing areas far from the city. Older areas in the inner city are taken over by new arrivals. They live there until their fortunes improve, at which time they will follow the grid out to more desirable and safer housing on the outskirts. This pattern has no fixed center. Any point on the grid can become important depending on what is located there. It can just as easily disappear into obscurity if economic development or public taste favors another location. New cities grow up at the intersections of the interstate highway system while the centers of older towns die from neglect. People want to know what opportunities they will find as they move out across the grid. And any corner can become a center.

c. The Cultural Patterning of Space

The circle and the grid cultures have developed two major systems for the patterning of space. The Chinese system connects all points and functions. If you look at a map of China that shows the railway system, the circle pattern is clearly visible, and different lines repeatedly come together at places of interest like Beijing, Wuhan, Shanghai, and Guangzhou. But the Western grid system separates activities by stringing them out. In China, there is a series of circular networks that build up into larger and larger centers. Each small center has its own channel to the next higher level. Generally the roads between centers do not go through other towns, because each town is connected to others by its own roads. Even the water passages which are necessary for the transportation of objects such as grains and stuff have been fetching from the southern provinces to Beijing, the center of China. The Sui Grand Canal system (隋朝大运河) which covers 2,350 kilometers, for example, was "a main artery to bring tax grain from the small towns to the political centre of gravity of the country." In contrast, the Western pattern strings out small towns like beads on a necklace

Unit 12 The Introvert-oriented vs. the Extrovert-oriented

along the routes that connect principal centers.

Both systems have advantages and disadvantages. For example, a mistake in direction in the circle system becomes more serious the farther one travels. In the grid system, baseline errors are of the 90-degree or 180-degree variety and are usually obvious enough to make themselves felt even by those with a poor sense of direction. If you are traveling in the right direction, even though you are one or two blocks off your course, the error is easily rectified at any time. Nevertheless, there are certain inherent advantages to the circle system. Once one learns how to use it, it is easier to locate objects or events in space by naming only one point on a line. Thus it is acceptable to tell a first-time visitor to meet you at the Qinhuai River Amusement Park (水木秦淮) not far from the Caochangmen Bridge west of Nanjing. That is all the information he needs. In contrast, the grid system involves at least two lines and a point to locate something in space. In the circle system, it is also possible to integrate a number of different activities in centers in less space than with the grid system. Thus, residential, shopping, marketing, commercial, and recreation areas can meet and be reached from central points.

2. Co-existence of the Circle Pattern with the Grid One

Cultural interactions enable the circle pattern to co-exist with the grid pattern in China today. Here let's consider buildings in Beijing where traditional architecture is based on the circle pattern and appears introverted in style with emphasis on the enclosing walls. Enclosing walls have two main functions: One is to protect the buildings inside; the other is to indicate that the buildings inside are very important and treasured. The ancient buildings in Beijing that have survived to this day fall roughly into three categories: palaces, temples and private residential houses. The Forbidden City is the largest and best preserved ancient palace complex now extant. It is the most representative ancient palace in China. On each of its four sides are high walls which protect the buildings inside. The Yonghe Palace Lamasery, popularly known as the "Lama Temple", is one of the most famous temples in Beijing. All the buildings in the temple are surrounded by a high wall. There are many courtyards inside. The entrances to all the courtyards are in the south, whereas the most important buildings are all in the north. The buildings in the Lamasery form many layers. Only by going through layer after layer of courtyards can the tourists see the centre of the Lamasery–the Sacred Hall of the Wheel of the Law (法轮殿). In the old alleys known as **hutong** we can also see the characteristic traditional Chinese architecture. The walls on both sides of the alley are very high and they serve to protect the private houses behind and highlight their importance. The private houses are mostly courtyard houses, with the most important room situated in the north of the courtyard. The center of a private house is protected by lower inner walls and other buildings as well as by the outer walls.

While traditional buildings are introverted in style, some modern ones are extroverted in Beijing. The layout of Zhongguancun might be a good example. There are no enclosing walls in the Zhongguancun Square which is completely open so that it is very easy for passers-by to access it. Hotels and apartment blocks there face the streets, not surrounded by other buildings. It is said that the three most famous construction projects in Beijing are the Olympic Stadium and Gymnasium, the National Grand Theatre and the new China Central Television Station. Their design purpose, which is to attract the attention of passers-by and make people want to get in, is completely different from that of the high walls of the Forbidden City.

Unit 12　The Introvert-oriented vs. the Extrovert-oriented

IV. A Contrast of Some Cultural Phenomena

Culture consists of a great many phenomena. These phenomena, like the cells that contain the secret of life, contain the genetic code–a nation's cultural code.

1. Candle Bundles vs. Baby Clothing

The practice of tying up newborn babies is very popular in many parts of China, especially the middle and lower reaches of the Yangtze River. Parents usually put their nude baby on a small fluffy quilt tenderly, straighten up its limbs before wrapping it in the quilt gently, and then tie up the bundle carefully with a cloth rope into something like a candle which is widely known as "candle bundle (蜡烛包)". They believe wrapping the baby in the candle bundle can make it quiet, self-disciplined, and not hyperactive when it grows older. Arguably, Chinese self-cultivation and introverted character start from the tied bundle, a Chinese baby's first clothing.

However, Western parents neither wrap up their babies tightly, nor let them be without any clothing. Instead, they choose soft fabrics as their newborn baby clothing, leaving babies' four limbs free of any restraint so that they can freely explore the new world they were born into.

2. Body Touch

a. Guy-girl Friendship

Extroverted Westerners can have affectionate guy-girl friendships without any romantic interest. If you are not kissing or holding hands, you're probably not dating. Chinese tend to have a much lower threshold of what is considered a relationship because most of us express ourselves in an introversive way. What Westerners might consider a normal guy-girl friendship can be read as definite interest in the other person by the Chinese. In particular, spending time alone with someone of the opposite sex is a strong sign of interest.

b. Hugging

Our introversion blocks us from explicitly expressing our love and closeness to others by using our body movements and gestures. Researches show that children who are often touched and hugged are psychologically healthier than those who get less touch and hugs. Everyone has a need for human touch. According to some statistics, Chinese children get far fewer hugs and kisses than their Western counterparts after they are more than 10 years old; almost no hugs and kisses are from traditional parents, not to mention from other sources. Except for holding hands, standing shoulder to shoulder or walking by linking arms, we don't have body touch with others until we are old enough to start dating. In other words, within a decade or even longer, we don't have much intimate human body touch.

Meanwhile, in extroversive Western culture, parents and their children, siblings, and good friends almost never stop hugging or kissing each other. It is widely known in this culture that "any speech cannot replace the expressions of our body."

Body touch is highly recommended by both sociologists and psychologists in China today, but we still rarely use body touch to transfer our intimate feelings and share our emotions. Is the fact a result or reason for our introversive culture?

3. Covering-up vs. Showing-off

Our observations can be used to justify the fact that extroversive Westerners seem disposed to show off while introversive Chinese cover up:

Traditional Chinese musical instrument *erhu* can produce beautiful music with the whole instrument closed from the inside, while its Western counterpart

Unit 12   The Introvert-oriented vs. the Extrovert-oriented

violin is hollow, with a big round opening.

Chinese steamed buns are closed without betraying their fillings, whereas an Italian pizza displays its content on the surface so that a consumer can make his or her decision by merely looking at the top.

The Chinese university campus is encircled by a high wall in order to create a serene and quiet atmosphere, while a Western one is open and accessible to anybody.

Our stay in Australia and the U.S. left us smiling a lot. After taking in the unfamiliar sight of women in their short shorts and short skirts and tank tops, we were astonished by how comfortable women felt displaying their cleavages and armpits. Imagine a young lady strutting her stuff like that on the street of Nanjing where we live! She would attract lingering glances for sure. Not that we hadn't seen bare bodies or some cleavages in Nanjing. Magazines and movies are full of them, with more and more entertainers daring to bare a lot. But spotting common women on the street in low-cut blouses is a bit tricky.

4. Modesty vs. Confidence

To be honest, we had a hard time responding to compliments. Those born before the 1980s, for instance, found it hard to say "thank you" and accept compliments like their Western counterparts. Compliments did make us feel good and proud, and we knew we welcomed it. But we had to be modest and correct others that we were not that good for we were told that there would always be someone better than us, and we had to learn to be humble and modest. To a certain extent, there is truth and value in that. Some Chinese do manage to be modest to avoid unnecessary jealousness. Imagine 100 people around you value high grades as good, and you have got it, they can be so jealous and just want to isolate you to feel better themselves. Can you handle that? So, to get on

well with others, some Chinese can be very self-deprecating. It is not unusual for a man to refer to himself as "a silly old egg (老糊涂蛋)" for the sake of modesty.

The cultural divide in modesty is very real. Western kids, exposed to the extroversive culture, are taught that "confidence will get you places (自信使人进步)." Chinese kids are taught by their parents born in the 1980s "modesty will get you places." Both follow their respective cultural training to make progress.

5. Handling the Deceased's Belongings

We have attended two burial ceremonies so far. One is Chinese and the other American.

At the Chinese burial ceremony, we saw the son of the deceased set fire to his personal belongings such as his expensive overcoats, woolen sweaters, bags, wallets, books, and pictures before putting his cell phone into his cinerary casket and sealing it up in his tomb with cement. In this way, almost all the traces the deceased had in this world were erased by his dear family with tears in their eyes so that he wouldn't start from scratch in the other world.

At a Western memorial ceremony (not very typical) we attended a few years ago, people gave thanks for the deceased's life and witness, sang songs, and then carved up some of his belongings. Every mourner had a share and went back home with a beautiful memory of the deceased and something once owned by him as a memento. As for his widow, she was grieved but was already talking about her plan for the future.

6. Answers to Questions like "Would You Like Something to Drink?"

"Would you like something to drink?"

A typical reply from a polite Chinese is "no, no, thank you" to show his humbleness even though he is very thirsty. A hospitable Chinese hostess should keep offering drinks until her guest says, seemingly embarrassed, "OK. Thank

Unit 12 The Introvert-oriented vs. the Extrovert-oriented

you very much. Sorry to trouble you."

A typical reply from a polite Westerner on this occasion is "yes, please" if he is thirsty, or "no, thanks" if he is not.

This cultural divide has made up many jokes. One of them is about an Australian gentleman's first visit to a traditional Chinese family. When he was served the first cup of tea, he drank it up and politely said, "Nice tea!" Seeing he liked the tea, his hostess said, "Drink more, then." and she refilled his cup out of hospitality before he had time to say "No, thanks." No longer thirsty, he still bottomed it up out of politeness. The hostess hastened to put another big glass of freshly-made tea before him, thinking to herself that he must be a big drinker. The Australian said, "No, no, no more." But his hostess insisted that he drink it up, assuming that he was refusing out of courtesy. Although unable to drink any more, he poured the tea down his throat and felt he was really full. His hostess was very happy to see her guest enjoy her tea so much and smilingly put another cup of tea before him and smilingly said, "Drink slowly (i.e. take your time)." But assuming it's a waste not to drink it all up, the man ended up going home with a stomach full of tea!

Further Reading

1. Ball, Philip. (2022). *The Water Kingdom: A Secret History of China*. London: The Bodley Head.
2. Hall, D. L. & Ames, R. T. (1995). *Anticipating China: Thinking Through the Narratives of Chinese and Western Culture*. Albany, NY: State University of New York Press.
3. Korieh, C. J. & Njoku, R. (2007). *Missions, States, and European Expansion in Africa*. London: Taylor & Francis Ltd.

4. Kroeger, O. & Thuesen, J. M. (1989). *Type Talk: The 16 Personality Types That Determine How We Live, Love, and Work*. New York: Dell Publishing Company.

5. Levathes, L. E. (1994). *When China Ruled the Sea: The Treasure Fleet of the Dragon Throne*. New York: Simon & Schuster.

6. Menzis, G. (2002). *1421: The Year China Discovered America*. New York: HarperCollins.

7. Thomson, L. (1998). *Personality Type*. Boston, MA: Shambhala.

8. 易中天 (2006),《闲话中国人》(第3版),上海:上海文艺出版社。

9. 乐黛云、张辉主编 (1999),《文化传递与文学形象》,北京:北京大学出版社。

Unit 13 Collectivism vs. Individualism

Private interests are vested in the group, that is, in the family or in the community, and not in the individual. True self-fulfillment for the individual lies in fulfilling social responsibilities to the greatest extent possible. In fact, the establishment of harmonious social relations is seen as an absolute necessity, without which any development is impossible.

—Jean Brick

Jean Brick, as an outsider who has come inside for some time, has observed the group-oriented Chinese values with keen cross-cultural awareness. For further thoughts: Discuss the satisfactions and difficulties of being a member of a group in China.

There is no such thing as society. There are individual men and women.

—Margaret Thatcher

What can we conclude from what former British Prime Minister Mrs. Thatcher said in a speech in 1987?

I. An Embarrassing Custom

An outsider may observe or get you (an insider) interested in looking for interesting things which have long been taken for granted in China. Take introduction and self-introduction for instance.

Tracy L. Steele, a dear and beloved friend who passed away in 2013, was an American historian. We met her when she was a visiting scholar at Nanjing University almost twenty years ago and soon we became friends. In 2007 she stayed with us for the Spring Festival, during which we took her to pay New Year visits to some of our former teachers and supervisors, introduced her to them and she enjoyed talking with them. Our apartment is on the fifteenth floor of a tall building inhabited almost exclusively by the teaching faculty of Hohai University, and we have to use the elevator a lot. Each time we get in the elevator, we run into some of our school colleagues whom we greet briefly and politely. To be frank, we have been doing this for many years without knowing what each other's name is, and have never tried to make any self-introduction, hence we know very little about each other except the fact that they work in Hohai University. We indeed do not feel uncomfortable about the situation that two people nodding or speaking terms don't know each other's name. It happens everywhere in this country. Neighbors, colleagues, acquaintances, or people from the same martial arts class greet each other and chat for a while when meeting on campus or in the shopping mall or classroom but they won't bother to ask about each other's name. That's truly the case. However, that doesn't necessarily mean names are sacred in China or knowing someone's name isn't important. The point is we feel it is rude to ask acquaintances their names. When we really need to know one's name, we can ask around, and then we will proudly say his or her name the next time we meet. Knowing others' names without asking them indicates we take them seriously.

Every time our neighbors talked to us in the elevator, seemingly ignoring Tracy, we could feel Tracy was upset for she had an open face. Not until then did we realize how embarrassing a custom it is not to make introductions or self-introductions in our daily life. We had the impulse to get Tracy into our conversation by introducing them, but resisted it in case we might embarrass our neighbors by asking them their surnames after having known them for so many years! Tracy told us later that she felt awkward not being recognized and being a part of the conversation although she knew Chinese are not good at introducing people. After all, the elevator was so small a space! Moreover, in her country it is nearly impossible for someone to know and interact with another person for many years without knowing his or her name.

This experience serves to highlight an interesting difference between Chinese and Western cultures. Western culture is often said to be individualistic, whereas China emphasizes collective, group relationships.

II. Collectivism and Individualism as Cultural Orientations

One possible consequence of collectivism is that people in China are more often addressed according to their role in a group such as **Director Zhang** (i.e. Mr. Zhang, the director), **Blacksmith Liu** (i.e. Mr. Liu, the blacksmith), and **Secretary Li** (i.e. Miss Li, the secretary) or their relationship to the person they know like **Mama Minchang** (i.e. **Minchang's mum**) and **Grandma Xiaoxi** (i.e. **Xiaoxi's grandma**). In the West where individualism is a principal value, people are more likely to simply address the other person by his or her first name like Tracy or Victor–a symbol of their individuality.

1. Collectivism

In traditional China, importance was attached to collective interests that could be divided into those of the small circle (blood-based), the intermediate circle (nation-based) and the large circle (world-based). In many cases group interests were placed above the individual's if they were in conflict.

a. Blood-based Groups

China is a country with a massively large population where people live in groups under the same roof based on biological and marital relations. Family loyalties and an emotional commitment to the village or the kin group took precedence over any sense of nationhood. The small interest groups present in all the workplaces (*danwei*) were nothing but an extension of such a group.

b. Nation-based Patriotism

Patriotism has been highly praised and eulogized since ancient times. The patriotic spirit has been inspiring Chinese people to put national interests above the groups' especially when the nation is in danger. As the end of the 19th century approached, many Chinese people, witnessing the aggressive behavior of the foreign imperialists, began to be more conscious of themselves as a nation and more determined to be united as one, and their fight against foreign invasion has been recorded in history books read by school children today.

c. *Tianxia* or World-based Great Harmony

As a concept of space, *tianxia* means the vastest space between the sky and the earth. In it, the soaring mountains, the plunging streams and placid lakes crossed by bridges, are observing the demands of *fengshui*, marshalling the flows and energies of nature to concentrate *qi*. And the circulation of the is believed to produce movement of life. As a political concept, *tianxia* means the country, the world as well as a harmonious political order transcending region and race. So the idea of *tianxia taiping* (i. e. world peace or national peace) proves to be the top of the Confucian political ideal.

We have always been educated in the spirit of patriotism as well as internationalism. "A public spirit should rule everything under the sun and a gentleman should put others' interests above his own when the great Way prevails (大道之行，天下为公)," said Confucius more than two thousand years ago. An ancient Chinese gentleman would consider it his primary aim in life "to cultivate his own moral character, put family affairs in order, administer state affairs well, and pacify the whole world (修身、齐家、治国、平天下)."(Zhengzi) A couplet from a Ming dynasty academy of classical learning (书院) says, "The sounds of wind, rain, and reading each come into my ears; the affairs of family, state as well as world are all kept in my mind." Fan Zhongyan, the Song dynasty poet, expressed his desire "to show concern over state affairs before others in the world and enjoy comforts after them."

Obviously the interests of the small circle, the intermediate circle and the large circle came above one's own, and one had to cultivate and exert himself in order to achieve the goal of serving the human community. In present-day China, collectivism remains an orthodox value, despite our changed attitudes toward the individual's role in society, social behavior, and values as a result of individualism introduced from the West. For example, many of us don't like to be separated from the crowd, solitude is still the most terrible punishment, and the collectivist saying "Extend your respect for your aged parents to all the aged, and extend your love for your own children to all children" is often on our lips. People today are still generally reserved with strangers and might not initiate conversations with strangers, but rules for addressing people remain. Children are all affectionately called "little brothers" and "little sisters". Adults (including strangers) are politely called by kids "uncle," "auntie," "grandpa" or "grandma."

2. Individualism

Western priority has been given to developing individual potentialities, realizing individual objectives and seeking individual interests. In the West, individualism is undoubtedly a positive core value; competition and independence are highly valued.

a. Competition and Success

In Western culture, an individual is moving forward continuously in his self-chosen direction for the sake of self-fulfillment. Suppose different people run parallel to one another, they will each smoothly attain their own aims in life. In such a society, maybe people are "selfish", but they stay out of each other's way and feel happy. However, if they stand in one another's way, the stronger will make the other go away or perish to keep moving on himself, conforming to the theory of "natural selection and survival of the fittest." Guided by competition-oriented individualism, everyone seeks independence and self-reliance, during which everyone feels insecure and makes unremitting individual efforts to achieve success at any cost, sometimes even at the expense of the interests of others.

b. Independence and Friendship

Among the ancient Greeks, many were able to make a living that didn't depend too strongly on others (such as those independent sea traders, pirates, grape growers, and wine producers). Today independence remains the Westerner's preference.

Emphasis on independence makes Westerners conclude that friendship is mostly a matter of providing emotional support and spending quality time together, so they feel uncomfortable in a relationship in which one is giving more and the other is dependent on what is being given. Conversely, Chinese friends give each other not only emotional support and concrete help. They even give each other money and might manage to help each other out financially over a long period of time. This is rarely part of Western friendship because it creates dependence and thus violates the principle of equality for most Westerners.

3. Attitudes Toward Collectivism and Individualism

Not all Westerners are happy with individualism and not all Chinese are satisfied with collectivism, but in general, Chinese attach more importance to collectivism, whereas Westerners focus more on individualism.

a. Pro-collectivist Chinese

For many Chinese people, individualism was equal to selfishness. The selfish behavior that people condemned was not necessarily at the expense of others. It was to place personal interests above those of the group or simply to devote much attention to one's own interests. This anti-individualist, pro-collectivist attitude is deeply rooted in Chinese tradition—although Daoism pays much attention to the individual pursuit of "cultivation of body and life" and individual freedom. After all, the value system of Daoism has not been the mainstream one. Since Confucianism became the orthodox ideology, a stress on the value of groups has been clearly reflected in the advocacy of the **ultimate public with no consideration of self** (大公无私), proverbs like **Two heads are better than one** (人多力量大) as well as folk tradition which provided cautionary tales to reinforce such community-minded behavior. One of the most familiar stories celebrates the power of collective action literally to move mountains. There was, the story goes, once an old man named Yugong (literally, **the Foolish Old Man**), who lived on North Mountain opposite the great peaks of Taihang and Wangwu, between the cities of Jizhou and Heyang. The northern flanks of the mountains blocked the road for travelers, who had to make a lengthy detour round them. This vexed Yugong, who called his family together and proposed that they clear a way through. The sons and grandsons liked the idea, but his wife objected, saying that the old man had barely enough strength to shift a tiny hillock. In any case, where would they put all the stones and earth?

Undeterred, Yugong and his sons and grandsons went out with pickaxes and began to hew at the rock and soil. When another neighbor mocked Yugong's plan, calling him a fool for spending his last years on this futile scheme, Yugong replied that, on the contrary, his success was assured. Certainly, he might die soon–but he has sons, and they have sons, and they too will have sons. His descendants will go on forever, but the mountain will never get any bigger, and so in the end his plan will triumph. To this, the neighbor had no answer. And truly Yugong's case seems unanswerable, for his philosophy has been justified time and again in Chinese history: given enough manpower, anything is possible.

But it should be pointed out that Chinese collectivism does not denote a negation of individual well-being or interests. Instead, it maintains that the group's well-being is the best guarantee for individual interests.

b. Pro-individualist Westerners

Cultural preference for individualism does not mean Westerners neglect the collective strength. Recently *jiti* (literally, the group or the collective) in Chinese vocabulary has been replaced by *tuandui* (literally, team or teamwork), a concept introduced from the West. Teamwork refers to a joint action by two or more people or a group, in which each person subordinates his individual interests and opinions to the unity and efficiency of the group. This does not mean that the individual is no longer important in Western culture; however, it does mean that effective and efficient teamwork goes beyond individual accomplishments. Today's Western businesses and organizations often go to great lengths to coordinate team building events in an attempt to get people to work as a team rather than as individuals.

Likewise, individualism doesn't stop Westerners from finding more about their family origins and traveling to the destinations where their ancestors originated from.

And the choice between individualism and collectivism at the level of society has considerable implications for many of the Western theories, especially economic theories. Economics as a discipline was founded in Britain in the 18th century. Among the founding fathers, Adam Smith (1723–1790) stood out above the rest. Smith assumed that the pursuit of self-interest by individuals through an "invisible hand" would increase the wealth of nations. This is an individualist idea from a country that even today ranks high on individualism. Since him, economics has remained an individualist science, and most of its leading contributors have come from strongly individualist nations such as Britain and the United States.

III. Collectivism and Individualism in Cultural Anthropology

To more clearly describe the two cultural orientations, it might be better to examine them within the context of cultural anthropology.

1. Collectivist Culture

According to Dutch cultural anthropologist Geert Hofstede, "Collectivist culture is a term used to designate the cultural trait of giving primacy to the goals and welfare of groups in the view of the world related to relationships with other humans." In other words, a culture in which the interests of the group prevail over the interests of the individual is collectivist. In this culture, the first group in one's life is the family into which he was born and grew up. There may be a number of people living under the same roof, for example, great-grandparents, grandparents, uncles, aunts, cousins, sisters, and brothers. This is the extended family where the child soon learns to think of himself as a part of "we" group or in-group. The in-group is the major source of one's identity and the only secure protection one has access to against the hardships of life, hence it is a good policy for one to remain loyal to it for a lifetime, and becoming disloyal is one of the worst things one can do. The "we" group is distinct from other people who belong to "they" group or out-group. The concepts of in-group and out-group have gone beyond families into many other departments such as workplaces, officialdom, and the neighborhood in a roughly group-based collectivist country.

Therefore, in a collectivist culture education aims to enable a child to live more harmoniously with others in a group. Everyone, however rich in wealth and high in social status, is in need of help and assistance at a certain point in time to live well, since in a collectivist society people are interdependent, finding it hard to live without help from others. In such a culture, the government was deeply concerned about the balance of public interests and private gains. Dyke maintenance represents an interesting case of how the government sought the balance. In the middle and late Ming dynasty administrators debated how best to divide responsibilities for this public good between the government, the landowners and the people, generally adopting the policy–reasonable within the social structures of the time–that the beneficiary should bear the brunt of the cost. Under the corvée labour system, every landowner was obliged to provide a certain number of workers for the task, the contributions determined by how much land they owned and how much revenue they were expected to get from it. It was in the interests of the peasants too, of course, but that didn't mitigate the toil.

2. Individualist Culture

Based on cultural data he collected in the 1970s from people working for IBM in over 40 countries, Dutch psychologist Geert Hofstede assumes that cultures in which the interests of the individual prevail over the interests of the group is individualist. In these cultures, most children are born into families consisting of one or two parents and, possibly, other children, while their relatives live elsewhere. This is the nuclear family where children soon learn to think of themselves in terms of "I". This "I"–their personal identity, is distinct from other individuals and these other individuals are classified to their group membership according to their individual characteristics or attributes rather than their relationships. The concept of "I" has gone beyond families into many other departments or sectors. So to speak, an individualist society is roughly individual-based. The creation of the English system of canals before the 18th century is an interesting case of how the aristocrats sought profits for themselves by facilitating the transportation of household products or farm produce.

Therefore, education in an individualist culture aims to enable children to be independent. No psychologically and physically healthy person should be encouraged to be dependent.

3. Differences and Cultural Discomforts

Different nations have different cultural traits just as different people have different characteristics. Key differences between the collectivist and individualist societies are summarized below:

In collectivist societies, one is integrated from birth into strong, cohesive groups that will protect him in exchange for unquestioning loyalty. In the groups, opinions are sometimes predetermined by group membership, collective interests often prevail over individual interests, the state dominates the economic system, companies are largely owned by families, collectives or the state, private life may be invaded by groups, law and rights may differ by groups, the so-called human rights rating is usually lower, the principle of egalitarianism often prevails over that of individual freedom, harmony and consensus tend to be ultimate goals, and patriotism is a noble ideal.

In individualist societies, one looks after himself or his immediate family first, everyone is expected to have his own opinion, individual interests prevail over collective interests, the role of the state in the economic field is restrained, companies are often owned by individual investors, everyone has a right to privacy, laws and rights are supposed to be the same for all, the so-called human rights rating tends to be higher, the principle of individual freedom usually prevails over the principle of equality, every individual is goal-oriented, and autonomy is ideal.

Cultural differences are often responsible for discomfort in intercultural encounters. For instance, Westerners are not expected to share snacks that they have with their friends. It is not considered rude to buy a bar of chocolate and eat it around your friends. In China, some people consider it bad-mannered not to share treats with friends and feel uncomfortable. During our stay in America and Australia, we noticed the most remarkable thing about visiting local households is that everyone is always thanking everyone else: "Thank you for reminding me. Thank you for passing me the salt. Thank you for teaching my son." To be frank, they sounded very hypocritical to us. Though we knew it was wrong, we just couldn't help feeling that way, because in China every family member has the obligation to serve and help at home and you don't have to thank them so frequently for carrying out their obligations.

IV. Collectivist and Individualist Perspectives of "Self"

If there are more people working on something, they are more likely to come up with a great solution even if they claim modestly they are mentally retarded since many heads are believed to be better than one (三个臭皮匠，顶

Unit 13 Collectivism vs. Individualism

个诸葛亮) in China. But for many people in the West, it could also be the case that "too many cooks spoil the broth (人多手杂反坏事)", even if they consider themselves "the best cooks in the world". Different cultures could be observed and judged from different perspectives of self by different people.

1. Chinese Sense of "Self"

a. Chinese View of "Self"

Chinese view of "self" is deeply rooted in the collectivist culture. First, Chinese view of self has been around for many years. "In the Confucian human-centered philosophy man cannot exist alone; all actions must be in the form of interaction between man and man."(Hu Shi) In other words, one exists within particular situations where there are particular people with whom one has the relationship of a particular kind.

Second, Chinese sense of self was mainly knitted into the cultural context. That is why we understand ourselves in terms of our relation with the family, workplace or society, e.g. **the second daughter of Mr. Zhu, the doctor** (祝医生的二女儿), **a Hohai professor** (河海大学的教授), or **Ai Man's neighbor**. Exposed to this cultural context, people have to keep a low profile in order to live well because there exists a prejudice against individualism. Take for instance the aphorism "The peg that stands out gets pounded down (枪打出头鸟)", "One tree far taller than others may fall victim to a strong wind more easily (木秀于林，风必摧之)", and "People are afraid of being famous and pigs are afraid of being strong." Individual distinctiveness is not particularly desirable. For some of us, feeling good about ourselves is likely to be tied to the sense that we are in harmony with the wishes of the group to which we belong. Since all actions are in concert with others, or at the very least affect others, harmony in relationships becomes a chief goal of social life, which requires one to forget his individual interests on some occasions and think in terms of collectivist interests.

Third, the self is connected, fluid, conditional, and hence highly dependent on situations. In ancient Chinese there are many expressions for **I**, depending on the speaker's relationship with the listener. When a minister spoke to his emperor, he customarily used ***chen*** (literally, your humble subject), which is closest to the trans-situational I; when the same man referred to himself in the presence of his parents he might say ***hai'er*** (literally, your child); when he talked to his son, he employed ***weifu*** (literally, your dad) which is equivalent to **I**.

Fourth, equal treatment was not assumed as desirable, since there were the concepts of in-group and out-group. People tended to be closer to in-groups and more trusting of them, drawing distinctions between in-group and out-group.

b. Modern Chinese Debate over Self and Group

In modern China, the debate over self and group seems to be quite confusing sometimes. On the one hand, the stress on individualism is unprecedented because of the introduction of Western ideas such as individual freedom and respect for individual rights, although individualism is undoubtedly against collectivism and holism. On the other hand, the group interests are still emphasized because of a need for harmony. In some sense, modern China is characterized by making attempts to unite the interests of individuals and those of groups. For example, Li Dazhao (1889–1927), the great Chinese politician, provided a theory of Great Harmony (大同思想) with individual freedom and thus won much applause from many people.

2. Western Sense of "Self"

Western view of "self" originates from ancient Greece. The ancient Greeks had a remarkable sense of self. They viewed themselves as unique individuals with distinctive attributes and goals. To modern Westerners, one has attributes or characteristics that are independent of circumstances or particular personal relations. This self can move from group to group and setting to setting without significant change. As beneficiaries of the ancient Greek civilization, modern Westerners have the same remarkable sense of self, as can be seen in all of the following statements made by them on different occasions:

"Each individual has his unique distinctive attributes. Moreover, each individual needs to be distinctive in important ways."

"Each individual is in control of his own life and feels better when his choice and personal behavior determine outcomes."

"Each individual is passionate about personal success and achievements and finds that relationships and group memberships sometimes get in the way of realizing their goals."

"Each individual strives to feel good about himself by achieving success through his own efforts."

"Each individual prefers equality in personal relations or when relationships are hierarchical, he prefers a superior position."

3. Manifestations of Different Senses of "Self"

a. In Self-introduction

Here is a typical Chinese self-introduction: "My surname is Zhu. I'm Sharon White's friend. Sharon's carpool friend Tracy Snow brought me here." Obviously, the focus is on relationships.

A typical English self-introduction is: "My name is Jane Will. I am a stay-at-home mom with a 5-year-old daughter Leah, and I am married to Tom. I recently received a referral for a beautiful 9-month-old girl and I am headed to Korea to bring her home." Evidently, the focus is on **I**.

b. In Self-description

"Tell me about yourself." A straightforward request, isn't it? The kind of answer largely depends on the society you are exposed to. Westerners will tell you about their personality traits (e.g. **hardworking, out-going**), role categories (e.g. **sales manager, programmer**), and activities (e.g. **I go boating a lot**). But our self-description depends much on the context (e.g. **I am on the teaching faculty of Hohai University, I am not a good mother because I am fun-loving with my friends, I am Joan Quin's pen pal**).

c. In Children's Primer

Americans over a certain age remember their primer *Daisy and the Doll*. It depicts a little girl Daisy, the only child of color in her classroom. Daisy was both embarrassed and angry when the teacher, in assigning poems to read and props to hold for a school program, singled Daisy out by giving her a doll with a black face. That moment was the first time someone had treated Daisy differently due to her skin color, and Daisy had trouble making sense of this experience. Ultimately, Daisy was able to use her courage and her talent as a poet to show her teacher, classmates, and the community the importance of speaking out about race and racial equality. This would seem the most natural sort of basic information to convey about kids–to the American individual thinking.

The first pages of the primer for many Chinese of the same age depict a little boy handing out bigger pears to his brothers. It begins: "Little Kong Rong gives bigger pears to his elder brothers. He says, 'I'm younger. Of course I should have a small one." Then he gives his younger brothers bigger pears and keeps the smallest one for himself, saying, 'I am older. Of course, I should give up bigger pears.'" This primer is about relationships with others, which seem important to convey in a child's first encounter with the printed words– natural for Chinese collective thinking.

d. About Distinctiveness

When North Americans are asked about their attributes and preferences, they report themselves to be unique, whereas Chinese are much less likely to do so. It isn't that we feel bad about our own attributes. Rather, there is no strong cultural obligation to feel that we are unusual. Plus, we don't like to be separated from crowds. The goal for the self in relation to society, as taught by our teachers and parents, is to achieve harmony and to play one's part in achieving collective interests.

Instead of teaching children how to blend harmoniously with others, Western parents encourage their children to be special and unique at schools in which each child gets to be a "VIP" for a day.

V. Interdependence vs. Independence

Collectivism or individualism as a cultural orientation may lead people to value either interdependence or independence.

1. Interdependent Chinese and Independent Westerners

Traditional Chinese are disposed to be interdependent, taking friends, family, the prosperity of the state, and even world harmony as sources of happiness. "There is an old saying, 'The world is the state.' As a matter of fact, the foundation of the world lies in the state, the foundation of the state the family, and the foundation of the family the individual (人有恒言，皆曰'天下国家。'天下之本在国，国之本在家，家之本在身)." (Mencius) In contrast, Westerners tend to be independent, taking independence as a great source of happiness. For them, "The most essential value of life is human independence."

In reality, every society and every individual is a blend of interdependence and independence. Therefore, it is quite easy to bring one or another orientation to the fore. And it is very possible that even if one's upbringing had not made him incline in one direction or another, the cues that surround him would make the person living in China behave in generally interdependent ways and the person living in Western societies behave in generally independent ways.

2. The Early Training for Independence and Interdependence

The training for independence or interdependence actually starts in the crib. It is common for Western babies to sleep in a cradle separate from their parents, or even in a separate room. But that is rare for Chinese babies. The Chinese baby is almost always with its mother and sleeping in the same bed with her. The close association with their mother is what some Chinese apparently would like to continue indefinitely, which is reflected in the interdependent relationship between mother and child, i.e. the child is dependent on its mother for care, love, food, drinks, advice, etc., and in turn, the mother will be dependent on her child for psychological and practical help when she is old and sick in the future, just as the saying goes, "Rear children for old age."

Independence for Western children is often explicitly encouraged. Western parents constantly require their children to do things on their own and ask them to make their own decisions, "Would you like to go to MGM or Magic Kingdom first?" so that both mothers and children are capable of living independently and having fun when children are around 18 years old and off hands.

3. Targeted Ad Campaigns

An important business implication of the differences that exist between independent and interdependent societies is that advertising needs to be modified for a particular cultural audience. Scholars have found that American advertisements emphasize individual benefits and preferences (e.g. **Obey your** thirst; **Don't leave home without it**), whereas Chinese ads are more likely to emphasize collective ones (e.g. **Feichang Cola, our own cola**; **Tianxiang Paint will give you a sweet home**). The individualist advertisements are evidently more effective with Westerners and the collectivist ones with Chinese.

4. Everybody, Somebody, Anybody and Nobody

Here is an interesting English story copied from wenweipo.com on Oct. 18, 2008:

Everybody, Somebody, Anybody and Nobody

This is a famous story about four people named Everybody, Somebody, Anybody and Nobody. One day there was an important job to be done and Everybody was sure that Somebody would do it. Anybody could have done it, but Nobody did it. Somebody got angry about that, because it was Everybody's job. Everybody thought Anybody could do it, but Nobody realized that Everybody wouldn't do it. It ended up that Everybody blamed Somebody when Nobody did what Anybody could have done.

Now, you must be smiling and reminded of the famous Chinese proverb which also means that everybody's business is nobody's business—**One boy is a boy, two boys half a boy, three boys no boy** (一个和尚挑水吃，两个和尚抬水吃，三个和尚没水吃). Smiles can be used to express happiness. Probably your smile at this moment may mean more after you finish reading the story.

Further Reading

1. Cante, F. & Torres, W. T. (2012). *Nonviolent Political Economy*. London: Routledge.
2. Clyne, M. (1994). *Intercultural Communication at Work: Cultural Values in Discourses*. Cambridge, UK: Cambridge University Press.

3. Hofstede, G. (2005). *Cultures and Organizations: Software of the Mind*. New York: McGraw-Hill.

4. Kluckholn, F. & Strodtbeck F. (1961). *Variations in Value Orientations*. Evanston, OH: Row & Peterson.

5. Medearis M. & Medearis A. S. (1983). *Daisy and the Doll*. Middlebury, VT: Vermont Folklife Center Book.

6. Schwartz, S. H. (1994). *Beyond Individualism/Collectivism: New Dimensions of Values*. Newbury Park, CA: Sage.

7. 范能濬编集 (2004),《范仲淹全集》(上、下),薛正兴校点,南京:凤凰出版社。

8. 梁羽生 (1993),《名联谈趣》,上海:上海古籍出版社。

Unit 14 Advocacy of *Jing* vs. *Dong*

Try the utmost to make the heart vacant, and be sure to hold fast to quietude(致虚极，守静笃).

—Laozi

What does Laozi advise us to do by holding fast to quietude?

If water is still, its clarity lights up the hairs of beard and eyebrows, its evenness is plumb with the carpenter's level; the greatest of craftsmen take their standards from it. If water, when still, is so clear, then how much more the quintessential spirit (水静则明烛须眉，平中准，大匠取法焉，水静犹明，而况精神).

—Zhuangzi

What is your understanding of Zhuangzi's remarks on still water?

Chinese college youths are considerably more mature than American students of the same age, for even young Chinese freshmen in American universities cannot get interested in football and motorcars.

—Lin Yutang

Why did Chinese youths appear more mature than their Western counterparts?

One should seek serenity to cultivate the body, thriftiness to cultivate the morality. Seeking fame and wealth will not lead to noble ideals. Only by seeking serenity will one reach far (夫君子之行：静以修身，俭以养德；非淡泊无以明志，非宁静无以致远).

—Zhuge Liang

Is what Zhuge Liang, the wise man in Chinese history, advocated still relevant today when fame and wealth seem to be criteria of success and many are trying all means to become famous and make big money?

The Americans are great missionaries. They have an irrepressible urge to convert others.

—Lee Kuan Yew

Singapore's former Prime Minister Lee Kuan Yew makes such a comment on the Americans in his book *The Wit & Wisdom of Lee Kuan Yew* published in 1992. Are you with or against him?

I. Introduction to Two Concepts

1. *Jing* vs. *Dong*

Jing (静) means non-action, motionlessness, stillness, serenity, quietness, stasis, tranquility, silence, smoothness, repose, etc. and *dong* (动) denotes the same with action, motion, movement, dynamic, activeness, etc. *Dong* and *jing* are basically understood correlatively in China. It is believed that where there is *dong* there must be *jing*; where there is *jing* there must be *dong*. In both Chinese and Western garden scenery, serenity is lodged in motion and motion arises from serenity. As one sits in repose in a pavilion, the clouds are floating, the water is flowing, birds are flying, and flowers are falling. And still water is in repose, but fish in it are moving. As stillness and motion interweave, they naturally create an aesthetic interest. For another instance, in our circle of friends, you may find some quieter on some occasions and more active and talkative on other occasions.

Regarding *jing* and *dong*, different cultures have different preferences. Some advocate that it is better to be *jing* while others hold that it is good to be *dong*.

2. Advocacy of *Jing*

Some cultures advocate *jing* (主静), and are inclined to maintain an unchanging nature. In these cultures, anything that might unbalance or disturb their equilibrium is likely to be discouraged. Instead, consensus-building, cooperation, togetherness, in-group, mass experiences, social sanctions and social regulation, structured socialization, peer loyalty, nation loyalty, sense of belonging, homogeneity, identity formation through allegiance to a group, etc. are more likely to be encouraged. To keep static or peaceful, these cultures employ numerous self-preservation mechanisms, strict hierarchy, obedience, discipline, and sometimes even discrimination (in gender, age, and familial affiliation). People exposed to these cultures prefer *jing* and are inward-directed or introverted, valuing the peaceful co-existence of their inner world with the outside.

3. Advocacy of *Dong*

Some cultures advocate *dong* (主动) and prefer to be pluralistic or heterogeneous. To keep dynamic or active, they encourage conflict as the main arbiter in the social, political and economic spheres (e.g. the invisible hand of the market and the American "checks and balances"), and favor contractual and transactional relationships, partisanship, utilitarianism, heterogeneity, self-fulfillment, fluidity of the social structures, freedom, rule of law, and democracy which has become "a game of money politics" in some Western countries.

People brought up in these cultures are apt to be outward-directed or extroverted and show an unusual love of actions.

II. Chinese Advocacy of *Jing*

A distinct aspect of Chinese culture is its advocacy of ***jing***. Chinese love serenity, seeking a poetic pastoral quiet life. The quietude, peace and harmony described in the "Peach Blossom Land" by Jin dynasty scholar Tao Yuanming have been pursued by Chinese people, some of whom meanwhile love **renao** on occasions like dinner parties and holiday gatherings.

1. Preconditions for Advocacy of *Jing*

A good living environment, stable family life, agrarian economy, doctrines of the three traditional Chinese teachings, etc. may have helped to develop Chinese love of *jing*.

a. A Good Living Environment

A good living environment is one of the preconditions for ancient Chinese to maintain an unchanging ritual and live a quiet and uneventful life. In very ancient times, cold winds from northern Siberia used to rush southward, carrying with them billions of tons of sand from the Mongolian Desert. When they reached the Yellow River, they became weak, bringing adequate rainfall and lots of sand to create about 150-meter-deep fertile topsoil for the Central Plains Region–the cradle of Chinese civilization and the birthplace of the Han nationality. With a fertile plain and a favorable climate, this region became a granary of the ancient Chinese who could settle down in one place for many generations.

Unit 14　Advocacy of *Jing* vs. *Dong*

b. An Ultra-stable Family-State

Living in one place for many generations was one of the preconditions for families to become bigger and bigger, especially in the Central Plains Region. One of the hundred surnames or **baixing** constituted one big family—the foundation of the state established much earlier in China than in the West. Hence, there has been in Chinese the concept of **guojia**, which implies that the state is an extended family in which interdependence and hierarchy are natural and essential. Running the state composed of many families therefore depended on the rulers' ability to keep peace within the ultra-stable family-state.

c. Agrarian Economy

Traditional Chinese culture arises from agriculture which has long been regarded as the basis of the economy. The rural-based agrarian economy relied on farming, hand labor, and manufacturing at home. This self-reliant and self-supporting economy resulted in an isolation and introversion in need of a spirit of opening up.

d. Confucian Emphasis on *Jing*

Chinese advocacy of ***jing*** is a part of the Confucian tradition. It is manifested in the doctrine of filial piety which traditionally limited Chinese travels and confiscated Chinese desire to leave home to seek more fortune outside by taking risks and adventures, for Confucius said, "A man does not travel to distant places when his parents are living, and if he does, he must have a definite destination (父母在，不远游，游必有方)." His disciple Zengzi defined the filial child this way: "He does not climb high, and does not tread on dangerous places (孝子不登高，不履危)." In one word, a filial son should live a quiet and safe life to please his aged parents.

The Confucian ideal family life has always been a quiet one, in which men are supposed to spend half of their time studying and half of their time tilling the field while women are supposed to spin and weave (男耕女织). The dream life is actually the "assumed" life of the early Zhou dynasty when life was the simplest and the needs of man were fewest. The worship of the ancients then became similar to the worship of simplicity and serenity, for the two notions in Chinese are closely related as in the phrase *gupu* (literally, ancient and simple).

According to the theory of virtue, another important Confucian doctrine, *jing* is the basis of exemplifying virtue. The *Great Learning*, one of the Four Confucian Classical Books, begins with the following sentences: "What the *Great Learning* teaches is to clearly exemplify illustrious virtue, to love the people, and to rest in the highest excellence. Only when one knows where to rest can he determine the object of his pursuit. Only with an object of pursuit can he achieve calmness of mind. Only with calmness of mind can he attain a tranquil repose. Only in tranquil repose can he deliberate carefully. Only through careful deliberation can he reach the desired goal (大学之道，在明明德，在亲民，在止于至善。知止而后有定，定而后能静，静而后能安，安而后能虑，虑而后能得)."

Dong Zhongshu, the famous Han Confucian scholar, drew widely from the other schools of philosophy and held that "the vastness of the Way arises from Heaven; Heaven is unchangeable and the Way is unchangeable (道之大原出于天，天不变道亦不变)," and encouraged the formation of an ultra-stable society where many generations could live in the same place so that a sense of deep root provided the kind of life ancient Chinese sought, which could create the feeling of being quiet, harmonious, stable, peaceful, and thus happy.

In order to remove selfish desires that may influence self-cultivation, Wang Yangming, the Ming dynasty Neo-Confucian scholar, suggested that one practice his type of meditation which he called "sitting still (静坐)". Obviously, he was inspired by the practice of *Chan* meditation in Buddhism. The purpose is to cultivate one's mind and nature (修养心性) so as to realize inner peace and balance with the outside world.

e. Daoist Cultivation of *Jing*

Laozi put forward the doctrine of "keeping quietude, valuing the supple, respecting the femininity, and taking no action (守静，贵柔，尊阴，无为)," based on which he came to the conclusion, "The heavy is the root of the light, and the quiet is the master of the unstable. Therefore, the sage travels all day, without putting down his heavy load. Though there may be spectacles to see, he easily passes them by. This being so, how could the ruler of a large state be so concerned with himself as to ignore the people? If you take them lightly you will lose your roots. If you are unstable, you will lose your rulership (重为轻根，静为躁君。是以君子终日行不离轻重。虽有荣观，燕处超然。奈何万乘之主，而以身轻天下。轻则失根，躁则失君)." The conclusion denotes that stability dominates the instability. Zhuangzi, the second important figure of Daoism, is famous for his concept of the mind's house (心斋), through which one is brought into harmony with nature and achieves peace by sitting and forgetting (坐忘). In *Human World* (《人间篇》) he states, "Only the Way can accumulate vacancy; the vacant is the mind's house (惟道集虚，虚者心斋)," believing only by maintaining the quiet and vacant of the mind can one attain the Way, because he held that the practice of "sitting and forgetting" could integrate one with nature.

Based on their observation and studies, both Laozi and Zhuangzi favored the notion of *jing* as the natural disposition of sages. After the fall of the Han dynasty, there arose the Neo-Daoist movement. Its central objective was to enjoy a long and serene life which, as taught by Laozi, may be attained through simplicity and tranquility, and as illustrated by Zhuangzi, through integration with nature, spiritual freedom, and indifference to life and death. This Neo-Daoist Movement assumed momentum in the third century BC and has continued to the present time.

f. Buddhist Emphasis on Inner Silence (涅槃寂静)

Ancient Chinese followed the life pattern of "using Confucianism to run the state, Daoism to cultivate body, and Buddhism to nurture mind (以儒治世，以道养身，以佛修心)." A silent mind/heart (心), freed from the onslaught of thoughts and thought patterns, is both a goal and an important step in spiritual development according to Buddhist philosophers. Inner silence is understood to be able to bring one into contact with the divine or the ultimate reality of this moment. The Buddhist tradition implies the importance of being quiet and peaceful in mind and spirit for transformative and integral spiritual growth to occur.

The mirror-like clarity of still water supplies the imagery for the state of mind/heart that a sage might attain (in ancient China the heart was considered the thinking organ).

2. Chinese Preference for *Jing*

In his poem *Admonishing a Son* (《诫子书》), Zhuge Liang, the famous military strategist of Shu during the Three Kingdoms period mentioned a couplet that had always bothered him: Without peace, there is no way to extend one's knowledge; Without tranquility, there is no way to clarify one's purpose (非淡泊无以明志，非宁静无以致远). Chinese people, especially scholars, like to enjoy a peaceful and serene life, describing a quiet man as being intelligent and introspective, and preferring a quiet stay at home after a long workday. If given a

Unit 14 Advocacy of *Jing* vs. *Dong*

choice, most of us would like to lead a quiet life and attend to our own business.

a. *Jing* as a Name of Objects

Maybe you have noticed the fact that Chinese parents like naming their children ***jing***. Take the famous singer Wang Jing and the renowned CCTV anchor Wen Jing for instance. They hope their kids will be serene and quiet for serenity is a good quality in this country. A young lady who is serene and quiet will be favored by her teachers, parents, supervisors, friends, etc. and a quiet boy will probably be good at his academic work at school.

In order to create an ideal environment for booklovers to do some reading and shopping, book sellers employ ***jing*** to name their stores, e.g. **Jing Zhai** (literally, Serenity Studio) and **Le Jing Ju** (literally, Studio of Happiness in Quietude).

Garden administrators use ***jing*** to name their gardens in order to attract more visitors who need a break from work, e.g. **Jing Yuan** (literally, Serenity Garden) and **Le Jing Yuan** (literally, Garden of Happiness in Quietness).

The public sign "**jing jing jing** (静 净 敬, freely, please be quiet, polite, and keep clean)" can be seen on many campuses, calling on children to keep quiet in public places, to be environment-friendly, and to respect parents, teachers and people who are older than them.

Despite the surface changes in customs, women's clothes, people's reading habits, the rhythm of life, etc., some conservative Chinese still retain a sneering smile for the hot-headed young person who is noisy, active, and in love with adventures and changes.

b. Chinese Idioms Denoting *Jing*

There are in Chinese many idioms denoting our love of ***jing***. They are used to express beautiful wishes for stillness, quietness, stability, tranquility, settlement, safety, peace, etc., as can be seen in idioms such as **Enjoy a tranquil and comfortable life** (岁月静好); **Bring peace and stability to the country** (安邦定国); **Live and work in peace and contentment** (安居乐业); **Settle down in one place** (安家落户); **Be safe and sound** or **Be uneventful** (安然无恙); **Hate to leave a place where one has lived long** (安土重迁); **Settle down and go on with one's pursuit** (安身立命); **Expire peacefully** (安然长逝); **Use quietude to control motion** (以静制动); and **Be prepared for everything with no change** (以不变应万变). A Chinese parent or teacher might use the expression **Hold your tongue** (静一静) a lot to shut up a group of noisy or hyperactive children.

c. Power of *Jing* in the Ancient Music

Ancient Chinese music is expected to create a sense of tranquility, serenity, peace, safety as well as beauty. The monophonic music reflects ancient Chinese concern for unity and harmony. Singers would all sing the same melody and musical instruments play the same notes at the same time. The famous "Empty City Scheme" is about how Zhuge Liang saved an empty city by playing the zither, an ancient musical instrument. During the Three Kingdoms period, Zhuge Liang was in the city of Yang Ping. He sent his general Wei Yan with the majority of the Shu soldiers to fight against the 200,000 strong Wei army led by General Sima Yi, leaving only 10,000 men behind to defend the city. However, due to miscalculation, the Shu army missed the Wei army. When the Wei army was about 60 miles from the city, Sima Yi learnt from his spy about Shu's strength that was left in the city. Zhuge Liang also received the news that the enemy was near, but it was too late to summon Wei Yan back. The town was in panic but Zhuge Liang remained calm. He ordered his soldiers to keep all the army flags flying and not to leave the tents without permission. He then

Unit 14 Advocacy of *Jing* vs. *Dong*

ordered men to open the gates and pretend to sweep the ground next to the gates. When Sima Yi arrived, he was shocked by what he saw. He knew Zhuge Liang was a good strategist with many tricks up his sleeve. So when he saw the gates were opened up, he suspected Zhuge Liang might have laid an ambush, waiting for him. His suspicion was further aroused when he saw Zhuge Liang sitting leisurely on top of the city wall playing the zither and sipping tea. Sima Yi paid attention to the chords played by Zhuge Liang and they were placid and calm, showing no signs of a troubled mind. He therefore, concluded that the empty city was definitely a scheme to lure his troops in. Sima Yi ordered his men to turn around and retreat. Thus Zhuge Liang salvaged the situation.

Incidentally, Buddhist music is also meant to create a sense of serenity, in which one could be gradually or suddenly enlightened. Hence, the simple recitation of Amitabha's name in the company of the same melody and musical instrument becomes the most common of all Buddhist practices in China and a tool popular with millions who seek liberation from the sufferings of this world (脱离苦海).

d. Chinese Preference for Steady and Taciturn Candidates

In selecting talents for leading positions, ancient Chinese preferred to see first of all whether the candidates were steady and taciturn (不苟言笑) or not, which has been a tradition since the Zhou dynasty. According to the *Yao Dian* (《尧典》) and *Shun Dian* (《舜典》), Emperor Yao was reverential, intelligent, accomplished, thoughtful, and mild. When Fang Qi recommended his son to be his successor, he said, "Your heir-son Zhu is highly intelligent." Yao said, "Alas! He is insincere and noisy. Can he do?" Later Shun was recommended, although he did not seem like promising material–a common man, his father was stupid, his stepmother arrogant, and his half-brother conceited. Yet Shun, a man with enormous emotional stability who did not allow his personal misfortunes or sufferings to affect his judgment made this difficult family live in harmony, and he performed his administrative duties with great skill. And above all, he was steady and taciturn (稳重寡言), and thus dependable. Proving equal to this demanding official role, he was invited to share Yao's throne.

e. Chinese Beautiful Wish for *Jing*

"Calm seas and tranquil breezes (风平浪静)" is the best wish for fishermen, or for the safety of a traveler or a person who is ready to travel. Jinghai Temple in Nanjing was built in 1402 when the famous navigator Zheng He came back from his second voyage to the Indian Ocean. In praise of his achievements in navigation and exchanges with other peoples and cultures, Emperor Cheng of the Ming ordered to build Jinghai Temple (literally, Calm-sea Temple), praying for the peace of the whole world. The temple was also built to show his gratitude and appreciation for the Sea God's protection of his great fleet, to ask for more mercy on travelers and to wish his people a tranquil and quiet life.

3. *Jing* as a Theme Popular with Chinese Poets

Jing is traditionally used by Chinese literati as a background in which they express their homesickness, ambition, pride, and uniqueness. Take *Jiang Xue* (*Fishing in Snow*) by Tang Poet Liu Zongyuan (773–819) for instance.

Fishing in Snow

From hill to hill no bird is in flight;

From path to path no man is in sight.

A lonely fisherman afloat

Is fishing snow in a lonely boat.

(Tr. by Xu Yuanchong)

Born in the Tang capital Chang'an, Liu Zongyuan was promoted very

Unit 14   Advocacy of *Jing* vs. *Dong*

rapidly in the civil government. He supported the reform efforts of Emperor Shunzong, fell into disfavor with the authorities when the emperor suddenly abdicated in 805. In exile, Liu Zongyuan turned his attention to literature. His autobiographical poem **Jiang Xue** composed during his exile is considered an example of how a few words can be used to convey a great deal of meanings such as his ambition, his uniqueness, and his perseverance. The poem has been the subject of numerous landscape paintings to exhibit the serene background, ambition and pride which characterize decent talented scholars or scholar-officials.

Jing is also employed by Chinese literati as a subject in which they express their idea of what the best life is, as demonstrated in this poem:

I asked the boy beneath the pine.

He said to me, "The Master's gone

Herb-gathering somewhere in this mount.

Cloud-hidden, whereabouts unknown."

This feeling for nature and stillness overflows in almost all Chinese poetry, and forms an important part of the Chinese spiritual heritage. Even as late as today, a call for the return of the traditional appreciation of the static beauty of harmony would be answered by many, because every Chinese has a desire for beauty since we are exposed to poems featuring serenity.

4. *Jing* as an Ideal Lifestyle

"Only after ***jing*** or tranquility can there come peace (静而后能安)," according to the *Great Learning*. It has long been believed that if one lacks tranquility, he could not clarify his purpose, thus unable to feel particularly peaceful or tranquil–even in his retirement. A life without peace was assumed to be pathetic in China. A retiree might have had his share of disappointments, humiliations and failures when he was in office, but if he can manage to retire with a little grace he will happily pursue a quiet life: in the evenings he wanders in the woods by moonlight listening to music and sits down in a quiet pavilion in the daytime watching the floating clouds. While the early autumn weather is still warm enough, he likes to settle in his study and read books like the *Classic of the Waterways*–descriptions of landscapes far away, to which he can now only travel vicariously. This is the ideal life many scholars dream to have when they leave office with a pension.

III. Western Advocacy of *Dong*

A distinct aspect of Western culture is its advocacy of ***dong*** (i.e. motion). Westerners tend to be more active, incessantly reaching out. A life of such is a life of strength, showing strength and discovery for most of them.

1. Ancient Greece and Advocacy of *Dong*

a. Ancient Greek Climate and Its Economic Activities

Ancient Greece could not possibly be as agriculturally productive as China. For one thing, there was the Mediterranean climate: hot dry summers and cold rainy winters, and the average annual rainfall in Athens was only 15.9 inches, and for another, there were few rivers in Greece, and most of the territory was broken up into islands and peninsulas that cannot receive the runoff of wetter mountains. Ancient Greece was thus wealthy off something else–sea trade, transportation, and even piracy, which led those who were in these professions to live a restless life by visiting different places, experiencing alien cultures and facing rapidly changing situations.

b. Sea Trade of Ancient Greece

Long coastline and being surrounded by water on three sides made it

Unit 14   Advocacy of *Jing* vs. *Dong*

possible for ancient Greeks to develop sea trade and transportation. To engage in trade, anyone needs something to get started, and Greek agriculture could provide a couple of starter products. Olive trees grew well in ancient Greece. Olives must be soaked in brine to be edible, but more importantly they can be pressed for olive oil. The oil is not very perishable, and could be stored and shipped easily to be sold at distant locations in exchange for food, fuel oil, or other purposes. Grapes as well grew well in ancient Greece. Grapes can be pressed and fermented to produce wine, another product that is not very perishable and can be stored and shipped.

Trade as a way of life would involve and foster considerable independence, being far away from all authorities at home, and it would involve dealing with all sorts of strangers, cultures, practices, and ideas.

c. Commodity Economy of Ancient Greece

Ancient Greece took advantage of its ecology and geography to develop its commodity economy, so commodity production and exchange characterized its economy. The Greek commodity economy helped to meet each other's needs, possessing the characteristics of openness to the outside, independence and equality, on the basis of which Western culture of extroversion was set up. Settled agriculture came to Greece almost two thousand years later than to China, but it quickly became commercial. Since the commodity economy arose out of equality and independence, this economy brought equality and democratic ideas to Western culture which advocates dynamic activities like discovery, invention, and adventures.

2. Scholars and Advocacy of *Dong*

Western love of *dong* owes much to Western philosophers and scientists.

a. Heraclitus

Ancient Greece has given Westerners more philosophy than any other place in the West by producing many philosophers. Heraclitus is one of them. The best-known aspect of Heraclitus' ideas is the omnipresence of change (一切皆流). There is, he said, nothing static in the universe, the mind, or the soul. Everything is ceasing to be what it was and becoming what it will be. This was a new idea. "All things flow; nothing abides," he wrote and "we are and we are not." His best-known remark is, "You cannot step twice into the same river, for other waters are ever flowing on to you." His system contains other hypotheses, but this is the most fruitful, and the one which commended itself most to his followers and successors.

b. Cratylus

If the world was in such constant flux that streams could change instantaneously, then so could words. Thus, Heraclitus' disciple Cratylus found communication to be impossible. As a result of this realization, Cratylus renounced his power of speech and limited his communication to moving his finger.

c. Nicolaus Copernicus

Nicolaus Copernicus (1473–1543) was the first astronomer to formulate a scientifically based heliocentrism, a theory that the sun is at the center of the solar system. His book *On the Revolutions of the Celestial Spheres* is often regarded as the starting point of modern astronomy that began the scientific revolution which encourages discovery and invention of new ideas.

3. Western Preference for *Dong*

a. Ancient Olympic Games

Ancient Greeks loved sports. What is astonishing, even to us today, is that during a celebration of the Games, an Olympic Truce was enacted to enable athletes to travel from their city-states to Olympia in safety; the entire Greek nation laid down its tools–including its arms if city-states were at war with one another–to participate in the Olympics as athletes or audience. The prizes for the victors were laurel wreaths, palm branches, woolen ribbons and sometimes even food for life. The modern Games held every four years is a continuation of the ancient Greek Olympics.

b. Ancient Greek Love of Fun

There is an ancient theater at Epidaurus in Greece. It can hold fourteen thousand people. Built into a hillside, the theater has a good view of mountains and pine trees. Its acoustics are very good after so many years. According to historical records, Greeks from the sixth to the third century BC traveled for long periods under very difficult conditions to Epidaurus merely to see plays and listen to people read poetry. They used to stay in the theatre from dawn till dusk for several days in a row and had great fun from the poetry reading and stage performance.

c. U.S. Presidents' Hobbies

Like us all, presidents need relaxation. Over the years, U.S. presidents have participated in a great variety of sports and hobbies while in the White House. Some were famous for their hobbies, such as Dwight Eisenhower for his golf, Ronald Reagan for horseback riding and John Kennedy for sailing and touch football. Gerald Ford even played football for the University of Michigan in the early 1930s. He was selected as Most Valuable Player in 1934 and was named an All-American, the only president to win this distinction. After college, he was offered contracts by several professional teams. President Barack Obama's favorite sport is basketball and he played varsity basketball in high school.

George Washington, true to the times and his class, enjoyed fishing and horseback riding. He found great relaxation in the out-of-doors, and enjoyed getting away from the pressures of office.

Washington's successor, John Adams, apparently had no specific hobbies during his term as President, and engaged in no sports. That may have had something to do with the portly Adams' nickname of "His Rotundity."

d. Western Preference for Active People

"All work and no play make Jack a dull boy" is one of the most often quoted proverbs, denoting that without time off from work, a person becomes bored and boring. If you work all day in this culture, few will be deeply impressed by your hard work. Instead, people will think you are a person of no life, a poor guy, and an overly introverted person.

e. Western Love of Adventures and Pursuit of Material Wealth

Traditional Western culture, composed of Greek, Roman and Christian cultures, holds that everything could be achieved through action and one's value could only be found in action. During the 1400s, some Europeans began to wonder what lay across the great oceans. Many decided to make dangerous journeys across the oceans in order to explore new lands for themselves, and one of them was Christopher Columbus.

Marco Polo traveled to China as a teenager and spent 17 years here. Upon his return, he wrote a book that describes all the wonders of China. Columbus read this book titled *The Travels of Marco Polo*. He too wanted to travel to the East. Columbus made four voyages across the Atlantic Ocean between 1492 and his death. During this period, new countries, a new continent and new civilizations were discovered for the very first time. As for why there were so great geographic discoveries in Europe, below are some possible reasons:

They wanted to explore new lands.

Unit 14 Advocacy of *Jing* vs. *Dong*

They intended to become rich by finding gold and silver.

They hoped to find new lands for their country to control.

They expected to find new people to convert to the Christian religion.

They wanted to prove that the world was round.

In one word, Western culture favors motion in the form of outward expansion or long-distance travel.

IV. Differences and Discomforts

1. Different Translation Strategies

In China, the best life or the most beautiful memory is experienced in a static state while in the West, in a dynamic setting. Chinese culture as a whole tends to be still, so anything relevant to stillness could be encouraged and hence prosper, which may illustrate why stillness is a favorite topic with classical Chinese poets and painters. Western culture as a whole is one of motion, so anything relevant to motion could be promoted and hence flourish. This difference might probably account for why Western translators adopt free translation to render classical Chinese poetry which is the aggregate of the Chinese cultural heritage, and sometimes go so far as to change the original theme of stillness into that of motion. ***Jing Ye Si*** by Tang poet Li Bai is one of the first poems most Chinese pre-school babblers can recite. Below are its two English versions translated by two scholars of different cultural and educational backgrounds.

A Tranquil Night

Abed, I see a silver light,

I wonder if it's frost aground.

Looking up, I find the moon bright;

Bowing, in homesickness I'm drowned.

(Tr. by Xu Yuanchong)

The Moon Shines Everywhere

Seeing the moon before my couch so bright

I thought hoar frost had fallen from the night.

On her clear face I gaze with lifted eyes:

Then hide them full of Youth's sweet memories.

(Tr. by W. J. B. Fletcher)

Obviously, the first version by Xu Yuanchong, a famous Chinese translator, is more faithful to the original. Xu chooses expressions like **tranquil** and **homesickness** in his version since *jing* is traditionally used by Chinese literati as a background in which they express their homesickness or ambition. However, the second version translated by Fletcher appears understandably unfaithful. Given the fact that a word-for-word translation into Chinese of **goodbye** which literally means "God be with you" according to English etymology may not be recognized as a parting in Chinese and the word-for-word translation into English of *zaijian* which means **see again** may not be regarded as a parting, it seems reasonable for the Western translator to translate by using dynamic expressions such as **shine** and **fallen** in accordance with his own culture in which tranquility is not associated with homesickness and serenity is not so strongly advocated.

2. Cultural Discomforts

In a normal discussion, Westerners (especially North Americans) usually appear active by interrupting each other. They seem to find silence uncomfortable and rude in conversations. Chinese do not generally interrupt one another. In group discussions, pauses and silence are valued by us. For some Westerners, Chinese silence is confusing, and sometimes upsetting.

Unit 14 Advocacy of *Jing* vs. *Dong*

Our friend Dr. Nancy Bush was invited to work for half a year at a Chinese university. She could tell that her students were very attentive in her classroom. They applauded warmly every time her lecture ended. However, Nancy was a little bit disappointed because no one asked her any questions, although she kept encouraging them to say something or anything. Somehow her students chose to sit back smiling or giggling but saying nothing. And they didn't avoid eye contact with her as she tried to persuade them to stand up and speak something! She grew upset and confused. Nancy's experience reminds Jifang of what happened to her when she was a freshman at Central China's Normal University 35 years ago:

"One day Mr. Brock who taught us Western Culture was ill. His wife came instead to teach us. In order to activate the atmosphere, she played a piece of music and suggested us dance to the music together with her, but all of us just sat there watching her and blushing with embarrassment. Then, she used imperative sentences to ask us to stand up and dance. Although we stood up, few of us followed her. Most of us felt shy, so we all fell silent, and I could see that Mrs. Brock was very frustrated."

Actually what Nancy Bush and Mrs. Brock experienced in China characterizes some Chinese students in their American lecture rooms. A few years ago, Li Ying, a graduate student studying psychology at an American university, became upset because of constant demand from her instructors that she should be more active by speaking or doing something in class. She was told repeatedly that failure to speak up could be taken as an indication of failure to fully understand the material and that speaking up and hearing the reactions from the instructor and classmates would help her to understand better. Li Ying refused to believe it. Instead, she felt that she and her fellow Chinese students would not benefit from being active in class because their way of understanding is not verbal, but silent. There is an age-old tradition in China of equating quietness rather than speech with digesting and accumulating knowledge, just as the aphorism goes, "He who knows does not speak, he who speaks does not know."

Further Reading

1. Buck, P. S. (2012). *The Good Earth*. Washington D.C. Washington Square Press.
2. Stewart, E. C. & Milton, J. B. (1991). *American Cultural Patterns: A Cross-Cultural Perspective*. Yarmouth, Maine: Intercultural Press.
3. Wu, Jian (1990). *Encountering the Chinese*. Yarmouth, Maine: Intercultural Press.
4. 崔瑞德、史乐民编 (2020), 《剑桥中国宋代史 上卷: 907–1279年》, 李永等译, 北京: 中国社会科学出版社。
5. 林语堂 (1998), 《生活的艺术》, 北京: 外语教学与研究出版社。
6. 罗素 (1976), 《西方哲学史》（下卷）, 何兆武、李约瑟译, 北京: 商务印书馆。
7. 饶尚宽译注 (2006), 《老子》, 北京: 中华书局。
8. 杨伯峻译注 (1980), 《论语译注》, 北京: 中华书局。

Unit 15   Implicitness vs. Explicitness

Saying few words fits in with Nature (希言自然).

—Laozi

What did Laozi mean by "saying few words"? Can saying few words help us tell China's story well?

二十岁的时候，老妈打电话，不等说完三句就恨不能挂了电话。三十岁之后，一听到妈的声音就禁不住哭出声来："妈呀，您老的所有担心现在都应验了……"

—Anonymous

The English version of the above is as follows:

At the age of twenty, while talking with my mother over the phone, I wanted to hang up before my mother had finished a few words. After thirty the voice of Mom invariably triggers my crying, "Mom, your worries about my marriage have all come true."

Why does the translator have to turn what is implied in the original into the explicit marriage reference in the English version?

The word for "bin" is "wastepaper basket" in America. They not only need to know what to put in it. They need to know not only it is paper, but "wastepaper." It is not just any paper. They kept throwing fresh paper away for a period before they introduced the "wastepaper basket."

—A stand-up comedian

According to the British comedian, Americans speak English but they've had to change it to make them understand it more explicitly by making a little bit more explanations. It's like they need instructions. Do you agree with him? Would you please give more examples to illustrate the differences between British and American English words?

I. "Half a Story"

Some non-Westerners complain that everything has to be explicitly talked about in some Western countries. Even the littlest thing has to be "Why, why, why?" "How, how, how?" "What, what, what?" And it's the speaker's or writer's responsibility to give definite and detailed answers to these questions instead of waiting for the listener or reader to come up with them.

At the end of 2007, as soon as she came back to her host university in The Woodlands, Texas with her son Minchang from their trip to New York City, Jifang went to visit her friend, Dr. Tracy L. Steele.

"Juliet and Nathan have been worried about you and Minchang. People feel I'm the person responsible for your safety here in America."

Noticing the displeasure in Tracy's tone, Jifang was kind of surprised and confused, "Why worry?" Juliet and Nathan were Jifang's neighbors in The Woodlands, a village near Houston.

"They say New York is not The Woodlands. You told them only half a story, Jifang. Why didn't you tell them the whole story? You should have told them you have a friend in New York, you have family there too, and you also have my brother and his family."

"But I had no time to give them more details about our plan and they

Unit 15 Implicitness vs. Explicitness

seemed to be in a hurry. I just asked them about the ferry to the Statue of Liberty and told them this was our first trip to New York. Wait a minute. Did I have to tell them all?"

As a matter of fact, Jifang knew she would not turn to anybody for help if anything should happen to her and her 13-year-old son in New York, because those people Tracy mentioned don't belong to the "we" group. Her New York friend Amy once worked at Hohai University as an English teacher, but they hadn't seen each other for four years. Her so-called family in New York is her husband's sister-in-law's sister who had migrated to New York two years before by marrying an American of Chinese descent who is much older than her, and she had seen that woman only once. And Tracy's brother? She had never seen him and his family who were on holiday in New York from Texas.

"Exactly. Everybody here thinks that I should be responsible for you. Half a story is misleading. They would judge me, Jifang."

Since then Jifang, a believer in the saying "when in Rome, do as the Romans do," has been careful about where she needs a little bit more explanation when talking with foreigners in English. One day after thinking about how to avoid telling half a story by speaking more explicitly, she chuckled and remembered how Tracy added information to her remarks when she talked to people who don't know much about China. She remembered Tracy added, "Jifang's father was a doctor" when she told her new friends "my father refused to give my son any medicine for his ADHD." She remembered Tracy explaining, "Nanjing is the capital city of east China's Jiangsu Province" when she told her new friends, "I'm from Nanjing." Having consulted many sources, Jifang eventually found herself on the journey to a new dimension–implicitness vs. explicitness.

II. Implicitness vs. Explicitness of Language

You may have found that language is not adequate to account for all of our thoughts. Problems of ambiguity (i.e. implicitness), lack of logical explicitness, etc. might serve as very good examples.

1. The Implicitness of the Chinese Language

A word, term, sign, symbol, phrase, sentence, or any other form used for communication, as a consequence of being implied or indirect, is called implicit if it is open to different interpretations and can be understood in diverse ways. The implicitness of Chinese may arise out of our distrust of words, layered expressions, etc.–a direct result of our synthetic thinking mode.

a. Chinese Distrust of Words

Lin Yutang acknowledged that "the Chinese distrust of logic begins with the distrust of words, proceeds with the abhorrence of definitions and ends with instinctive hatred for all systems and theories." Our distrust of words is revealed in what our parents taught us when we were little, such as **When you listen you should pay attention to the tone just as you should pay attention to the rhythm when you listen to the gong** (听话听声，锣鼓听音), which means "You should figure out what is implied," and **Examine a man's language and observe his countenance** (察言观色), which means "Learn what one is thinking by observing his face." When we want to convey something we are reminded to remember the policy of **"It can only be implied, not expressed in words"** to increase the readability. The distrust of words is also displayed in pop lyrics such as **Everything is clearly expressed in silence** (尽在不言中), and presents in aphorisms like **The ability to listen is golden; the ability to speak convincingly is silver** (会听是金，会说是银) because many Chinese believe

"The intention of the drinker lies not on the wine, but on other purposes (醉翁之意不在酒)." Therefore, for the sake of convenience or to save time, polite or shrewd people love saying "Do whatever you want" or "Suit yourself (随便)," leaving the other party to figure out for himself what is on their mind, and hence "Do as one's host thinks fit (客随主便)" becomes a polite pet phrase.

Distrust of words is one of the reasons why some ordinary Westerners who bear no grudge against China find it difficult to learn Chinese.

b. Expressions That Defy Easy Translation

There are many Chinese expressions that would invite misinterpretation if there were no context. It's always wise to stay mindful of the words for "some Chinese terms are so complicated in meaning that there are no English equivalents for them and they therefore have to be transliterated." This warning is especially pertinent in discussing Chinese philosophical concepts such as *qi*. What perhaps most distinguishes *qi* from cognate ideas in other cultures is its dependence on flow. In the system of traditional Chinese medicine, the unobstructed flow of *qi* is essential for health. "When fluent *qi* takes form, the order is generated therein," says Xunzi. According to the 4th century-BC philosopher Guanzi, "Water is the blood and *qi* of the earth; it resembles what flows through the veins and arteries." The *Shuowen Jiezi Dictionary* defines *qi* as "cloud vapour." The traditional form of the modern character is also associated with clouds, water vapour and mist: it is really "steam," rising from the cooking pot full of rice. That is the beauty of the Chinese language, in which the characters may occasionally blend the metaphysical with the practical not just conceptually but visually, and thereby connect profound and abstract concepts with the daily routine. Today *qi* which defies easy translation can be translated as energy, air, gas or breath; *tianqi* (weather) is literally "Heaven's breath."

Many commonly used expressions seem hard to be translated appropriately without consulting the context. Does "jiang hao zhongguo gushi (讲好中国故事)," for instance, mean "tell good Chinese stories" or "tell China's story well"?

c. Layered Expressions

Words in Chinese are not just semantic signifiers. They are distillates of Chinese thought, saturated with association and ambiguity, ready to unfold layers of meaning that differ according to context. That is why it is better, in any case, to call them characters, not words: their form and content are inextricably entwined. The little sayings that Chinese people love to quote are a kind of philosophical distillate: ideas, stories, legends, concentrated beyond the reach of literal translation. They tend to be "layered," although the superficial message becomes apparent immediately. But as you re-read, you discover deeper meaning. **"Datie hai xu zishen ying** (打铁还须自身硬)" would be a good example. Its superficial message is that **It takes a good blacksmith to make good steel** or **It takes a good blacksmith to forge good tools**. Then you will find deeper connotations: **To forge iron, one's own self must be strong**; **If you want to work with iron, you have to be tough yourself**; or **To be forged into iron, the metal itself must be strong**. More examples of layered proverbs may help to more clearly explain why Chinese seems ambiguous to some people:

Qianlizhidi, kuiyuyixue (superficial message: a thousand-mile dike is destroyed by ant nests; deeper meaning: Neglecting something. small may result in big troubles.)

Bu zuo kuixin shi, bu pa gui qiaomen (superficial message: A clear conscience never fears midnight knocking; deeper meaning: A quiet conscience sleeps well even in thunder.)

Er bu xian mu chou, gou bu xian jia pin (superficial message: A dog

Unit 15 Implicitness vs. Explicitness

won't forsake his master because of his poverty; a son never deserts his mother for her homely appearance; deeper meaning: A mother never looks ugly to her son; Be grateful and faithful.)

Yu bu zhuo bu cheng qi (superficial message: Gems unwrought can do nothing useful; deeper meaning: No one can achieve anything without education and learning.)

Read and re-read the proverbs above and you will find them open to different interpretations and can be understood in different ways–to the bafflement even of the foreign students who can decrypt the individual meanings.

d. Chinese Synthetic Thinking Mode

Closely associated with intuition and thinking in terms of images, the synthetic or holistic mode of traditional Chinese thinking has determined the quality or state of implicitness, which is synonymous with **ambiguousness**, **cloudiness**, **equivocalness**, **indefiniteness**, **nebulousness**, **obscurity**, **uncertainty**, **unclearness**, and **vagueness**.

Intuitive thinking is a special process of obtaining knowledge about the whole situation. This thinking takes place very quickly with much information, transcending the restrictions imposed by the pursuit of clarity. It seeks integral and absolute knowledge, so it is qualitative, not quantitative. Lack of quantitative analysis results in ambiguity, which features Chinese, for instance, the concept of *dao* is ambiguous since, according to Laozi, *dao* is invisible and indescribable.

Thinking synthetically helps to form the habit of communicating through symbolic expressions, hints and allusions expecting listeners and readers to grasp the meaning by reading between the lines. Many readers may have read a public sign "**My love, when you miss me, remember to take good care of the green grass** (记得绿罗裙，处处怜芳草)" which means " Keep off the grass."

The ambiguity of thinking encourages neglect of logical clarity and lexical-semantic "accuracy," which makes a combination of linguistic units in Chinese paragraphs appear casual. There are many expressions used by many including linguists in spite of logical ambiguity such as **kaixin** (开心 literally, to open heart; freely, to be very happy) and **jiuzai** (救灾 literally, rescue disaster; freely, disaster rescue). Obviously, only a few representative words combined together are enough. Therefore, the basis of Chinese grammatical rules is meaning, not form; thus we like to say, "He who says the least says the most."

Synthetic thinking mode instructs us not to depend very much on quantitative instructions. For instance, we learn cooking not by following recipes with precise quantitative descriptions, but by intuitively acquiring our mothers' or our masters' technique after repeated imitations, so we don't use measuring cups. Another example is traditional Chinese painting. We seek close resemblance in spirit when we paint instead of accurate likeness in appearance. In fact, intuitive feeling and fuzzy beauty are held in great esteem in almost all forms of Chinese art such as poetry, drama, and painting.

2. Explicitness of the English Language

A word, term, sign, symbol, phrase, sentence, or any other form used for communication, is called explicit if it can be interpreted in only one way. Therefore, explicitness is synonymous with **certainty**, **clarity**, **clearness**, **definiteness**, **explicitness**, and **lucidity**.

a. Logical Thinking

Comparatively speaking, English is more explicit. Its explicitness may arise out of logical thinking, the opposite of Chinese holistic or synthetic thinking. Logical thinking is a learned mental process, in which one uses reasoning consistently to come to a conclusion. Problems or situations that involve logical thinking call for structure, for relationships between facts, and for chains of reasoning that make sense. The basis of all logical thinking is sequential thought. This process involves important ideas, facts, and conclusions. To think logically is to think in steps, involving both qualitative and quantitative analysis, but putting more emphasis on the study of the latter. The quantitative emphasis endows English with explicitness and accuracy. For instance, they like using expressions such as **Don't beat about the bush**; **Let's get down to business**; **Let us be clear**, and **Get to the point.** They write explicit public signs like **Keep off** rather than **The grass smiles and asks you to take the sidewalk** (小草微微笑，请君走便道) or **The grass has life. so please be merciful** (小草有生命，脚下请留情). Westerners, exposed to relatively explicit languages, try to get at things very clearly, asking or explaining what, why and how much while we show more interest in dealing with things using metaphors or intuitive comparisons.

b. Need for Clarity

Many Westerners believe that God has made man a creature of time and therefore, a creature of number, so they tend to depend on very explicit words and exact quantitative instructions. For instance, they learn cooking by following recipes with precise quantitative descriptions. They are trained on how to make their case in 30 seconds or less.

They seek accurate likeness in appearance when working on oil paintings, e.g. every inch of canvas is filled up and even the wrinkles on the dress can be seen.

They are alert to embroidery (奢华语言) and exaggeration in communication, afraid they become lies and demean their language.

They avoid confusion of facts with opinions, believing when these two things get conflated, one is listening to the wind and it is difficult to listen.

III. Implicit Traditional Chinese

The implicitness or ambiguity of traditional Chinese has been much discussed by scholars at home and abroad. Some like Hu Shi held that implicitness was producing a country of lazy-bones while others advocated using implicitness in creative work.

1. The Beauty and Ugliness of Implicitness

a. The Beauty of Implicitness in Classical Chinese Poetry

Implicitness, sometimes known as plurisignation or multiple meaning, is a central concept in the interpretation of poetry. Oriental Studies Master Ji Xianlin defended it as a source of poetic richness rather than a fault of imprecision during an interview in 1996.

Chinese, a language of parataxis (意合), does not stress the form, its structure can be incomplete, and its verbs are not so salient, especially in classical Chinese poetry, which requires the reader or listener to involve his own personal experience in Chinese poetry interpretation and appreciation. Take for example "Standing near the hut in the moonlight, I hear the cock crowing, and get a sense of some steps of passers-by before me on the bridge (鸡声茅店月，人迹板桥霜)" composed by Tang poet Wen Tingyun. We can understand the two lines on the basis of our own experiences and see a man who, away from home, misses his family in late autumn. This understanding owes much to the free and ambiguous expressions employed by Wen. Suppose the expressions were clear and explicit, our aesthetic fancy might be greatly reduced. Wang Guowei in *Comments on Ci* (《人间词话》) brought up with **yijing** (literally, poetic excellence) and **guya** (literally, classical grace) theory, coining phrases like

Unit 15 Implicitness vs. Explicitness

context with me (有我之境, freely, context with an explicit actor) and **context without me** (无我之境, freely, context without an explicit actor) employed in classical Chinese poetry. According to him, "采菊东篱下，悠然见南山" provides a "context without me," and its beauty lies in the ambiguity of the actor. If translated into English, however, the actor should be added as in "While picking asters 'neath the Eastern fence, my gaze upon the Southern mountain rests," otherwise the translation will not make any sense to the target reader, thus leaving no imaginative space and decreasing the original poetic beauty of implicitness.

As a great example of literature highly succinct in writing, classical Chinese poetry is full of vivid images in limited space of lines that produce pictures in the minds of readers or listeners, so it is essential to exert our imagination when reading and appreciating a classical Chinese poem. Take for instance two lines from a poem by Wang Wei (701–761): "I would ask you to drink a cup of wine again; West of the Sunny Pass no more friends will be seen (劝君更尽一杯酒，西出阳关无故人)." Obviously, the second line is the cause and the first one is the effect, but there is no word in the original lines to join them, so we have to comprehend these two lines by firing or unfolding our imagination. The following is a lyric by the Yuan poet Ma Zhiyuan (c.1250–1321), entitled ***Qiu Si*** (*Autumn Thoughts*):

Autumn Thoughts

Over old trees wreathed with rotten vines fly evening crows;

Under a small bridge near a cottage a stream flows;

On ancient road in the west wind a lean horse goes.

Westward declines the sun,

Far, far from home is the heartbroken one.

(枯藤老树昏鸦，小桥流水人家。
古道西风瘦马，夕阳西下，断肠人在天涯。)

(Tr. by Xu Yuanchong)

Old trees, **rotten vines** and **evening crows** arranged one after another in a sequence in the original, give us much freedom of thinking and great enjoyment. The implicitness is not bad, is it? Only two verbs can be found in the original poetry *xia* (下, i.e. set down) and *zai* (在, i.e. be), which is unimaginable in English. The famous American poet Ezra Pound, influenced by Chinese poetry, composed poems in the Chinese way, became very popular for a period of time and then went into oblivion because Chinese poetic lines without verbs appear ambiguous and thus beautiful, but English, as an inflectional language, stresses the importance of grammar and form–hypotaxis and thus lines without verbs are ambiguous and hence undesirable and incomprehensible.

Ancient Chinese poets used implicit language to produce vivid images for aesthetic purposes. Take for instance the two famous lies of poetry "How much sorrow, pray, can a person carry? Like the spring torrent flowing eastward, without tarry (问君能有几多愁，恰似一江春水向东流)." The two lines are from a *ci* poem composed by Li Yu (937–978), a poet emperor of the Later Tang dynasty. In this poem spring water in the river implies endless melancholy.

As an art of language, Chinese poems use words in extraordinary ways for expression and description. A story goes about Wang Anshi (1022–1086), a famous poet and statesman of the Song dynasty, who racked his brains for perfection in the choice of words. Originally, he used words explicitly in the line of his poem and it was read as "The vernal wind has reached the southern shore again (春风又到江南岸)." But he did not feel satisfied with its explicitness. After looking desperately for the right word, he found that the adjective "green" should be the best choice because it is so colorful and imaginable a description of "the southern region of the Yangtze" in spring when being tentatively used as a verb, much better than any explicit verbs such as ***dao*** (到, i.e. reach), ***guo*** (过, i.e. pass by), and ***ru*** (入, i.e. enter) he had weighed. In this way he finalized the line as "The vernal wind has greened the southern shore again (春风又绿江南岸)."

There are many implicit, typical and poetic expressions in classical Chinese poetry which can arouse rich literary associations. For example, **the moon** can be associated with homesickness; **weeping willows** may evoke memories of departure. And there are also some culture-loaded words that can call forth specific feelings among Chinese people and their implicitness can't be reproduced in any other language. So it is unimaginable to separate classical Chinese poems from traditional Chinese culture. In this sense, Chinese poems cannot be translated into any other language. As a carrier of culture, classical Chinese poetry reflects the history, tradition and civilization of China and the living environment, thinking mode, values and tastes of its people in ancient times. Its implicit beauty is rooted in the fertile soil of Chinese culture, brimming with Chinese scent.

b. Ugliness of Implicitness

The reader or listener responsibility system which was born out of the implicitness works against efforts to make everything clear, offering ambiguous explanations, which created many negative effects, too.

Wang Yangming (1472–1529), the leading figure in the Neo-Confucian school of Mind, is regarded as one of the four greatest masters of Confucianism in history along with Confucius, Mencius and Zhu Xi because of his contribution to the revival and development of Confucianism. Nevertheless, the language in which he expressed some of his ideas was so ambiguous that almost immediately his school diverged on some basic issues.

Bu haoyisi, one of our pet phrases, is open to many interpretations, but it is safe for us to use it and it can save us a lot of trouble in countless difficult situations. When we're late for a meeting, we can say *bu haoyisi* (Sorry. I am late). When we reach for the last cookie on the plate while others are watching, we say *bu haoyisi* (Sorry, but I need one more). When we bump into someone on the subway, we say *bu haoyisi* (Sorry for bumping into you.). When we are caught beating the traffic light, we say *bu haoyisi* (Sorry for breaking the traffic rule). When we take things that don't belong to us, such as taking briberies, we say *bu haoyisi* (Sorry for this). *Bu haoyisi* has created people without bottom lines. With *bu haoyisi* as a pretext, some of us put away all rituals or our faces and do what we really want to do such as enjoying undeserved fruits, help or kindness from others. The intention is to use the phrase as a smoke screen to hide the bad scars on our bodies.

Arguably, the implicitness of language has ruined many dreams since ancient times. *The Butterfly Lovers* is a case in point. The story is about a young woman named Zhu Yingtai from Shangyu, Zhejiang, who disguised herself as a man traveling to Hangzhou to study. During her journey, she met Liang Shanbo, a scholar from Kuaiji in the same province. They felt like old friends at first sight. Therefore, they gathered some soil as incense and took vows of brotherhood in the pavilion of a thatched bridge. For three years at school, they shared the same room where there was only one bed and two quilts. Yingtai slowly fell in love with Shanbo, but Shanbo did not see any traces of female characteristics in Yingtai. Time flew by quickly. One day Yingtai received a letter from her father asking her to return home. As a filial daughter she had no

Unit 15 Implicitness vs. Explicitness

alternative but to pack her belongings immediately and bid farewell.

Liang Shanbo, being Yingtai's sworn brother, accompanied Yingtai for 18 *li* to send her off. On the way, Yingtai implied to Shanbo that she was female. For example, she compared themselves to a pair of mandarin ducks (love birds), but Shanbo did not catch on to her hidden meaning. Finally, Yingtai had an idea: She told Shanbo that she would be a matchmaker and match make Shanbo with her sister. Before the two parted, Yingtai reminded Shanbo to pay a visit to her home so that he could propose marriage. Liang Shanbo and Zhu Yingtai reluctantly took leave of each other at the pavilion where they had first met.

When Shanbo arrived at Yingtai's home, he discovered her true gender, but it was too late. Yingtai told Shanbo that her parents were forcing her to marry Ma Wencai, a rich spoiled young man although she had hinted to her parents about her love for Liang Shanbo and her determination to marry none but him. Liang Shanbo was heartbroken. His health soon deteriorated until he died in his office as a county magistrate.

On the day Yingtai was to be married to Ma Wencai, whirlwinds prevented the wedding procession from escorting Yingtai beyond Shanbo's tomb. Yingtai left the procession to pay her respects to Shanbo. She begged the grave to open up. Suddenly there was a clap of thunder, and the tomb opened. Without hesitation, Yingtai leapt into the grave to join her beloved Shanbo. A pair of beautiful butterflies emerged (the spirits of Zhu Yingtai and Liang Shanbo) from the tomb and flew away, which symbolized the union of the couple.

Westerners find it difficult to understand *The Butterfly Lovers*. It is hard for them to imagine the life of traditional Chinese young ladies from rich or academic families, not to mention the implicit way they expressed themselves. Zhu Yingtai, an ancient woman restricted by the time she lived, could do nothing but imply to Shanbo her real gender and feelings and hint to her parents about her own plan.

2. Impacts of Implicitness

Implicitness plays a mixed role in China. Co-existing with its ugliness, its greatest beauty lies not only in producing many touching poems but also in creating social harmony.

a. Social Harmony

We often hear people say something like **Whatever we do, it's OK to be just about right. What is the use of being precise and accurate? It's better to be a confused man, just as Zheng Banqiao said.** Qing poet and painter Zheng Banqiao (1693–1765), a representative of the Eight Eccentric Painters of Yangzhou, did say "难得糊涂 (literally, The rare quality is confusion)," but it has been misinterpreted by many. What Zheng Banqiao really meant can be taken as not to be over-calculating on personal gains or losses. Instead of encouraging people to be over-calculating, he encouraged them to compromise and tolerate if necessary to lead a still and harmonious life. It can be said that implicitness, compromise, and tolerance are sources of Chinese peace and stability, which helped ancient Chinese civilization to continue.

Regarding the continuity of Chinese civilization, it is essential to mention traditional Chinese medicine established on thousands of years' accumulation of *jingyan* (literally, experience) which is hard to be explicitly explained. When consulting a practitioner of traditional Chinese medicine, people are inclined to believe that the more *jingyan* he has, the more resourceful he will be. Partly owing to *jingyan*-based medicine, Chinese civilization continues.

b. Mr. Cha Buduo

The greatest ugliness of implicitness is reducing all human activities to the

Unit 15 Implicitness vs. Explicitness

level of immaturity, producing lazybones, so great scholars like Hu Shi and Lu Xun severely criticized the practice of implicitness. "Mr. Cha Buduo" written by Hu Shi explicitly unmasks the ugliness of ambiguity. Excerpts of the article are as follows:

Do you know who is the most well-known person in China?

The name of this person is a household word all over the country. His surname is Cha and his given name is Buduo, which altogether means "About the Same". He is a native of every province, every county and every village in this country. You must have seen or heard about this person. His name is always on the lips of everybody because he is representative of the whole Chinese nation.

...

When Mr. Cha Buduo was about to breathe his last, he uttered intermittently in one breath, "Live or die, it's about…about…the same…. Whatever we do…it's OK…to be…just…just about right….Why …why… take it…so seriously?" As soon as he finished this pet phrase of his, he stopped breathing.

After Mr. Cha Buduo's death, people all praised him for his way of seeing through things and his philosophical approach to life. They say that he refused to take things seriously all his life and that he was never calculating or particular about personal gains or losses. So they called him a virtuous man and honored him with the posthumous reverent title Master of Easy-going.

His name has spread far and wide and has become more and more celebrated with the passing of time. Innumerable people have come to follow his example, so everybody has become Mr. Cha Buduo. But lo,

China will hence be a nation of lazybones!

Unfortunately, Mr. Cha Buduo Hu Shi severely criticized many years ago survives Hu and is converting more people. Despite this disappointing fact, some people are doing their best to remove the bad influence of Mr. Cha Buduo. For instance, to overcome the ugly aspects of implicitness, Beijing volunteers launched many specific and explicit campaigns such as "**Use explicit and standardized language to welcome the Winter Olympics** (规范语言迎冬奥)" before the 2022 Beijing Winter Olympic Games, setting up a good example for us to follow.

IV. Explicit Westerners

There are two newly-established disciplines in the West. One is known as Fuzziology (模糊学), and the other, Chaos Theory (混沌学) which is fuzzier or more ambiguous. Despite this fact, Western languages like English are known for their emphasis on explicitness. Western culture highly values logical and analytical thinking, which inevitably further boosts explicitness.

1. Westerners in the Eyes of Non-Westerners

To the Western marketing people in China, their Chinese counterparts are ambiguous and even unprincipled. But from the marketing perspective of many non-Westerners, Westerners seem so accurate that they appear insensitive and rigidly boorish. Some say, "The Westerner is very explicit. He wants a 'yes' or 'no.' If someone tries to speak figuratively, he is confused."

An Iranian said in his blog, "The first time my British professor told me 'I don't know, I will have to look it up,' I was shocked. I asked myself 'Why is he teaching me?'"

In our communication with Western scholars, we have found that we have to give further information when mentioning very Chinese stuff. When we discuss a Chinese celebrity, e.g. **Bai Juyi**, we have to add **the famous poet of the 8th century**; when mentioning **Qin Shihuang**, we have to add **the first emperor of the Qin dynasty, who united China for the first time in Chinese history in 221 BC**; when talking about **Xinhai Revolution**, we need to add **the 1911 Revolution which overthrew the last dynasty before establishing China's Republic**; when explaining **the Great Leap-forward**, we should add **a movement which attempted to have a high-speed development in the late 50s**; when it comes to **common prosperity,** we have to add **a future where prosperity is shared by everyone in the country** or **affluence shared by everyone both in material and cultural terms**. If not provided with explicit background information, they would be confused and some of them would deliberately distort the fact.

2. Western Preference for Explicitness

We came across an interesting English story the other day. It goes:

There was a man who planned to rob a convenience store. His plan was to give the clerk a ten-dollar bill. When the clerk opened the cash drawer to make the change, the would-be thief would grab all the money. The man's plan worked perfectly. The clerk set the $10 bill on the top of the cash register and opened the drawer. The thief pushed the clerk back and grabbed all the money in the cash drawer–a grand total of $4.34. Since he had left his $10, he lost $5.66 on the transaction.

Interesting, isn't it? What interests us is not the story itself, but the accuracy of the amount mentioned over and over in the story.

Western love of accuracy and explicitness involves a scientific spirit. When we translate from Chinese to English we sometimes have to take this fact into

consideration. For instance, the implicit Chinese saying **It is better for the doer to undo what he has done** (解铃还需系铃人) is usually rendered into an explicit expression: **Whoever started the trouble should end it**. In like manner, when we translate from English to Chinese, special attention should be paid to this fact as well. Take for instance the translation of the following passage from *Tess of the d'Urbervilles*:

It was a typical summer evening in June, the atmosphere being in such delicate equilibrium and so transmissive that inanimate objects seemed endowed with two or three senses, if not five. There was no distinction between the near and the far, and an auditor felt close to everything within the horizon. The soundlessness impressed her as a positive entity rather than as the mere negation of noise. It was broken by the strumming of strings.

Version 1：那是一个典型的六月黄昏。大气的平衡如此精微，传导力如此敏锐，就连冥顽的无生物也有了知觉——如果不是五种知觉的话，也有两三种。远和近已失去了差异，地平线以内的声音都仿佛近在咫尺。这一片寂静在她耳里并非是消极的默无声息，而仿佛是一种积极的实际存在。而这寂静却被拨弄琴弦的声音打破了。

Version 2：这是六月里特有的夏日黄昏。暮色格外柔和静美且极富感染力，连那些冥顽之物都仿佛平添了几分灵性，有了各种知觉。远近一切，难分彼此；天际间任何一丝声息，好像就在耳边，那是一种实实在在的感受，不想这静寂却被瑟瑟的琴声打破了。

Version 1 above is a word-for-word translation. It seems faithful to the original, but sounds awkward to Chinese readers for it runs counter to our aesthetic concepts and expressing habits. The original passage is a beautifully written description, in which the wording of accuracy is very striking. For example, scientific and thus explicit expressions like **equilibrium**, **transmissive**,

inanimate objects and two or three senses, if not five are used by the author to convey the beauty of explicitness. However, the Chinese emphasis on the beauty of implicitness makes the word-for-word translation of Version 1 sound absurd and funny. So different ideas about what is beautiful and what is not should be considered in the translation process. That's to say, it is necessary to freely translate explicit English expressions into implicit Chinese ones sometimes, turning the charm of explicitness into the beauty of implicitness just as the translator of Version 2 does.

V. High-context vs. Low-context

Communication is contextual, which means that communication does not happen in isolation and it must happen within a setting or context. Implicitness in everyday communication is usually resolved by their context. Therefore, the dimension of implicitness and explicitness is context-dependent: The same linguistic item (be it a word, phrase, sentence) may be ambiguous in one context and less ambiguous in another. The preference for ambiguity or implicitness can cause high-context communication, whereas the love of explicitness may lead to low-context communication.

1. Definitions

A high-context communication is one in which most of the information is either in the context or internalized, and little is in the coded, explicit, transmitted part of the message. Sources of high-context communication are neighbors, personal relationships, best friends, family members, etc. because they share context. Chinese people are disposed to be high-context communicators as compared to Westerners.

When people do not share context, they depend more on low-context sources of information. A low-context communication is one in which most of the information is in the explicit codes in order to make up for what is missing in the context. People in most Western countries communicate primarily through language codes. They look for and receive information from low-context sources like newspapers, textbooks, lectures, roadmaps, announcements, instruction sheets, and public signs.

2. "All Are High-context Communicators Sometimes"

High-context communication is economical, fast, and efficient. It works very well when the people communicating understand the meanings in the context. Everyone, the Chinese or Westerners, communicates in this way on some occasions. The most common example is communication between roommates on campus. They are so familiar with one another that a glance or a turn of the head carries more meanings than many words possibly could. In the intimacy of these relationships, people "discount" what the other person is saying if what is said is not consistent with the context, as can be seen in the article below entitled "Verbal Shorthand" from the widely read magazine *Smithsonian*:

Verbal Shorthand

I don't know why it is, but people who have been married for a long time tend to cut corners when it comes to spoken language. In fact, if it weren't for pronouns, I don't think many of us could communicate at all. A single word may convey several meanings, thoughts or requests, but somehow each partner knows exactly what the other is saying at any given time.

My wife and I are guilty of using such verbal shorthand. For example, the other evening I asked her if she would please hand me the thing. She knew immediately that I wanted the TV remote.

If she asks me to turn it down, I know she means the TV, if it's on.

Unit 15 Implicitness vs. Explicitness

Otherwise, she's talking about the thermostat. See what I mean? "It" covers many bases. My wife may say, "Please put it back together when you are through." I understand she is referring to the newspaper.

"It's about time for it to come," I might proclaim. This could mean the mail, the paper, the bus, or the cab we called, depending on the time and context. While in the laundry room, she might remark, "We've got to get a new one before long." "Yes," I reply. "It's given us many years of service." We both mean the washing machine. If she calls from the laundry room and inquires, "Is it on yet?" she means, are the commercials over and is the program starting?

She may say: "You would think he would be cold out there without a coat." If she is looking out our north window, I know she means Harry next door. If the south window, it's neighbor Bob. But when she asks, "Has he been out yet?" she means Earl, our dog.

When I exclaim, "I've had it for now!" my wife knows that I'm frustrated with whatever project I've been working on and am ready for a map. When she says, "You'd better do something for that," I know that she has heard me sneeze. When she's in another room and admonishes, "That will spoil your appetite," she's heard the rustle of my candy-bar wrapper.

If I head toward the garage, she may say, "Don't forget to fill it up." She means the car. But if I'm in the backyard and she says the same thing. I know she means the birdbath. When she says, "I think you can do better than that," I have either just finished mowing the lawn, trimming the hedge or (in winter) shoveling the sidewalk and driveway.

When my wife proffered a box of assorted chocolates the other evening and asked which I preferred, I said, "The one in the corner." I got the one

I wanted. I didn't have to say, "the chocolate, nougat and caramel-covered macadamia nut cluster." She knew.

And so it goes. Somehow we manage to subsist on this sparse diet of words. Tonight, after the dinner dishes had been washed, dried and put back in the cabinets, she asked sweetly if I would carry out the garbage. I was a bit taken aback. The first noun today, and it's garbage.

(From "Verbal Shorthand," August 2001, *Smithsonian*)

The article above is about a high-context communication between an American husband and his wife. From the article, we can conclude that all are high-context communicators sometimes. However, while high-context communication is fast and efficient, it takes a long time to learn. That's why high-context communication can bring people together. Naturally, we feel close to those with whom we can communicate in this way.

3. Differences Between Low-context and High-context Communicators

Low-context communicators pay less attention to messages sent non-verbally. They think communication is the exchange of verbal messages, though aware of some non-verbal behavior such as facial expressions, voice and tone. So when they respond, they respond to what people say, paying little attention to the situation, the roles of participants and other factors that make up the context of the communication. For this reason, they often fail to notice things such as the status of the people they are communicating with, what the other person is not stating, and social rituals not expressed in words, expecting what other people say to be informative. On the contrary, high-context communicators pay less attention to messages sent verbally. They seldom fail to notice such things as the status of the listener or speaker, what is implied, and implicit social rituals. Therefore, people from different cultures often misinterpret each other. For instance, when a host from the high-context culture says, "We welcome you to come again," the low-context guest may interpret this as an actual invitation rather than identifying it as a polite parting.

Low-context communicators assume that the speakers and writers are responsible for the success of communication, and expect them to make meanings explicit, whereas listeners and readers are supposed to ask for clarification or further information. That is the reason why it is a custom in the West for a lecturer to spare some time to answer questions at the end of his lecture. In more informal situations a speaker will specifically encourage listeners to interrupt to ask questions. However, people from high-context cultures don't say things clearly or specifically; instead, they derive meanings from the context—what we might call "reading between the lines." High-context communicators expect listeners or readers to take more responsibility for interpreting the meaning of messages. They assume that speakers or writers do not always express their meaning fully or precisely in words. It is up to the listeners or readers to interpret the meaning of words by paying attention to the context in which they are produced, which can explain why there are one thousand versions of Lin Daiyu (the heroine of *The Story of the Stone*) among one thousand readers.

VI. "Chicken and Duck Talk"

"Chicken and duck talk (鸡同鸭讲)," a neutral Cantonese expression, is often used to refer to communicators who don't understand each other.

1. In the Advertising Industry

Cultural differences have been attached great importance by many people, especially those in the advertising industry.

Owing to its successful promotion campaign, Nesta Coffee is selling well in China, and its consumers like the way the commercial slogan "The taste is great (味道好极了)" is pronounced and presented. For the Chinese, to know one celerity or a beauty enjoys drinking Nesta Coffee is enough because many of us habitually take the communication between us and the celebrities and beauties on the TV screen as a face-to-face talk, a source of high-context information exchange. As for how great it tastes, that is not our concern since different people have different taste buds. What we shall do is buy and drink it and see what it is really like.

However, Nesta Coffee's advertising campaign did not enjoy the same success in Germany. When Germans heard "It tastes great," their first response was: "How great?" They won't buy it unless they are given an explicit answer.

2. At the Workplace

In Chinese culture, people want to save face for both themselves and others, so we would not express our ideas directly. However, in the West, unless you express yourself clearly and directly, others cannot understand you. When a Chinese answers "We must give it more thought" to a request at the workplace, he is turning down a request that cannot be met. He is implicit because he does not want to disrupt the relationship with the person making the request and expects the other person to interpret his answer as a polite refusal. But his Western coworker may keep asking him why he must give it more thought. In a similar situation, many Westerners would not hesitate to say, "Sorry, it can't be done." For this reason, when low-context Western communicators encounter Chinese implicitness in the workplace, they feel they are being deliberately lied to.

Unit 15 Implicitness vs. Explicitness

3. At the Dinner Table

Different ideas about what is beautiful and what is ugly have left some Chinese hungry at a Western dinner table, for Chinese politeness calls for three refusals before one accepts an offer, but the Western host takes "no" to mean "no" whether it is the first, second or third time. However, some Westerners have left the Chinese table with a bursting stomach, for Western politeness requires them to praise their Chinese hostess' cooking skills and the hostess may take the praise as a sign of a big appetite and thus offers more for fear that her guest should leave her dinner table hungry or thirsty.

Differences between the two cultures are sources of misunderstandings. A low-context hostess, if complimented for her cooking skill, is likely to say, "Oh, I am so glad you like it. I cook it especially for you." But a high-context hostess would instead apologize for "Nothing to eat" out of politeness with an apologetic smile on her face before saying, "I just cooked some dishes at random and they are not very tasty (随便做几个菜，不好吃)." Upon that, the low-context guest will probably feel confused and a little bit upset: Why do you invite me to your family and have bad food, then?

4. A Painful Communication Breakdown

Maybe you are good at English, but due to different cultures, you may find yourself failing to communicate well. Let us look at the following dialogue:

Mr. Jefferson: It looks like we were going to have to keep working on the project on Saturday.

Mr. Zhang: I think so.

Mr. Jefferson: Can you come in on Saturday, Mr. Zhang?

Mr. Zhang: Yes, I think so.

Mr. Jefferson: That'll be a great help.

Mr. Zhang: Yes. Saturday's a special day, you know.

Mr. Jefferson: What do you mean?

Mr. Zhang: It's my wife's birthday. We will have a birthday party.

Mr. Jefferson: How nice. I hope you all enjoy it very much.

Mr. Zhang: Thank you. I appreciate your understanding.

Mr. Jefferson: See you Saturday.

The conversation taking place between a Western boss and his Chinese employee indicates that Mr. Zhang, though good at English, experienced a painful failure in intercultural communication. From the very beginning, he wanted to tell the boss that he didn't want to work on Saturday. However, direct refusal is impolite for good-mannered Chinese like him, so he chose to refuse implicitly by saying "I think so." Unfortunately, the boss didn't understand him and went on to ask him a question which could be answered only by "Yes" or "No." In order to save the boss' face, he had to answer, "Yes, I think so." The answer in Chinese just means "I hear what you say, but I don't want to work on Saturday." If he was willing to work, he would say "Sure" or "Of course, I will." But the boss misunderstood him again. Even after he told the boss that Saturday was his wife's birthday, the boss didn't know what he really meant. Here Mr. Zhang violated the principle of explicitness or straightforwardness in Western culture while the boss needed some knowledge about Chinese rules of etiquette. In Western culture, "explicitness" is regarded as a polite manner of communication, whereas indirectness or implicitness is more appreciated in Chinese culture, especially when requests are made.

Further Reading

1. Beiswinger, G. (August 2001). "Verbal Shorthand," *Smithsonian*. Washington

DC.

2. Blackman, C. (1997). *Negotiating China: Case Studies & Strategies*. Sydney: Allen and Unwin.

3. Hall, E. T. & Hall, M. R. (1987). *Hidden Differences: Doing Business with the Japanese*. Garden City, NY: Anchor Press/Doubleday.

4. Harvard Business School (2004). *Face-to-face Communications for Clarity and Impact*. Boston, MA: Harvard Business School Press.

5. Rosenberg, M. B. (2013). *Nonviolent Communication: A Language of Life*. Encinitas, CA: PuddleDancer.

6. 包惠南、包昂编著 (2004),《中国文化与汉英翻译》,北京:外文出版社。

7. 郭志族、郭京龙 (2005),《谎言研究》,北京:中国社会出版社。

Part V
Different Cultural Standards

We are familiar with concepts like gold standard and silver standard, but some of us may have little idea about cultural standards (文化本位).

Cultural standard is a combination of all forms of perception, thought, evaluation and action which are regarded by the majority of the members of a particular culture as normal, typical and obligatory. According to the central cultural standards that regulate wide areas of thought, evaluation and action, personal behavior and the behavior of others are judged and regulated. The individual and group-specific manner of handling central cultural standards for behavior regulation can vary within a certain range of tolerance. Manners of conduct outside the given limits are rejected and discredited. Those who behave in a different way are seen as outsiders.

In one word, cultural standards give orientation, influence the perception of one's material and social environment as well as the evaluation of things and persons, and thus guide one's actions and behavior. The table below shows previous research findings on cultural standards in China, Germany and the U.S.

Chinese Cultural Standards	German Cultural Standards	U.S. Cultural Standards
Peace	Conflicts/war	Conflicts/war
Egalitarianism	Inegalitarianism	Inegalitarianism
Good human nature	Evil human nature	Evil human nature
Rule of Individuals	Rule of Law	Rule of Law
Harmony	Focus on practical issues	Individualism
The concept of face	Importance of rules & regulations	Goal orientation
Etiquette	Directness	Directness
Relationship	Differentiation of interpersonal distance	Equality of chances
Groups	Importance of hierarchy and authority	Interpersonal openness

In this part, we are to explore the first four dimensions.

Unit 16   Peace vs. Conflict

He who is good at being an officer does not boast of his martial prowess; he who is good at fighting does not resort to rage; he who is skillful at defeating enemies does not wrestle with them; and he who is skillful at managing his men has a modest attitude toward them.

—**Laozi**

The quotation from Laozi embodies the peace-loving cultural tradition of the Chinese nation. Is it still relevant today?

He that makes a good war makes a good peace.

—**An English aphorism**

What does a good war mean to you and your international teachers of English?

Great things can be reduced into small things, and small things can be reduced into nothing.

—**A Chinese aphorism**

Chinese recognize the necessity of human efforts but also admit the futility of it. This general attitude has a tendency to develop passive defense tactics. On this general principle, all Chinese disputes are patched up in the same way as the aphorism above advocates. Would you please cite some examples to illustrate its use in your life?

I. Great Names and Different Cultural Standards

In Europe, empires were built by plundering the land; in China that benefited you little unless you had a means of making it productive. To guarantee the means of agrarian production and distribution, you needed to mobilize huge numbers of people: it was a peaceful environment that really mattered, which reveals one of the fundamental differences between Chinese and Western cultures: peace vs. conflict. It should be noted that "peace" in this unit is identical to **passiveness**, **harmony**, **stillness**, **stability**, and **serenity**, while "conflict" here is synonymous with **plundering**, **aggression**, **war**, **confrontation**, **discord**, **debate**, **fight**, and **strife**.

1. Chinese Philosophers and Peace

Chinese cultural standard of peace largely originates from the three philosophies–Confucianism, Daoism and, later, Buddhism.

a. Confucian Doctrine of Harmony as the Most Valuable Principle

Confucianism has been the dominant ideology of Chinese society since the Han time practiced "rejecting other schools of thought, respecting Confucianism only (罢黜百家，独尊儒术)." Many of its doctrines encourage peaceful efforts. For instance, the doctrine of rites or ritual (*li*) which includes everything from funeral ceremonies to offerings of food and wine to ancestral spirits declares, "In observing the rites, seeking peace is the most valuable principle (礼之用，和为贵)."

The Confucian idea of peace or harmony has greatly influenced many departments of Chinese society, such as city construction and relations with ethnic minorities. Emperor Cheng (1360–1424) of the Ming dynasty had his new capital city built around the Forbidden City which radiated symmetrically from

Unit 16 Peace vs. Conflict

a central axis. This symmetrical requirement is an extension of the harmony concept of Confucianism. Under the influence of Confucianism, Beijing was built with an axis line that ran north to south and through the center of the Forbidden City.

The harmony concept of Confucianism is also present in relations with ethnic minorities, one of the top concerns of the ruling class. To cement relations with ethnic minorities, Liu Bang, the first emperor of the Han dynasty, though at the pinnacle of Han society, sent daughters of the Liu family to their rulers as their wives, which started a tradition of marriage-for-peace policy (和亲). The story of Zhaojun's matrimonial journey is a continuation of this policy. And the marriage of the Tang Princess Wen Cheng and Tibetan King Songtsän Gampo can be regarded as a perfect example of Chinese peace-loving by nature, given the fact that the Tang dynasty was very powerful. There were altogether 20 princesses of this kind during the 289 years of the Tang dynasty. From historical records, except six of these "princesses," all the others were not the daughters of the emperors but the girls in the royal clans, most of whom were emperors' nieces or the daughters of officials with outstanding service to the royal family. Though most of these princesses were "fake ones," their families all had close relationships with the royal family Li, and their status had no marked difference from those of the "genuine ones."

b. Laozi's Harmony Theory

Laozi encouraged harmony, discouraging argument. To him, "a good man does not prove things by argument; he who proves things by argument is not good (善者不辩，辩者不善)." For the sake of harmony, a man is required to swallow up humiliation without making any complaint. "He who bears the humiliation of the whole state can be the lord of the country (受国之垢，是

谓社稷王)." To maintain peace and harmony, Laozi stressed the importance of taking precautions and said, "Deal with things before they happen, and get things in order before the onset of their disorder (为之于未有，治之于未乱)."

c. Buddhist Peace and Compassion

The Buddhist doctrine of peace teaches that whether we have global peace or global war is up to us at every moment. The situation is not hopeless and out of our hands. If we don't do anything, who will? Peace or war is our decision. The fundamental goal of Buddhism is peace, not only peace in this world but peace in all worlds. According to the Buddha the first step on the path to peace is to understand the causality of peace. When we understand what causes peace, we know where to direct our efforts. No matter how vigorously we stir a boiling pot of soup on a fire, the soup will not cool. When we remove the pot from the fire, it will cool on its own, and our stirring will hasten the process. Stirring causes the soup to cool, but only if we first remove the soup from the fire. In other words, we can take many actions in our quest for peace that may be helpful. But if we do not first address the fundamental issues, all other actions will come to naught. Buddhism stresses peaceful minds that can lead to peaceful speech and peaceful actions. If the minds of living beings are at peace, the world will be at peace. Meditation in Buddhism can help people to find inner peace. But it is up to us to master this technique since it is hard and requires a lot of patience.

Meanwhile the Buddhist doctrine of nonviolence expresses belief in the sacredness of all living creatures. Buddhist philosophers show compassion, mercy, leniency, generosity, and indulgence, calling on the multitude never to kill or injure any living creatures.

2. Western Elites and Conflict

The formation of the Western cultural standards of conflict owes a lot to the elites of its society like great philosophers, economists, and politicians.

a. Philosophers and Their Doctrines of War

Heraclitus, probably the most significant philosopher of ancient Greece until Socrates and Plato, was the first one to come up with the doctrine of war. To him, "Strife is the origin of everything and war is the father of all things." So he deemed it necessary to understand that war is common, strife is customary, and all things happen because of strife and necessity. He said, "We must know that war is common to all and strife is justice, and that all things come into being through strife necessarily." Meanwhile he held that strife is absolute while harmony is relative. Heraclitus disliked Homer, declaring that Homer should be driven out of the races and whipped because Homer prayed for peace, not knowing when the strife was gone everything would die.

For Socrates who was once an army man, philosophy as critical inquiry is itself a kind of war. Given the stakes involved, nothing could be more critical than bringing philosophy as war to bear on the topic of war.

Likewise, many of the ancient Greek philosophers saw that harmony and discord depend upon one another. One way of naturalizing and thus justifying war is to claim that conflict and strife constitute the very order of things. Greek thinking greatly influenced the entire Western world so that many public festivals throughout ancient Europe had to do with preparing boys to be warriors, girls to be mothers.

Like Heraclitus, Hegel held that two forces, love and strife, peace and war, interact together. His *Philosophy of Right* is one of the great works in political philosophy and its importance to contemporary philosophy has been ongoing. In the book he points out, "War is the state of affairs which deals in earnest with the vanity of temporal goods and concerns–a vanity at other times a common theme of edifying sermonizing." Hegel is notorious for "rationalizing" war to the point of glorifying it. He advocated war as a good thing and held that the rationality of war reveals itself in the way sovereign states relate to each other. Hegel realized that there are many ways for states to recognize one another: treaties, border agreements, and alliances. But the one paradoxical way is in the case of war: "It follows that if states disagree and their particular wills cannot be harmonized, the matter can only be settled by war." In one word, Hegel regarded war as a healthy system, necessary to ensure the domestic health of a nation.

Friedrich Wilhelm Nietzsche (1844–1900), although different from Hegel, also agreed about the central role played by conflict and war.

b. Social Darwinists and Their Doctrines of Conflict

By the last quarter of the 19th century, the English naturalist Charles R. Darwin (1809–1882) promulgated his theory of natural selection, of "survival of the fittest," which was being applied to human societies known as social Darwinism. Social Darwinism is a belief, popular in the late Victorian era in England, America, and elsewhere, which states that the strongest or fittest should survive and flourish in society while the weak and unfit should be allowed to die. The theory was chiefly expounded by Herbert Spencer, whose ethical philosophies always held an elitist view and received a boost from the application of Darwinian ideas such as adaptation and natural selection. Thus, in the evolution of mankind, those civilizations which failed to respond to the challenges of external forces would lose the struggle for survival. The process was relentless and through it the species evolved.

Social Darwinism gave support to Western colonization (outward expansion). Western imperialist nations felt they needed colonies in order to maintain their status as great powers. Meanwhile, they could justify their colonial activities by considering them altruistic attempts to provide the natives with the secrets necessary to succeed in the brutal struggle for survival. In this way, Darwinism gave Westerners a great excuse to adopt conflict as one of their cultural standards.

c. Politicians, Economists and Their Doctrines of Conflict

Western society has been promoting conflict as the main arbiter. Its politicians such as the founding fathers of the U.S. used narrow conflict in their political system so as to avoid dictators. All the Western countries base their politics on political partisanship, allowing different parties to compete against each other for people's support in order to reduce government corruption and supervise one another.

Meanwhile, economists brought up the concept of "the invisible hand of the market" to explain the function of the market on the demand and supply of commodities. To avoid uncertainties, people are encouraged to use contracts to establish transactional relationships. At the same time, "the visible hand of management" is expected to take action.

The West today thinks of itself as the most cosmopolitan of all cultures, because for 200 years, the West has been so dominant in the world that it's not really needed to understand other cultures and other civilizations because at the end of the day, it could, if necessary, by force get its own way.

II. External Factors and Cultural Standards

Although the elites mentioned above are extremely wise, their success depends much on external factors such as their upbringing and education. It can be said with certainty that the formation of cultural standards owes a lot to external factors. Here factors such as ecology, social practice, and traditions are to be discussed.

1. Natural Environment

a. Natural Environment of Ancient China

Natural environment of the Central Plains Region–the cradle of Chinese civilization, primarily consisting as it does of relatively fertile plains, low mountains and navigable rivers, favored agriculture and made centralized control of society relatively easy. Generally, agricultural people need to get along with one another–not necessarily to like one another–but to live together in a reasonably harmonious fashion. This is true wherever irrigation is required, as in the Yellow River Valley of northern China, particularly true for rice farming, characteristic of southern China, which requires people to cultivate the land in concert with one another.

b. Natural Environment of Ancient Greece

Natural environment of ancient Greece–the cradle of Western civilization, on the other hand, consisting as it does mostly of mountains descending to the sea, favored hunting, herding, fishing, trade and even piracy. These occupations require relatively little cooperation with others. According to Hegel, the inhabitants living along coastlines are brave and adventurous, daring to open up new sea routes and make more progress. In fact, with the exception of trade, the economic activities ancient Greeks took part in did not strictly require living in the same stable community with other people. Settled agriculture came to Greece almost two thousand years later than to China, and it quickly became commercial. The soil and climate of Greece were congenial to wine and olive oil production and, by the sixth century BC, many farmers were more nearly businessmen than peasants. The Greeks were therefore able to act on their own to a greater extent than the Chinese. Not feeling it necessary to maintain harmony with other fellows at any cost, the ancient Greeks were in the habit of arguing with one another in the marketplace, debating in the political assembly, and resorting to war to solve their conflicts or problems. As legend has it, when Socrates was in his forties or so, he began to go around Athens asking people he met these questions: "What is wisdom?" "What is piety?" Sometimes people would try to answer him. Then Socrates would try to teach them to think better by asking them more questions which showed them the problems in their logic. Often this made people angry. Sometimes they even tried to beat him up.

2. Social Customs

Cultural standards also stem from social customs while creating them.

a. Competitive Activities

In ancient times, attending the Olympics or debate was a special occasion for Greeks. During the Olympic Games the entire Greek nation laid down its tools and many even went on a long journey for the sole purpose of participating in the Olympics as athletes or audience. Hence many Greek vases and wine goblets exhibit pictures of battles, athletic contests, and bacchanalian parties.

b. *Chuanmen* or Visiting Each Other

When Greeks had fun at the Olympic Games, theatres, or markets, the Chinese of the same period were visiting with friends and family. Visits meant to show respect for the old or friends were especially important during the major holidays. Hence in paintings on Chinese screens, embroidery work, porcelain, woodcarving, etc., families having fun together or visiting each other is a popular theme.

3. Tradition of Debates

Within the Chinese social group, any form of confrontation, even debate, was disfavored. Although there was a time called the period of the "contending hundred schools of thought," during which polite debates occurred, mainly among philosophers, anything resembling public disagreement was discouraged. But the whole rhetoric of argument or debate is regarded as second nature to Westerners. North Americans began to express opinions and justify them as early as the show-and-tell sessions of kindergarten.

III. Cultural Standards and Their Unique Products

1. Old Rogues, Fatalism, Harmony, and Pacifism

Old rogues, fatalism, harmony, and pacifism are unique products of a culture with peace as one of its cultural standards.

a. Old Rogues

Old rogues are popular in traditional China, according to Lin Yutang. Some of the young men liked being referred to as "an old rogue," because that means in others' eyes they appeared mellow and good-tempered and many girls' mothers preferred them for their future sons-in-law. An old rogue usually has a rich knowledge of the vicissitudes of life, thus has formed his peculiar shrewd philosophy, working against action. They can not only recite but also put to practice proverbs like **By losing that pawn, one wins the whole game** (丢卒保车); **A true hero never incurs present risk** (好汉不吃眼前亏); **Take a step backwards in your thought** (退一步，海阔天空), and **Of all the thirty-six alternatives, running away is the best** (三十六计，走为上策). Life is then for them full of second-thoughts and the "thirty-sixth alternatives." You can predict how they will respond because they tend to act in their own best interest.

This roguery, traditionally a peaceful force in China, has permeated the whole fiber of Chinese thought and can be found in our blood. It has been helping to establish a stable, still and harmonious environment.

b. Fatalism

Fatalism (宿命论) was a great source of peace and contentment in traditional China. A talented young man ambitiously tried hard to climb up the social ladder despite all kinds of hardship, torture and "eating bitter." The expression "eating bitter" describes putting up with difficulties. But with time passing by, when he became old but remained poor, he would convince him that it is Heaven who has decreed such a result, he could at once, through an act of understanding, become a happy husband, contented father, and then proud grandpa. For him his youthful struggle or "eating bitter" was a "predestined fate", and he had to do as the proverb says, "You can fight against Heaven, earth and man, but you have to be obedient to your predestined fate." With that understanding, he valued his remaining years, knowing all the time that Heaven is looking on.

c. Harmony

It is known to many that it was the ancient Chinese who invented dynamite. Then, how did they use it? They used it to make firecrackers which exploded on major holidays to create a festive atmosphere instead of employing it in the process of making weapons and warships as the Westerner did. Why so? Because our ancestors went out of their way to avoid wars and conflicts since harmony is the greatest source of peace and contentment in China. The Confucian emphasis on harmony as the ideal of life is usually written on red paper and pasted on all house-doors on the Eve of Spring Festival: "Harmony brings good luck (家和万事兴)."

d. Pacifism

Pacifism was regarded as a virtue of the Chinese people. The proverb **It's better to be a dog in a peaceful time than be a man in a chaotic period** (宁

为太平犬，不做乱世人) reveals our love of peace. On many occasions when a man was wronged, offended, bullied, humiliated or enraged, if he could hold his tongue or keep his temper, he was expected to rise higher or do something great in the future, as the saying warns, "A man who cannot tolerate small ills can never accomplish great things (小不忍，则乱大谋)." As a people, we hate war, believing good people never fight, for "good iron is not made into nails, and good men are not made soldiers (好铁不做钉，好男不当兵)."

In fact, pacifism could also become a vice of cowardice. The responsibility for the family we are born with makes us sober and ready to compromise. Before adventures, most of us have a wife and babies to think about, and aged parents to remember. When wronged or humiliated, we comfort ourselves, "A real man can bend and stretch (大丈夫能屈能伸)." In such a society, pacifism has no reason not to exist; people seem ready to tolerate unfairness and bitterness.

2. Heroic Code, Chivalry, Competition and Cold War Mentality

A culture with war or conflicts as one of its cultural standards has its peculiar products such as heroic code, chivalry, competition, and Cold War mentality.

a. Heroic Code

Heroic code has something to do with the Homeric heroes who have been respected and honored since the Homeric epic. The heroic code which governs the conduct of the Homeric heroes is a simple one: The aim of every hero is to achieve honor, that is, the esteem received from one's peers. Honor is essential to the Homeric heroes so much so that life would be meaningless without it. As you will notice in reading the *Iliad*, when a hero is advised to be careful to avoid a life-threatening situation in battle, his only choice is to ignore this warning. A hero's honor is determined primarily by his courage and physical abilities and to

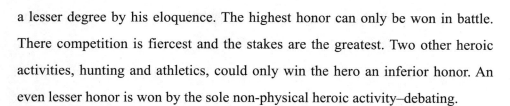

a lesser degree by his eloquence. The highest honor can only be won in battle. There competition is fiercest and the stakes are the greatest. Two other heroic activities, hunting and athletics, could only win the hero an inferior honor. An even lesser honor is won by the sole non-physical heroic activity–debating.

b. Chivalry

Chivalry is the generic term for the knightly system of the Medieval Times (the 5th to the 15th century) and for virtues and qualities it inspired in its followers. It first appeared with military activities against non-Christian states. During the Medieval Period, Western Europe aggressively sought to expand its area of control. The first orders of chivalry were very similar to the monastic orders of the era. Both sought the sanctification of their members through combat against "infidels" and protection of religious pilgrims, and both had commitments that involved the taking of vows and submitting to regulation of activities.

The thirteenth-century conventions of chivalry directed that knight's honor, serve, and do nothing to displease ladies and maidens as members of the noble class, socially as bearers of arms, economically as owners of horse armor, and officially through the religious-oriented ceremony. While some were knighted on the battlefield, most spent years as a squire, practicing the art of war while serving his master.

After the Crusades, knights continued to show their prowess and skills in medieval tournaments.

Today chivalry is reflected in rules of etiquette and specific things like opening and holding doors for women or running errands for women.

c. Competition

Westerners believe that competition occurs naturally whenever two or more parties strive for one goal which cannot be shared. For example, humans, like animals, compete over water supplies, food, and mates. When these needs are met deep rivalries often arise over the pursuit of wealth, prestige, and fame. In the West, the election campaign is often associated with competition as most candidates are in competition with at least one over the same group of voters.

Many people in the West hold that competition originates internally and is biologically motivated. It exists to further the survival of an individual or species. Social Darwinists state that competition is moral and necessary for the survival of the species. Moreover, competition is believed to be able to give incentives for self-improvement. For example, if two shoemakers are competing for business, they will hopefully lower their prices and improve their products to increase sales.

Over the years, competition has greatly released Westerners' potentiality and energy, and helped to develop Western economic and political civilization. Meanwhile, it is also because of competition that the two world wars erupted in the first half of the 20th century.

d. Cold War Mentality

The cultural standard of conflict or war explains why there is the Cold War mentality, even in the 21st century when the real Cold War has already ended.

The Cold War that arose from the intense competition influenced nearly all aspects of Western political and cultural life from 1946–when the former British Prime Minister Winston Churchill announced the descent of an Iron Curtain separating the Soviet Union and her Eastern European satellite states from the non-communist West–to the disintegration of the Soviet Union in 1991. Throughout this period, the rivalry between the two superpowers was expressed through military coalitions, propaganda, espionage, weapon development, industrial advances, and competitive technological development, e.g. the space race. Both superpowers were engaged in costly defensive spending, a massive conventional and nuclear arms race, and numerous proxy wars so that the Cold War influence on Western political life was deep and long-lasting.

Today, some politicians in some Western countries are still using the Cold War thinking. The U.S. Defense Department in 2015 issued an annual report on China's military power, continuing to peddle the so-called "China threat." It said that China was developing weapons that could disable its enemies' space technology, such as satellites. The "China threat" theory is not in accordance with the facts and seriously interferes with China's internal affairs.

Under the influence of the Cold War mentality, some scholars in some Western countries are selling their theory of conflicts, refusing to shed the Cold War mentality. The influential political scientist and former Harvard professor Samuel Phillips Huntington (1927–2008) is best known for his views on the so-called clash of civilizations. Huntington argued that conflicts in our post-Cold War world would be rooted in cultural and religious differences among major civilizations, rather than ideological rifts between nations.

The Cold War mentality is a reflection of Western concern that some civilization is to replace it. This over-alertness explains a reason why there is among some Westerners a phenomenon of "seeking the enemy." It seems that they have to find an opponent. Otherwise, they are not sure of their trend and direction.

IV. Better Ways to Know Each Other

The cultural standard of harmony has been pushing the Chinese to go on with the policy of peace. When asked how to treat people who are not so kind, many cite this dialogue between two Tang Buddhist monks:

> A monk asked, "If one slanders me, insults me, sneers at me, despises me, injures me, hates me, and deceives me, what should I do?"
>
> "Only bear with him, yield to him, let him, avoid him, endure him, respect him, and ignore him. And after a few years, you just look at him," replied the abbot.

The peace made through this kind of pacifism has been regarded as the highest product of Chinese intelligence. But as a Chinese proverb goes, "The tree may prefer to be calm, but the wind refuses to subdue (树欲静而风不止)." Despite China's persistent stand for dialogue and cooperation, some countries have time and again provoked confrontation and antagonism, taking China as the main target for their attack. In spite of that, the policy of "peace with differences reserved" will be carried forward by the Chinese government and its influence as a force of peace and harmony in the world will grow. On many occasions, President Xi highlighted China's commitment to peace, development, equity, justice, democracy and freedom, which are common values of humanity, pointing out that drawing ideological lines or dividing the world into different camps or rival groups will only make the world suffer.

Further Reading

1. Brislin, R. W. (1990). *Applied Cross-Cultural Psychology*. Newbury Park, CA: Sage Publications.
2. Hegel, G.W. F. (1991). *Philosophy of Right*. Cambridge, UK: Cambridge University Press.
3. Kluckholn, F. & Strodtbeck, F. (1961). *Variations in Value Orientations*. Evanston, OH: Row & Peterson.

4. Rosenberg, M. B. (2013). *Nonviolent Communication: A Language of Life*. Encinitas, CA: PuddleDancer.

5. Tannen, D. (1998). *The Argument Culture: Moving from Dialogue to Debate*. New York: HarperCollins.

6. 阿·托克维尔 (2020)，《论美国民主（英文版）》（下卷），沈阳：辽宁人民出版社。

7. 冯波 (2003)，《中西哲学文化比较研究》，北京：北京广播学院出版社。

8. 冯友兰 (2013)，《中国哲学简史》，涂光译，北京：北京大学出版社。

9. 明恩溥 (2011)，《中国人的气质》，刘文飞、刘晓旸译，南京：译林出版社。

Unit 17   Egalitarian vs. Inegalitarian Distribution

Refrain from exalting capable men, so that the people shall not compete (不尚贤，使民不争).

—Laozi

What do you say to this aphorism?

The law cannot make all men equal, but they are all equal before the law.

—Frederick Pollock

How shall we understand the remark made by the noted British jurist?

From shirtsleeves to shirtsleeves is only three generations.

—Andrew Carnegie

This saying has been attributed to Andrew Carnegie (1835–1919), a manufacturer and philanthropist. Shirtsleeves denote the need to work hard for one's living. Does the Chinese proverb "It takes three generations to make a gentleman" express the same idea?

I. Hate-the-rich Mentality

"Hating-the-rich" is an abnormal psyche, which encourages the thinking that if you have more, then I must have less. Misconducts of some affluent people as well as the illicit channels they are using to accumulate their wealth will undoubtedly add a further irritant to the discontent of the less fortunate.

Unit 17 Egalitarian vs. Inegalitarian Distribution

Such terms as **corrupt rich**, **stinking rich** and other much harsher things are often used by ordinary people to describe those "wealthy but bad guys" in their eyes. Actually, the mainstream public is not hostile towards wealthy people. If one can get rich quickly through hard work, the general public response will be admiration, not hatred. But in real life some people get rich overnight in illegal ways. In such cases, the public will naturally question their behavior and despise them, and their so-called "hate-the-rich" mentality is not targeted at all the wealthy people, but only at those who have acquired their wealth through illegal means such as tax evasion, taking bribery, and injuring the consumers' right.

However, an undeniable fact is that a handful of people do have a blind prejudice against the rich. They have been openly declaring, "The rich are not benevolent (为富不仁)." The root cause of this prejudice may be that the age-old system of egalitarian distribution has been broken and their psychological balance is thus destroyed. Some of them even go so far as to want the system of egalitarian distribution to return. Will egalitarianism come back, then? To answer this question, it's better to know what egalitarianism really means in the first place.

Egalitarianism is a trend of thought in economic, political and social philosophy. An egalitarian favors equality of some sort: People should get the same, be treated the same, or be treated as equals, in some respect. Egalitarian doctrines tend to express the idea that all the persons are equal in fundamental worth or moral status. Because in both China and the Western societies the term "egalitarian" is often used to mean equality in the distribution of income, wealth, and resources, "egalitarianism" used in this unit is referred to **only as a concept in economical thought**.

II. Traditional Chinese-style Egalitarianism

The egalitarian concept is characterized by a passion for equality at least in distribution and a strong sense of solidarity with other people. It figured prominently in traditional Chinese culture.

1. Philosophers and the Pursuit of Plenty

Egalitarian distribution was regarded as an economic issue by pre-Qin period Legalists, Confucianists, and Daoists, who agreed that people in all communities should have the same standard of living and be equal in the distribution of resources, although, in practice, many of the philosophers were more in favor of the concept "pursuing plenty (求足)" and worked hard to systematically elaborate on its necessity and significance.

a. Guan Zhong

The book named after Guan Zhong, the Legalist minister of the powerful state of Qi during the Spring and Autumn period, illustrated the importance of "pursuing plenty" this way: "One cannot tell the difference between what is honorable and what is shameful until he has plenty of food to eat and plenty of clothes to keep warm; one cannot know ritual until he has plenty of food and clothes for future use (衣食足而后知荣辱，仓廪实而后知礼仪)." Obviously great priority was given to plenty.

b. Confucianists

"The wealth of the country is measured by the abundance of its people (国之称富者，在乎丰民)." The *Analects* makes it clear that it is necessary to enrich people before educating them: "If the ordinary people have plenty of food and clothes, the king will surely find himself in possession of plenty of belongings (百姓足，君孰与不足)."

Unit 17 Egalitarian vs. Inegalitarian Distribution

In the *Xunzi*, the last great Confucian scholar of the pre-Qin period Xun Kuang promulgated his theory of "pursuing plenty" by informing the rulers, "People's desire should be satisfied and their demands should be met (养人之欲，给人以求)." Clearly, plenty rather than egalitarianism was his main concern.

c. Why Not Accept "Pursuing Plenty" as the Orthodox?

But why was the theory of "pursuing plenty" out and egalitarian distribution in?

First, the schools of the pre-Qin period philosophy differed in value systems, but unanimously wanted people to be happy with what they had and live harmoniously with one another, however poor and simple their life might be. This expectation was in conflict with the concept of "pursuing plenty," but in agreement with the idea of pursuing egalitarian distribution.

Second, in an agrarian economy where sources of income were few, the concept of "The more sons, the more blessings" and the need for more human resources boosted population growth. In a populous country, it was impossible to attain plenty. On the contrary, the goal of egalitarian distribution could be more easily achieved.

Third, Buddhist and Daoist literature propounded an egalitarian view, which, to some extent, encouraged people to favor the egalitarian ideal and disfavor the theory of pursuing plenty, although the two religions did not uphold the equal status of women. For instance, Buddhist doctrine of five obstacles (五障) maintained that women were incapable of becoming a Buddha.

2. Egalitarian Practice in Traditional China

a. Misinterpretation of One of Confucius' Doctrines

In a populous poor agrarian economy, it was impossible to pursue plenty, and hence pursuing egalitarian distribution (求均) as an economic ideal became the only alternative available to people. For a long time, the doctrine "Don't worry about being scanty, but do worry about being unequal (不患寡而患不均)" has been misinterpreted because it provided no context. Confucius didn't mean he advocated egalitarian distribution. Instead, he was talking about an ideal. For him production was more important than distribution and the pursuit of plenty more significant than pursuing egalitarian distribution. But because of the misinterpretation, equalitarian distribution was passionately pursued by many. As a consequence, if not equally rich, being equally poor merely made people poorer and poorer.

b. Wang Mang's Practice of the Egalitarian Ideal

Egalitarian distribution had been so beautiful a dream that Wang Mang (45 BC–23 AD) tried hard to make it come true.

In 22 BC, Wang Mang managed to usurp power, declaring himself the emperor of the Han. With great passion he began a series of radical reforms. The most radical one was his effort to set up an equal land-holding system. This project included the nationalization of all land, abolition of private land-holding system, prohibition of trade of land, etc. But people in power were not ready for such a reform that suggested egalitarianism. Soon Wang Mang's brief reign became unpopular with all social classes of the nation and in the end he even lost the backing of the Confucian bureaucracy which had earlier supported him because of his impractical attempts. Without the support of the people, his measures, however effective theoretically, were doomed to failure, but his egalitarian land reform inspired the later reformers.

c. Egalitarian Practice Before China's Opening-up and Reform

Egalitarianism greatly impeded Chinese economic development before

1976. Take the practice of **Iron Rice Bowl** for instance. The "Iron Rice Bowl" was the name of the Chinese social security system that guaranteed food, housing and social benefits for everybody. The benefits were especially good for people who worked for the state. The cradle-to-grave social security system of the state offered everyone free education and low-rent housing, guaranteed lifetime jobs, pensions, and workers' holiday camps, subsidized theaters and concerts, and free medical and dental care, organized tours and trips, provided workers with kindergartens, sports stadiums, holiday centers, summer camps for children, cultural centers, sports facilities, and rest and rehabilitation spas. Women were given a year's paid maternity leave, access to free day-care centers and free abortion on demand. Once you held the "iron rice bowl," you would feel safe because the iron bowl was not easy to break, regardless of how much you did or what poor performance and bad work habits you had. This egalitarian policy in the distribution of incomes created many sluggish and unenterprising people.

III. Western-style Inegalitarianism

In the Western societies, although people believe "The end makes all equal, since there is no medicine against death." But they are not in favor of economic egalitarianism. "Inegalitarianism" is an economic concept often used to refer to a position that favors, for any of a wide array of reasons, a greater degree of inequality in income and wealth across persons.

1. Aristotle's Inegalitarian Distribution Theory

It is agreed that inegalitarianism originates from Aristotle, who established the idea by analyzing justice.

a. Concept of Justice

For Aristotle, justice is a virtue obtained from the law and its administrators. In the legal sense, whatever laws are laid down, they are assumed to be just. Law covers the whole field of virtuous action so that in this general sense justice is an inclusive term equivalent to righteousness.

b. Distributive Justice and Corrective Justice

For Aristotle, one can be wicked without being greedy and greedy without being otherwise wicked. He divided justice into two types. One type of justice, distributive justice (分配正义), is concerned with the distribution of money or honor or other resources that are divided among all who have a share in some public organization. In cases of distributive justice, things must be distributed equally. Equal distribution must be determined carefully. Things should be distributed so that individuals get their share based on merit. Thus, if things are to be divided based on some property, each individual should receive a portion proportional to their possession of that property. The other type of justice is corrective justice (修正正义). This justice governs personal transactions between individuals, whether mutually agreeable (voluntary) or forced upon a particular party (involuntary).

In the Western cultural tradition, egalitarianism is not so popular a concept partly because of Aristotle's emphasis on distributive justice.

2. Three Great Principles of Western Civil Law

In 1804, the three great civil law principles were established in the French Civil Code (1804): unlimited ownership of private possessions, free contract, and neglect of duty (私有财产神圣不可侵犯、契约自由、过错责任原则). The three principles lay solid and stable foundation for French civil law, so the Code can survive after about two centuries and is being used in France until now.

According to the three principles, no man should benefit from his injustice, pacts must be respected, and private possessions should not be violated. To improve efficiency and realize fairness, most Western countries follow the three great principles in the distribution of resources and wealth–a manifestation of the inegalitarian qualities of Western culture.

IV. Egalitarianism and Inegalitarianism in China and the West

1. "Birth Can't Make a Great Person"

While in the West, nobility was commonly a matter of birthright, the Confucian gentleman (***junzi***) was not necessarily high-born. He acquired his status from his attitude: he cultivated virtuous, humane behavior. Anyone could in principle become a gentleman–and while, inevitably, the chance to do so was increased by advantages of birth, nevertheless this egalitarian ideal did occasionally mean that men from humble backgrounds could achieve distinction. (Of course, that says nothing about the dearth of opportunity for women to attain similar rank, which was as lamentable in China as it was in the rest of the world.) As the saying goes that birth can't make a great person while his endeavor can (将相本无种，男儿当自强), we believe that no man is born successful or great, so any man can become a great asset to his country as long as he studies and works hard. The imperial examination system (科举制度) exemplified this belief by effecting a qualitative selection and enabling talent to reproduce and propagate itself. With the imperial examination system in the Sui dynasty put into effect, the door had been opened down to 1905 for all men to rise from poverty to power, fame, and hence wealth as long as they studied hard.

As far as the Western European and Anglo-American philosophical tradition is concerned, there is one significant source of egalitarianism–the Christian notion that God loves all human souls equally and gives love to all humans equally. In spite of this, the *Bible* says, "Jesus looked up and saw some rich people tossing their gifts into the offering box. He also saw a poor widow putting in two pennies. And he said, 'I tell you that this poor woman has put in more than all the others. Everyone else gave what they didn't need. But she is very poor and gave everything she had.'" It seems that Jesus, although equally loving every Christian, is not against the inegalitarian distribution in wealth.

2. Efforts to Break with Egalitarianism

Before China's reform and opening up, workers received nearly the same amount of wages regardless of their contributions. In spite of a frugal living they led, people seemed happy. But a society without producing wealthy people is never progressing on the healthy track. In 1979, the egalitarian practice of "eating from the same big pot" was officially stopped and there arose a gap between the poor and the rich and uneven distribution. About this, Deng Xiaoping (1904–1997) stated that the problem of the poor-rich gap and unfair distribution shall be particularly brought up and resolved at the end of this century when China will have reached a moderately prosperous level. He aimed at an egalitarian welfare in the end, i.e. establishing a system requiring the "stratum and regions which got rich first" to feed the "late wealth-winning" strata and regions. To this end, Deng Xiaoping urged Chinese people during his 1992 tour of south China to be more emancipated in our thoughts, more courageous in reform and opening up to the outside world, and quicker in our development steps and on no account to allow our opportunities to slip through our fingers.

Today, the term–"common prosperity"–has become a new catchphrase in China. At recent high-level meetings on financial and economic affairs, China's top leaders pointed out that common prosperity is not egalitarianism.

It is by no means robbing the rich to help the poor as misinterpreted by some Western media. Protecting legitimate private property has been written into China's Constitution. Moreover, common prosperity refers to affluence shared by everyone both in material and cultural terms. It is not just an economic issue and far from simply redistributing wealth. In the process of achieving common prosperity, strengthening anti-monopoly efforts, cracking down on illegal gains, and encouraging charitable donations are all internationally accepted means of regulation and adjustment. Those moves do not mean that capital or private companies, in general, are a target in the pursuit of common prosperity, but serve as a warning against unfair business practices.

Further Reading

1. Aristotle, trans. by J.A.K. Thomson (1976). *Ethics*. London: Penguin Books.
2. Bond, M. H. (1996). *Handbook of Chinese Psychology*. Hong Kong: Oxford University Press.
3. Buck, P. S. (2012). *The Good Earth*. Washington D.C.: Washington Square Press.
4. Davies N. (1997). *Europe: A History*. New York: Harper Perennial.
5. Hofstede, G. (1980). *Culture's Consequences, International Differences in Work-related Values*. Beverly Hills, CA: Sage Publications.
6. 赵焕祯校注 (2006),《曾国藩家书》, 武汉: 崇文书局。

Unit 18　Good vs. Evil Human Nature

Men are born to be good. It is education and practice that set them apart (人之初，性本善。性相近，习相远**).**

—Wang Yinglin

The Three-Character Classic or San Zi Jing was attributed to Wang Yinglin (王应麟). It is not one of the traditional five Confucian classics. It is rather the distillation of the essential Confucian thought, expressed in a way that is suitable for teaching young children. It is written in couplets of three syllables for easy memorization. Do you agree with the beginning lines of the book on human nature? Why or why not?

I. Definition of Two Concepts

In the *Mencius*, there is an account of Mencius' dispute with a scholar named Gaozi, who claimed that "human nature is like whirling water." To this, Mencius responded:

"…Man's nature is naturally good just as water naturally flows downward. There is no man without this good nature; neither is there water that does not flow downward.… Man can be made to do evil, for his nature can be treated in the same way." Mencius had a better understanding of human nature than Gaozi, so he has been considered the victor in this famous debate on human nature.

1. Human Nature

What is human nature, then? A passage from the National College English

Unit 18 Good vs. Evil Human Nature

Test Band IV of January 2004 puts it this way, "For most thinkers since the Greek philosophers, it was self-evident that there is something called human nature, something that constitutes the essence of man. There were various views about what constitutes it, but there was agreement that such an essence exists— that is to say, that there is something by virtue of which man is man. Thus man was defined as a rational being, as a social animal, an animal that can make tools, or a symbol-making animal." In other words, human nature is the concept that there is a set of inherent distinguishing characteristics, including ways of thinking, feeling and acting that humans tend to have.

The concept of "human nature" has often been used as a shield behind which the most inhuman acts are committed. In the name of human nature, for instance, Aristotle and many European thinkers up to the 18th century defended slavery. In order to prove the rationality and necessity of capitalism, Western scholars have tried to make a case for acquisitiveness, competitiveness, and selfishness as innate human qualities. Often, one refers cynically to "human nature" in accepting the inevitability of such undesirable human behavior as greed, cheating, lying, and even murder.

2. Good and Evil

The phrase "good and evil" in religion and ethics refers to the location of objects, desires, and behaviors on a two-way spectrum, with one direction being morally positive or good, and the other morally negative or evil. "Good" is a broad concept and difficult to define, but typically it deals with an association with life, continuity, happiness, desirability, or human flourishing. "Evil" is often defined as the opposite of good. Depending on the context, "good and evil" may represent personal judgments, societal norms, or claims of absolute value related to human nature or transcendent religious standards.

There is no consensus so far over whether either good or evil is intrinsic to human nature.

II. Human Nature and Education

1. Different Ideas about Human Nature

In China where Confucianism is widely accepted, people are believed to be basically good in nature, hence young children are believed to be pure and innocent but may become mean and bad as they grow older and have more contact with society where there might be bad influences. Because of this possibility, it is the obligation of those in authority, such as parents, caregivers, educators, public figures, and civil servants to protect the morality of those under their care and to be role models of virtue themselves, and hence we are apt to idealize our parents, professors and honored historic figures and present and regard them as models.

In the West where the belief that "we have all sinned and fall short of the glory of God" is a widely accepted truth, many people believe man is basically evil in nature, and even the greatest figures are believed to have flaws but may become good as they grow older and receive moral education. Former American president Bill Clinton's sex scandal conforms to the Western expectation that great men can be ruined by something bad inherent in nature. On the other hand, some Westerners assume that good and bad exist side by side. For them the categories of good and bad appear everywhere in society. The point is the good should be praised and the bad eliminated to the minimum possible. However, Western people agree unanimously that it is necessary to confess the bad you do. You should admit to your mistakes and shortcomings. This is the first step to become good. Even Clinton was forgiven for his lying desperately about his extra-marital affairs with a White House intern after he publicly admitted to having had an "improper relationship" and promised not to do it again.

2. Common Expectations for Education

Although the direction of moral changes is likely to be from good to bad in China, and from bad to good in the West, China and the West share common expectations for education.

a. School Education

Chinese and Westerners agree that education should be a good moral influence on children. Confucius said he educated without any care about the students' social classes, thus bringing moral education to all young men, poor or rich. The ancient Greek philosopher Aristotle also emphasized education and stated, "The roots of education are bitter, but the fruit is sweet." In fact, the Chinese expect schools and universities to be places of virtue. That can explain why a news report about an immoral educator or a scandal relevant to a university professor can become very sensational in China. However, Westerners do not expect particular institutions to be more virtuous than other institutions, believing that good and bad are found everywhere, within each person, and therefore within each organization. In their thought, it is as possible to be a virtuous businessman as it is to be a virtuous professor if proper education is provided to improve human nature, increase the good and reduce the bad.

b. Older People as Role Models

Both traditional Chinese and Western cultures stress the role of older people in education. The Chinese saying **What kind of father must have what kind of son** (有其父必有其子；上梁不正下梁歪) means the same as the English proverb **Like father, like son**. The set phrase **to instruct somebody not only in words, but also by deeds** (身教言传) is synonymous with **Children are**

what the mothers are, and the idiom **Talented students are trained by strict teachers** (严师出高徒) is identical to **Like teacher, like the pupil.** The equivalence of these idioms shows that both cultures emphasize the role of older people in educating the younger generation.

c. Friends as Influencers

It is widely believed in China that one will unconsciously become good if he hangs out with good people. As Confucius put it, "To live with good people is like staying in a room of orchids where, after a long time, one would naturally be sweet-scented; to associate with bad people is like living in a dried-fish shop, where one would unavoidably become imbued with the odor (与善人居，如入芝兰之室，久而不闻其香，即与之化矣；与不善人居，如入鲍鱼之肆)." Therefore, it is important to choose friends for Chinese.

In like manner, Westerners are careful in choosing their friends, which finds expressions in English proverbs like **A man is known by his friends**; **Birds of a feather flock together** and **If you live with a lame person you will learn to limp**.

d. Art's Role as the Educator

Opera, for instance, in traditional Chinese or Western society was used as a vehicle to spread knowledge and ethical teachings. Most operas were based on historical events, folklore or classical novels. They promoted traditional values and moral principles such as punishing the evil and eulogizing the good, loyalty and kindness and denunciation of the ungraceful.

Artistic works like paintings also play the role of educators. Human profiles were used in the Western medieval Biblical paintings as a method to glorify the Holy Family, narrate biblical stories or spread messages from God. In China Tang dynasty officials even tried to bring paintings into Confucian ideology.

The Court of the Song dynasty published an official guide to paintings. This raised criteria not only for human profiles but also for landscape and object paintings. The subjects were used as references to people in order to deliver moral messages. For example, peonies and peacocks represented wealth and fortune; pine trees, bamboo, plum blossoms and orchids represented elegance and integrity; and pine trees and cypresses symbolized loyalty and never giving up.

III. Theorization of Assumptions about Human Nature

1. Chinese Philosophers in the Theorization of the Assumption Concerning Human Nature

Ancient Chinese philosophers emphasized the innately good by nature and managed to theorize this assumption.

a. Confucius

Confucius held that men are pretty much alike by nature, but it is learning and practice that set them apart (性相近也，习相远也). His theory of human nature abolished the status distinctions of a feudal society, and replaced them with a new classification by educational level because education was assumed to raise man to a higher moral status. Meanwhile by prescribing rules of behavior for the educated people–the gentleman or *junzi*, Confucius declared that man, good by nature, needed education to bring out his moral qualities, and the *junzi*, both by example and teaching, would lead society and state to moral harmony, because he firmly believed, "The gentleman understands what is right; the inferior man understands what is profitable (君子喻于义，小人喻于利)." For Confucius, "the gentleman makes demands on himself; the inferior man makes demands on others (君子求诸己，小人求诸人)." And he declared, "The resolute scholar and humane person will under no circumstances seek life at the expense of their humanity; on occasion they will sacrifice their lives to preserve their humanity (志士仁人，无求生以害仁，有杀身以成仁)."

b. Mencius

Confucius' view was later developed by Mencius who theorized issues untouched by Confucius. As the first philosopher to systematically elaborate on the good human nature assumption, Mencius advocated that man, as a rational being, is endowed with four dispositions **ren, yi, li** and **zhi** (humanity, righteousness, propriety and wisdom), a reflection of being good by nature. He went on to illustrate his theory that man is endowed with good human nature from birth by using the example of a child falling into a well and the rescuer's psychological reaction: "When I say that all men have a mind which cannot bear to see the suffering of others, my meaning may be illustrated thus: Even nowadays, if men suddenly see a child about to fall into a well, they will without exception experience a feeling of alarm and distress. They will feel so: not as a ground on which they may gain the favor of the child's parents, nor as a ground on which they may seek the praise of their neighbors and friends, nor from a dislike of the reputation of having been unmoved by such a thing (所以谓人皆有不忍之心者：今人乍见孺子将入于井，皆有怵惕恻隐之心；非所以内交于孺子之父母也，非所以要誉于乡党朋友也，非恶其声而然也。)." Mencius observed that the rescuer's reaction was spontaneous and had no other motive. He went on to say that good human nature is innate and should be developed:

"From this case, we may perceive that the feeling of commiseration is inherent in man, that the feeling of shame and dislike is inherent in man, that the feeling of modesty and complaisance is inherent in man, and that the feeling of approving and disapproving is inherent in man (由是观之，无恻隐之心，非人也；无羞恶之心，非人也；无辞让之心，非人也；无是非之心，非人

Unit 18　Good vs. Evil Human Nature

也。)."

For Mencius, the four dispositions are undoubtedly innate. In his words, "We are born to be endowed with **ren**, **yi**, **li**, and **zhi**, which are not imposed on us from the outside (仁义礼智，非由外铄我也，我固有之也。)." While Mencius placed emphasis on the four innate dispositions of man, he also knew fully well one's character depended much on upbringing and education, that is, on external factors. He said, "In good years most children are good, while in bad years most of them abandon themselves to evil. It is not owing to their natural powers conferred by Heaven that they are thus different. The abandonment is owing to the circumstances by which they allow their mind to be snared and drowned in evil (富岁，子弟多赖；凶岁，子弟多暴，非天之降才尔殊也，其所以陷溺其心者然也。)."

c. Importance of the Innately Good Human Nature Theory

The theory of good human nature took up a predominant position in traditional Chinese culture, which greatly influenced the ancient concepts of traditional Chinese politics and law and became the theoretical starting point of humane government (仁政) which ushered in the rule of individuals.

2. Western Scholars in the Theorization of the Assumption about Human Nature

The theory of innately evil human nature is a denial of the good human nature theory. The traditional Western assumption about human nature is that humans are basically evil. Those who have contributed to this theory are many. The most influential are authors of Thomas Hobbes, Georg Wilhelm Friedrich Hegel (1770–1831), and some Western jurists.

a. Christian Scholars

According to Christian scholars God created Adam and Eve, the human ancestors, and allowed them to live in Paradise, but told them never to have the fruit in the Tree of Knowledge. But driven by their greed, they ate the fruit. Then in anger, God drove them out of the Garden of Eden. Because they sinned all their offspring would be born with original sin and should atone for their crime as soon as they were born. This Biblical story means humans do evil as part of their nature, hence laying the foundation for the establishment of the theory on innately evil human nature.

St. Augustine (354–430), who was born 905 years after Confucius, defended the doctrines of original sin and the fall of man in systematizing Christian thought and thus reaffirmed the necessity of God's grace for man's salvation and further formulated the Church's authority as the sole guarantor of the Christian faith.

b. Hobbs' View of Evil Human Nature

In *The Leviathan*, the great British philosopher Thomas Hobbes (1588–1679) illustrates his views of human nature. Hobbes believed that humans are born to be selfish and in the face of limited wealth, human relationship would become that of one wolf and another wolf.

According to him, human beings naturally desire the power to live well and they will never be satisfied with the power they have. He also believed that all people are created to be equal, and that everyone is equally capable of killing each other because although one man may be stronger than another, the weaker may be compensated for by his intellect or some other individual aspect. Hobbes held that the nature of humanity leads people to seek power. When two or more people want the same thing, they become enemies and attempt to destroy each other, starting the war. There are three basic causes for war–competition, distrust and glory. In each of these cases, men use violence to invade their enemies' territory either for their personal gain, safety or glory. Without a common power to unite the people, they would be in a war of every man against every man as long as the will to fight is known. He believed that this state of war is the natural state of human beings and that harmony among human beings is artificial because it is based on an agreement. If a group of people has something in common such as a common interest or a common goal, they would not be at war and united. One thing he noted that is consistent in all men is their interest in self-preservation. Therefore, he concluded that humans are selfish, thus bad and evil by nature.

c. Hegel's Theory of Evil Human Nature

German philosopher Georg Wilhelm Friedrich Hegel came up with a theory on evil human nature, too. According to him, the theory of evil human nature is greater than that of good human nature, implicitly stating that evil nature has played an important part in the development of history.

Hegel influenced writers of widely varying positions, including both his admirers (e.g. Bauer, Marx, Bradley, and Sartre) and his detractors (e.g. Schopenhauer, Nietzsche and Russell).

d. Russell's Theory of Evil Human Nature

According to Bertrand Arthur William Russell (1872–1970), the most influential philosopher of the 20th century, moral evil or sin is derived from the instincts that are transmitted to humans from the human ancestry of beasts. This ancestry originates when certain animals became omnivorous and employed predation in order periodically to ingurgitate the flesh as well as the fruit and produce of other once-living things to support metabolism in competition with other animals for scarce food-animal and food-plant sources in the predatory environment. Therefore, the simple fact that humans must eat other life or else starve, die and rot is the probable primordial origin of contemporary and historical moral evil, i.e. the bad things humans do to each other by lying, cheating, slandering, thieving and slaughtering.

e. Jurists and the Rule of Law

Western jurists have established the rule of law on the theory of evil human nature, believing humans are born to be selfish and discriminatory and therefore conflict and fight against each other, and hence it is essential to set up a series of regulations and laws to solve human conflicts and disagreement in order to ensure the stability of society, to which we should be alert.

f. Sigmund Freud's Theory of Human Nature

The traditional Western view of human nature showed up in modern theories that seem to have nothing to do with religious beliefs. In his psychological theories, Austrian psychiatrist Sigmund Freud included the idea that infants are controlled by primitive desires and learn to control them as the personality develops. This contrasts sharply with the Chinese view that children are pure and good and learn to do bad things as a result of contact with bad influences in society. Typically, Westerners stress the ability of people to change for the better. Now they are more likely to assume that education and other good influences will save them.

To sum up, human nature is believed to be basically good in China, and therefore education is valued to protect and keep people's virtue inherent in nature, some systems are established to reward good behavior, and virtuous rulers are expected to find the most virtuous people to help them run the state. For Westerners, human nature is basically evil, and therefore education is valued to help get rid of evil, some watchdogs are used to find evil and fight against it, bad behavior is punished, and people should believe God so that they can be saved from their evil nature.

IV. Human Nature Theories and the Rule of Ethics vs. Law

1. Rule of Ethics

The concept of "the rule of ethics," a cultural heritage handed down by Confucianism, was built on the idealistic assumption that human nature is innately good. The theory of good human nature emphasizes the rationality and necessity of moral government, but it is short of a forewarning mechanism. Moreover, the rule of rites and ethics is very likely to be turned into the rule of individuals who are apt to take law as an art.

2. Rule of Law

The Western concept of law was built on the hypothesis that human nature is basically bad. The theory of evil human nature emphasizes the possibility of evil, so it is not short of a forewarning mechanism.

The American founding fathers believed that people are selfish, coveting more and more property and that leaders lust after more and more power, and they assumed such human nature is unchangeable. In the 4th U.S. president James Madison's words, "If men were angels, no government would be necessary." Therefore, the founders fragmented the American government's power, which is reflected in the three concepts they built into the structure of government–federalism, separation of powers, and checks and balances. With the three concepts, the founders expected conflict and invited the parts of government to struggle against each other in order to limit each other's ability to dominate all. Meanwhile, they hoped for a "balanced government." The national and state governments would represent different interests. The House would represent the common people and the large states; the Senate, the wealthy people and the small states; the president, all the people; and the Supreme Court, the Constitution. Although each part would struggle for more power, it could not accumulate enough to have absolute control over the others. Eventually, its leaders would have to compromise and adopt policies in the best interests of all the parties. In this way, the founders expected the narrow conflict to produce broader harmony. To them, the legislative branch of government and media journalists should keep an eye on the president, state governors and other government officials to make sure they do not do anything evil. If some wrongdoings were discovered, the person should be punished or removed from office.

Further Reading

1. Hofstede, G. (2001). *Culture's Consequences, Comparing Values, Behaviors, Institutions, and Organizations Across Nations*. Thousand Oaks, CA: Sage Publications.
2. Russell, B. (1945). *The History of Western Philosophy*. New York: Simon & Schuster.
3. Twitchett, D. & Fairbank, J. K. (1978). *The Cambridge History of China*. NY: Cambridge University.
4. 冯友兰 (2016),《中国哲学史》, 北京: 商务印书馆。
5. 黄建军译注 (2015),《荀子译注》(精编本), 北京: 商务印书馆。
6. 梁漱溟 (2010),《东西文化及其哲学》, 北京: 商务印书馆。
7. 梁漱溟 (1987),《中国文化要义》, 上海: 学林出版社。
8. 梅仁毅主编 (2002),《美国研究读本》, 北京: 外语教学与研究出版社。
9. 杨伯峻译注 (1960),《孟子译注》, 北京: 中华书局。

Unit 19　Rule of Individuals vs. Rule of Law

The law cannot make all men equal, but they are all equal before the law.

—Frederick Pollock

Is what British jurist Frederick Pollock declared more than 100 years ago still relevant in today's global community?

The rule of law is better than the rule of any individual.

—Aristotle

Do you agree with Aristotle? Why or why not?

I. Rule of Individuals in Traditional Chinese Thought

Chinese advocates of the rule of law may differ on many things, but at least agree on this historical fact: In governing the state, traditional China practiced "the rule of ethics and rites (以德治国，以礼治国)." Based on the principle of "promoting ethical standards without resorting to punishment (明德慎罚)" and a theory of rule by self-restraint (自我约束), Confucianism advocates "the rule of rites" (礼治) and "the rule of ethics" (德治), which unavoidably ushered in the rule of individuals (人治) with Chinese characteristics.

1. Confucian Advocacy of the Rule of Rites and Ethics

a. Rule of Rites

The rule of rites is largely marked by protecting the hierarchical system, in which the higher position one is in, the more virtuous and thus more powerful one should be. For instance, the patriarchal hereditary system of the Zhou time provided noblemen of all levels with rights to enjoy independent administrative, legal, and judicial privileges in their own fiefs, which emphasized the role of the ruler with extraordinary abilities as an individual as well as a role model of morality.

Among the five Confucian classics, there is a special book on rites–the *Book of Rites* expected to be the controlling document on civilized behavior. In the Confucian world view, the rule of law is applied only to those who have fallen beyond the bounds of civilized behavior. Civilized people are expected to observe proper rites. Only social outcasts are expected to have their actions controlled by law. Thus the rule of law is considered a state of barbaric primitiveness, prior to achieving the civilized state of voluntary observation of proper rites. What is legal is not necessarily moral or just. In identifying the importance of the rule of rites, Confucius pointed out, "Respectfulness, without the rules of rites, becomes laborious bustle; carefulness becomes timidity; boldness becomes insubordination; straightforwardness becomes rudeness (恭而无礼则劳，慎而无礼则葸，勇而无礼则乱，直而无礼则绞。)." Accordingly, a superior ruler should cultivate the qualities of a virtuous man. Only then would his morality influence the ministers around him. The ministers in turn would be examples for others of the lower ranks, until all men in the state were permeated with noble, moral aptitude. The same principle of trickle-down morality would apply to every aspect of life. So Confucius further pointed out, "If a man lacks the human virtues, what has he to do with ritual? If a man lacks the human virtues, what has he to do with music (人而不仁，如礼何？人而不仁，如乐何？)?"

Unit 19 Rule of Individuals vs. Rule of Law

But how should the rites be observed? The answer is by observing rites of Five Relationships or ***wulun***. Each individual shall clearly understand his social role, and each shall voluntarily behave according to the proper observance of rites that meticulously define such relationships. No reasonable man shall challenge the rites of the Five Relationships. It is the most immutable fixation of cultural correctness in Chinese consciousness. The Five Relationships governed by Confucian rites are those of: sovereign to the subject, parent to child, elder to younger brother, husband to wife and friend to friend (君臣、父子、兄弟、夫妇、朋友). These relationships formed the basic social structure of Chinese society. Each component in the relationships assumed ritual obligations and responsibilities to the others while he enjoyed privileges and due consideration accorded by the other components.

b. Rule of Ethics

The rule of individuals in ancient China was ethics-centered and could only be founded on ethics just as Confucius said, "The government of King Wen and King Wu is displayed in the records. Let there be the right men and the government will flourish. But, without the right men, the government will decay and cease (文武之政，布在方策。其人存，则其政举；其人亡，则其政息。)."

As time went by, the rule of rites and ethics gave impetus to the formation of the rule of individuals which was applied to traditional Chinese politics bit by bit.

2. Confucian Doctrines of Governance

a. Rule of Individuals

What Confucianism held conflicted with the Legalist school (法家) which advocated the rule of law and stressed the dominant role of laws in governing people during the contention of a hundred schools of thought (百家争鸣). Their debates which focused on individuals and laws played a decisive role in governance. In debating with Legalists, Confucianists stuck to the rule of rites and ethics, putting forward such basic doctrines as follows:

First, "Governance or administration depends on individuals (为政在人)." Confucius said, "If one promotes the straight and sets them on top of the crooked, they will be submissive; if one promotes the crooked and sets them on top of the straight, they will not be submissive (举直错诸枉，则民服；举枉错诸直，则民不服。)." He proposed using virtuous people to rule the country and enforce the law. For Confucianists, good or bad governance was decided by the ruler, particularly the top leader. They hoped that rulers could be as virtuous and wise as sage-kings Yao, Shun, King Wen, King Wu and Duke of the Zhou, the *dao* (way) of Yao and Shun should be followed, and the system of King Wen and King Wu should be imitated (祖述尧舜，宪章文武). In other words, they valued the politics of wise men, believing prosperity or chaos of a state was brought about by virtuous or evil rulers, just as Confucius declared, "Administration depends on individuals." If the ruler is in his position his policy might be practiced, but once out of his position, his policy might go unnoticed (人亡政息). Mencius echoed Confucius' theory on the rule of individuals by pointing out, "It's good to put only those who are humane in high positions (惟仁者宜在高位)." He said, "Kindness is not enough to govern a state, and law is not enough to restrain oneself (徒善不足以为政，徒法不能以自行。)." These sayings show that Mencius paid great attention to the virtuous quality of the ruler, and that he advocated equal importance of virtue and law in administering the state.

Second, "Only rulers can bring stability to the state, but no laws can make the state stable (有治人，无治法。)." This view was illustrated by Xunzi in the third century BC, who valued law and its significance more than any other pre-Qin Confucian thinkers (先秦大儒), since he maintained that human nature is innately bad. But when comparing "individuals" and "law" in governing the state, he regarded the individuals (rulers) to be more important, promulgating the famous doctrine, "There are only rulers who bring stability to the state, but no laws that can make the state stable." To prove this theory, Xunzi gave three reasons: First, law is important to running a state (法者，治之端也), but law is made by gentlemen, and therefore decided by them (君子者，法之原也); second, even if there is a good law, it is gentlemen who enforce it, otherwise law is nothing (得其人则存，失其人则亡); third, state affairs are so complicated and changeable that laws cannot cover all or flexibly adapt to changing situation (法不能独立，类不能自行), and hence it depends on the flexible handling of man. Inspired by his research, Xunzi concluded, "There has been chaos even with good laws; but since ancient times there has been no chaos under the leadership of gentlemen (故有良法而乱者，有之矣；有君子而乱者，自古及今，未尝闻也。)." Hence from the perspective of jurisprudence, Xunzi provided interlinear explanations for "the rule of individuals" and "the rule of law."

The third is the Confucian concept of "true rulership responding to people's needs (政在得民)." Mencius believed that it is humanity and a sense of obligation that characterize the true ruler. According to him, the reason why the ruler exists is that he brings the ruled peace and prosperity, educates them, and leads them by exemplifying virtue; if the ruler neglects his duty, or worse, oppresses his people, he is not a true ruler, and the people have right to overthrow him. The belief that people are of the first importance while the ruler is of the least importance (君轻民贵) caused the *Mencius*, one of the Confucian Four Books, to be regarded by some rulers as a "dangerous" book.

b. Rule of Law

The Confucian doctrines of the rule of individuals were bequeathed to later dynastic rulers and became the core of orthodox ideology. The assumption that individuals of virtue are able to play a more significant role in running the state does not mean that Confucianists belittled the role of law, or negated law and the significance of "the rule of law." As a matter of fact, not only Xunzi gave great priority to law and rites (礼法并重), the Confucius and Mencius also called on people not to violate laws and rites. Confucius even came up with the doctrine of "rectification of names (正名)," an undertaking that was essential to ensure social stability and rule by law. Mencius was against "those who are high above ordinary people do not follow righteousness and *dao,* and those who are low in their social position do not follow the law (上无道揆，下无法守)." They put forward the important legal principle "Do not give privileges to relatives when governing a country or enforcing the law (执法不避亲)," which indicates that they strictly abided by the principle that everybody is equal before the law. However, Confucius also mentioned concealment between father and son, although it is not concerned with law enforcement, but about giving witness. He pointed out the testimony given by relatives is not reliable. This is not contradictory to the principle that everybody is equal before the law; it is simply human nature. The Confucian legal idea is also reflected in its requirement for fair punishment. Confucius was strongly against using the law for purposes of revenge, and Mencius proposed severely punishing the tyrant. To ensure everybody was equal before the law, Confucianism advocated that punishment should fit the crime, nobody should be above the law, and equal punishment for all guilty of the same offense (法度严谨，执法不避亲，不避贵). These are ancient Chinese expressing forms of equal legal rights and fair justice, and they have a great influence on modern legal and human rights concepts in China.

II. Rule of Law in Traditional Western Thought

Law is believed to be one of the pillars of Western civilization and can ensure sound government, commercial confidence, and orderly society.

1. Solon and the Rule of Law

Scholars found that the concept of the rule of law originated from the reforms of Solon of ancient Greece. In 594 BC, Solon (c.630 BC–c.560 BC) divided Athenian society into four classes based on wealth. The two wealthiest classes were allowed to serve on the Areopagus (the council of elders). The third class was allowed to serve on an elected council of four hundred people. This council was organized according to the four tribes making up the Athenian people; each tribe was allowed to elect one hundred representatives from this third class. This council of four hundred served as a kind of balance or check to the power of the Areopagus. The fourth class, the poorest one, was allowed to participate in an assembly; this assembly voted on affairs brought to it by the council of four hundred, and even elected local magistrates. This class also participated in a new judicial court that gradually drew civil and military cases out of the hands of the wealthiest people, the Areopagus.

Solon's new state perished soon, but invented the concept of the rule of law. Later he was considered by the Athenians the great hero of their state and his reforms were pointed to as the basis of their state.

2. Theorization of the Rule of Law

The thought of the rule of law was not theorized until Aristotle whose rule of law theory is based on negating Plato's rule of individuals and later developed by Roman jurists.

a. Plato's Rule of Supremely Virtuous Individuals

Plato, the most renowned thinker in Western history, enjoyed the same position in the West as Confucius in ancient China and East Asia. He advocated "the politics of wise man," and belittled the role of law. Nevertheless, in his later works, he began to believe that law was the second best choice, only inferior to "the politics of wise man" or "the rule of a supremely virtuous individual," moreover he was inclined to admit that law was omnipotent.

b. Aristotle and the Rule of Law

Among all the Greek thinkers, Aristotle advanced the richest and most profound thoughts of law. For example, he deemed that the law restricts both the common people and the men in power. His thoughts include that the rule of law is better than the rule of individuals; the rule of law means people generally obey the law which should be well enacted; the law reflects justice, which means a kind of equality. For Aristotle, "a central function of the law is to compensate for the imperfect and random judgment of men," since he believed that law is order and good law is good order.

c. Early Greek Vision of Law

The early Greek philosophers had a vision of law as a system of rules whose source lay outside of the ruler himself. For them, the law was inherent in the natural order or arose from the timeless customs of the people, although for the Christian philosophers, law came from God. Accordingly, if a king were to rule according to law, he would be constrained and his powers would be limited.

d. Ancient Roman Jurists

Jurists in ancient Rome, inheritors of ancient Greek culture, strongly advocated the rule of law. Besides developing well-legislated law, especially the private law reflecting advanced simple commodity production relationships, they had done a lot of job in theorizing the rule of law. By using concepts like **natural law**, **reason**, and **justice**, they managed to illustrate the nature of law and stressed the authority and significance of law. For instance, Marcus Tullius Cicero (106 BC–43 BC), the famous Roman philosopher, statesman, and constitutionalist, developed Plato's idea that law as a divine order in the sky is articulated by the philosopher-king, but borrowed from Aristotle the belief that everybody has an innate knowledge of the divine law. He argued that all laws that differ from this universally known divine law are not real laws, but only the instruments of men in rebellion against the divine law. Cicero wrote, "According to the law of nature it is only fair that no one should become richer through damages and injuries suffered by another." He insisted that laws should be interpreted in a liberal sense so that their intention may be preserved and he said explicitly, "The magistrates are the ministers for the laws, the judges their interpreters, the rest of us are servants of the laws, that we all may be free." Many people accept implicitly and without questioning the truth of Cicero's aphorisms just as **When men are pure, laws are useless; when men are corrupt, laws are broken**, **The laws of each are convertible into the laws of any other**, **If there were no bad people, there would be no good lawyers**, **We are in bondage to the law in order that we may be free**, and **Liberty consists in the power of doing that which is permitted by the law**.

There also existed the concept of the rule of law in Medieval Europe. Peter Lombard (1100–1160), a scholastic theologian, held that one is not to be punished as a sinner unless there are written rules to refer to, which had been developed into the principle of "the rule under written law".

The ancient Greek and Roman theory on the rule of law has a far-reaching influence on the Western law culture.

3. Institutionalization of the Rule of Law

Out of their reflection on Western social history, the European Enlightenment thinkers held the banner of "reason, democracy and the rule of law" and worked on theoretical issues such as what is the rule of law, why there is a need for the rule of law, and how to practice the rule of law. Their efforts ushered in the institutionalization of the law theory.

a. British Jurists

In Britain jurists like John Lock (1632–1704) and A.V. Dicey (1835–1922) put forward and proved with great passion the necessity of institutionalizing the rule of law.

John Locke was the first to talk about the division of power, especially between the legislative power of the parliament and the administrative power of the king. He did not claim the need for the separation of judicial power, but realized its importance in setting up a system of mutually limiting and balancing powers and authorities. From the outset, Locke openly declared the remarkable theme of his political theory: In order to preserve the public good, the central function of government must be the protection of private property. According to him, the actions of every human agent–even in the unreconstructed state of nature–should be bound by the self-evident laws of nature. Understood in this way, the state of nature vests each reasonable individual with an independent right and responsibility to enforce the natural law by punishing those few who irrationally choose to violate it. Because all are equal in the state of nature, the proportional punishment of criminals is a task anyone may undertake.

Dicey is believed by some to be the first one in history to explicitly elaborate on "the rule of law." He declared obliterating dictatorship, the superiority of law, equality of all classes and all people before the law, etc. as the basic principles of institutionalizing the rule of law.

b. French Jurists

As the center of the 18th century Enlightenment Movement, France produced influential figures like Jean-Jacques Rousseau and Baron de Montesquieu who helped to institutionalize the rule of law.

In *On Spirit of Laws* and other writings, Montesquieu (1689–1755) proposed theories as follows:

1) The theory of natural origins of society. According to him, human society and its laws are not invented at will, but are formed naturally, based on human nature and natural laws. He agreed neither with the theory of social contract nor Hobbes' theory of mutual conquest.

2) Geographical and environmental theory. He held that laws and other social systems contributed to national character and the material environment.

3) Division of power. To him dividing political authority into the legislative, executive, and judicial powers means the most effective way of ensuring liberty. He argued that these three powers must be assigned to different individuals or bodies, acting independently; otherwise, they would give rise to misuse of power and corruption. The core of his political theory is to argue for the separation of political power into three parts, according to who holds power and the attitudes towards the law of those holding the power. The three political systems are: republican, monarchical and totalitarian.

Montesquieu's most important contribution is the concept of the division of power. Both the 1789 *Declaration of Human Rights* and the later constitution of France acknowledged his theory. Its application became a weapon in the struggle against feudalism and autocracy, making a major contribution to the historical development of the Western world.

c. American Jurists

Thomas Paine (1737–1809) and Thomas Jefferson (1743–1826) totally accepted French and British theories on democracy and the rule of law and actively put them into practice in America. The American founders established the idea of a written constitution, first in the Articles of Confederation and then more prominently in the Constitution itself. They felt that a constitution should be a fundamental law above all other laws–not a mixture of customs and laws.

III. Rule of Law in China Today

The rule of law has been regarded by Western scholars as a central aspect of modernity. Since the rule of law was the basis of the first unification of China in 221 BC, modernity occurred about 2,300 years ago in China.

1. Why Were Rites & Ethics More Important Than Law in Traditional China?

The rule of law did not have a precise definition, and its meaning varied between different nations and legal cultures. Generally, however, it can be understood as a legal-political regime under which the law restrains the government by promoting certain liberties and creating order and predictability regarding how a country functions. In the most basic sense, the rule of law is a system that attempts to protect the rights of citizens from arbitrary and abusive use of government power. But why were rites and ethics regarded as more important than law in traditional Chinese culture?

a. Confucian Answer

Confucius stated, "If the people are led by law, and uniformity is sought by punishments, they will try to avoid the punishments, but have no sense of shame. If they are led by morality, and uniformity is sought by rules of ritual, they will have a sense of shame and, moreover, will become good (道之以政，齐之以刑，民免而无耻；道之以德，齐之以礼，有耻且格。)." This remark can be understood as follows:

Although both would accomplish the goal of governing the people, the rule of ethics and the rule of rites were superior to the rule of law because the former created in people an understanding of right from wrong so that people would voluntarily follow the rules and do the right things. On the other hand, the rule of ethics and rites might win over the hearts of people, while the rule of law would achieve superficial obedience by the people. The effect of ethics and rites was achieved through teaching and persuasion, and was therefore adopted by rational governments. However, the effect of law was through oppression by forces and was therefore adopted by authoritarian governments. The root of ethics and rites was believed to be the innate nature of the sages and the natural order of the world. And the root of the law was believed to be the power men used to secure their political positions. All of the above means that the law did not have the legitimacy of ethics and rites.

The Confucian *Book of Rites* was expected to be the controlling document on civilized behavior, not law. In the Confucian worldview, the rule of law should be applied only to those who have fallen beyond the bounds of civilized behavior. Civilized people were expected to observe proper rites. Only social outcasts were expected to have their actions controlled by law. Thus, the rule of law was considered a state of barbaric primitiveness, before achieving the civilized state of voluntary observation of proper rites. What was legal was not necessarily moral or just.

b. Semantic Answer

A powerful Confucian argument for rejecting rule by law has its root in Semantics. In Chinese vocabulary, law has always been equated with punishment. According to Confucianism, everybody must be punished according to the law if found guilty, whether the felon was from the royal family, a high-ranking government official or an ordinary person. If the emperor's father was found guilty, he could not enjoy the privilege of going unpunished. Confucius strictly practiced this legal principle when he served the State of Lu and was highly praised by the people. If law simply means punishment, naturally it is inferior to ethics and morality. No wonder ancient Chinese people viewed law with hostility: They believed that law would not only betray human ethics and morality, but also destroy the order of the world.

2. Benefits of the Rule of Law

Building a rule-of-law state is becoming an irreversible trend in all democracies throughout the modern world. What are the benefits of the rule of law, then?

The benefits of the rule of law depend on how the rule of law is defined. For Christian philosophers, the rule of law is identified with the triumph of the substantive commandments of God; to Chinese people, it is valuable because it is equivalent to good government, and it is a must for peaceful development, economic growth, clean government, cultural prosperity, social justice and a sound environment. More generally, the advantages of the rule of law are the advantages of whatever rules are to be implemented, for example, the guarantee of basic human rights such as the right to life, the freedom of thought, the right to get an education, privacy and personal liberty. The narrower procedural definition of the rule of law has virtues as well.

3. Future Trends of the Chinese-style Rule of Law

China first incorporated the rule of law into its Constitution in the 1990s. The sentence "exercise the rule of law, building a socialist country governed according to law (依法治国，建设社会主义法治国家)" was added to the Constitution in 1999. The concept which is now an important Party mission and crucial to the current reform campaign as China enters the "deep-water zone" where problems that remain are all difficult ones, is of its own particular trends.

a. Inclination to the Rule of Ethics

Conceptually our society today is still inclined to the rule of ethics, and the core of the construction of spiritual civilization remains to be the construction of morality. If we go through materials on spiritual civilization, we would find many expressions of the same viewpoint. In practice, we also witness the spirit of ethics permeate all aspects of our society.

b. Gradual Shift from the Rule of Individuals to the Rule of Law

The rule of law in China co-exists with the rule of individuals, which is most obviously revealed in *guanxi*. The existence of *guanxi* is unavoidable, since China is gradually changing from an agrarian civilization based on the rule of ethics to the market economy based on the rule of law.

c. Rule of Law with Chinese Characteristics

China has over 240 laws covering almost every aspect of political and social life. Under the leadership of the CPC Central Committee, China is marching to the future. The quintessence of this future society can be simply summarized as the socialist rule of law with Chinese characteristics. Because only under the conditions of the socialist rule of law can we transcend the traditional rule of ethics and rites, overcome the shortcomings of the Western-style rule of law, and truly realize a harmonious society.

Further Reading

1. Pattberg, T. (2009). *The East-West Dichotomy*. New York: LoD Press.
2. Raz, J. (1979). *The Authority of Law–Essays on Law and Morality*. Oxford: Clarendon Press.
3. Russell, B. (1945). *The History of Western Philosophy*. New York: Simon & Schuster.
4. 郭齐勇主编 (2005),《中国古典哲学名著选读》,北京:人民出版社。
5. 亨利·基辛格 (2011),《论中国》,胡利平、林华、杨韵琴、朱敬文译,北京:中信出版社。
6. 祝吉芳编著 (2010),《中国传统文化经典英语导读》,Jack Franklin,王华宝审校,南京:河海大学出版社。
7. (2022),《中华人民共和国民法典》,北京:法律出版社。